SPSS for Windows
Made Simple

Paul R. Kinnear & Colin D. Gray

*Department of Psychology,
University of Aberdeen*

 LAWRENCE ERLBAUM ASSOCIATES, PUBLISHERS
Hove (UK)   Hillsdale (USA)

Reprinted 1995

Lawrence Erlbaum Associates, Publishers
27 Palmeira Mansions
Church Road
Hove
East Sussex, BN3 2FA
UK

British Library Cataloguing in Publication Data

A catalogue record for this book is available from the British Library

ISBN 0-86377-350-8

Printed and bound in the UK by Redwood Books, Trowbridge, Wiltshire from camera-ready copy supplied by the authors

CONTENTS

Contents

CHAPTER 3   INPUTTING AND EDITING DATA *22*

Contents

Contents

PREFACE

By exploiting the advantages of a graphical, rather than command-driven, operating system, *SPSS for Windows* has taken a further significant step towards a truly interactive mode of use: command-writing has been largely dispensed with, and the analyses are selected from drop-down menus on the screen. The choice of an item from a menu brings to the screen a dialog box for completing the specification of the command.

This book is an introduction to the use of *SPSS for Windows* for the analysis of data in the social and biological sciences. Although there were already available excellent texts, both on *SPSS* itself (eg Norussis, 1993) and on *Windows* (Microsoft, 1992), there was an evident need for an introductory book, written from a social science perspective, that would serve as a preparation for the more comprehensive treatments.

Like its predecessor *SPSS/PC+ Made Simple*, *SPSS for Windows Made Simple* is the product of many years of teaching experience. There is an abundance of illustrative material and worked examples, which include annotated *SPSS* output listings and actual screen images of application windows and dialog boxes. These are accompanied by comments clarifying the points that have arisen most frequently from students' queries during practical classes. As the title suggests, the emphasis is upon simplicity rather than comprehensiveness; nevertheless, the range of problems and techniques covered is much wider than in comparable introductory texts.

It is anticipated that readers will have varied experience of computing and the use of computing packages. Chapters 1-4 introduce the reader to the PC, the Windows operating system, the preparation and exploration of data sets and to some basic statistical concepts. At various points, the reader is informed of the material that is about to be presented, so that the experienced computer user can skip the block (or chapter) concerned. Chapter 5, though short, is important, because it provides a guide to the remainder of the book by first introducing some general guidelines for choosing a statistical test and then indicating the locations of the various methods. The remaining chapters are relatively self-contained, each dealing with a particular test or procedure, with preliminary comments about its use and specification of the conditions that must be satisfied for its correct application. Chapter 6 describes techniques for comparing the averages of two samples of scores. Chapter 7 introduces the topic of analysis of variance with a consideration of the completely randomised ANOVA. Chapter 8 describes the completely randomised factorial ANOVA. Chapters 9 and 10 consider the ANOVA for experiments with repeated measures on some (or all) of their treatment factors. The measurement of statistical association in various kinds of data is described in Chapter 11. Regression, simple bivariate and multiple, is the topic of Chapter 12. Chapter 13 discusses the application of log-linear models to the analysis of multi-way contingency tables. Chapter 14, on discriminant analysis, describes how category membership can be predicted from knowledge of an individual's scores on other variables. Finally, Chapter 15 concerns the use of factor analysis to identify the psychological dimensions that are held to underlie performance on batteries of tests of ability or personality. At the end of the book, there is a course of Exercises, covering all the topics considered in the text. Wherever possible, the opportunity is taken to amplify and illustrate important points. There is also a comprehensive Index.

We are fortunate indeed to have had the advice, help and encouragement of John Lemon, Senior Computing Adviser at the Computing Centre at Aberdeen University, who has kindly read the manuscript at various stages of preparation, and given us the benefit of his experience with SPSS. We also thank John Thom and Elizabeth Ray for their helpful advice on the production of the illustrations.

We are also grateful for the help and encouragement we have received from our colleagues within the Psychology Department. In particular, we have had first class technical support from Edward Stephen and James Urquhart, who ensured that our PCs and printer always had the necessary capacity for the enormous processing loads they would be required to carry, and from Peter Bates, who prepared illustrations for Chapters 1 and 2. We would also like to thank Caroline Green for working through the Exercises and making so many helpful observations. Throughout the project, we have been sustained in our efforts by the interest, encouragement and support of our Head of Department, John Shepherd.

Finally we would like to thank all those people who, though too numerous to mention individually, have contributed helpful advice or comments.

Paul R. Kinnear and Colin D. Gray.

May 1994.

CHAPTER 1

THE PERSONAL COMPUTER

1.1 INTRODUCTION

1.1.1 To The Reader

We anticipate that our readers will vary considerably in their computing background. Some will certainly be experienced in the use of computing systems and packages; but, others, just as certainly, will be newcomers to computing. Should you be in the former category, you will probably wish to skip the remainder of this chapter, which is about computer basics (with just a little history), and move directly to Chapter 2; indeed, if you are already a **Windows** expert, Chapter 3 might be your best starting point. If you are not an experienced user, however, we suggest you begin with this chapter, and familiarise yourself with some computing terminology, with the layout of the PC computer keyboard, with the nature and functions of an operating system and with the organisation of files and directories.

1.1.2 How computer use has changed : interactive computing with SPSS

Recent years have seen dramatic changes in computers and in computing. Just ten years ago, most computers were of the **mainframe** type, operated by users at remote terminals. Early

1

mainframe computers were of massive proportions and one could easily occupy a large part of a building. At the time, such bulkiness was essential: in those days, the possibility that any small **desk-top** machine could possibly process the amount of information required for large scale statistical computation would have been unthinkable. Yet today's small **personal computers (PCs)** are more powerful than some of yesterday's mainframes.

This new physical accessibility has been paralleled by an equally dramatic change in the way in which computers are used. Computers are designed to obey sets of instructions known as **programs** (in the jargon, programs are **software**, machines are **hardware**), the writing of which follows a set of syntactic rules known as a **programming language**. For some years, however, there have been available pre-written sets of programs known as **packages**, one of the earliest of which was the *Statistical Package for the Social Sciences (SPSS)*.

The early mainframe packages used **batch** processing, whereby there could be no input from the user once a program had started to run: the assignment, or **job** had to be completely (and correctly) specified beforehand. In this mode of operation, it was some time before the user knew whether the run had been successful. In batch processing, a premium is placed upon knowledge of the syntax of the **control language** by which the programs in the package are accessed. This contrasts with **interactive processing**, in which the user receives prompts and feedback on a more or less continuous basis, thus avoiding the soul-destroying list of error messages that could result from even a small syntactic error in a job submitted for batch processing. The advent of interactive processing has increased the 'user-friendliness' of computing packages (and the enjoyability of computing) enormously.

1.2 COMPUTERS IN GENERAL

A computer is a device for processing information. This processing has three aspects:
   (1)   **Input** of information to the system.
   (2)   **Central processing** of information by the system.
   (3)   **Output** of information from the system.

There are several ways of inputting information into a computing system. All of these, however, are controlled by the operation of a **keyboard**, which resembles that on a typewriter. Information can be typed in directly from the keyboard; but it can also be retrieved from storage. Among the output devices of a computing system are the **visual display unit (VDU)**, on the screen of which can be seen the computer's responses to the user's commands. An invaluable modern input device is the **mouse**, which allows the user to control the position of a pointer on the VDU screen. The mouse is one of the mainstays of modern interactive computing. There is also the **printer**, which produces a permanent print-out, or **hard copy**, of the work that the computer has done.

An important aspect of computing is the retention of information in memory, both in the **short term** (that is, for the duration of a computing session) and in the **long term** (indefinitely). Information is stored in units called **files**, which are patterns of electromagnetic disturbance on the surfaces of structures known as **disks**, the latter being driven by hardware called **disk drives**. (For additional back-up storage, electronic recording tape is sometimes used.)

By the operation of a disk drive, information is stored in and read from files on disk. There are two main types of disks:

    (1)   **Floppy disks**, which are physically accessible to the user and hence portable.

    (2)   **Hard disks**, which are an integral part of the hardware and cannot be withdrawn by the user.

A disk drive operates in two modes:

    (1)   In **write mode**, it transfers information to files on a disk.

    (2)   In **read mode**, it extracts information from files on a disk.

There are different kinds of floppy disk drives, designed to handle disks of varying size and storage capacity: the modern, **3½″ floppy disk** has a rigid plastic container; the older, **5¼″ floppy disk** had a bendable cardboard sleeve.

Disks also vary in their storage capacity. A **high-density** 3½″ disk stores more information (1.44 Megabytes) than does a **double-density** disk (720 Kilobytes). Although a high-density disk drive can also read from and write to a double-density disk, the converse does not hold: a double-density disk drive can neither read from nor write to a high-density disk. Although, on some machines, it may appear possible to do this, the resulting files are usually unreadable.

The construction of a file (particularly one containing a large data set, or an extensive piece of writing) may require many hours of work. Floppy disks (and hard disks too) can occasionally be damaged, or **corrupted**, so that the information they contain is lost. This, we assure you, is a highly unpleasant experience and probably very bad for the blood pressure. The moral is clear: always duplicate important files on **back-up disks**: it is well worth the trouble. (If the option is open to you, **back up on a hard disk as well**: it is best not to entrust valuable files to floppy disks alone since the latter do not take kindly to rough handling, or applications of tea or coffee.)

Before a new floppy disk can be used to record material, it must be **formatted**, that is, prepared for use with a specific **operating system** (see below for an explanation of this term). This procedure will be described later.

There are different kinds of PCs: some are **stand-alone** machines, intended for independent use; others are part of a **computer network**, in which the user's PC is one of several that are linked to a central machine known as a **file server**. In either case, however, the procedure for operating SPSS for Windows is basically the same, barring a few minor details, such as the manner in which one enters and leaves the system, and how one prints the output.

1.3 THE PC COMPUTER KEYBOARD

To use a computer effectively, the user must become accustomed to the layout of the keyboard. Ideally, this section should be read at a real keyboard, where the various items can be identified with the descriptions in the text.

1.3.1 Arrangement of the keys on a PC keyboard

To the proficient typist, the PC keyboard will look very familiar. In fact, the letter keys are arranged exactly as they are on an ordinary typewriter: from left to right, the letters of the top row appear in the order Q,W,E,R,T,Y, ... ; and, as on a typewriter keyboard, there is a row of number keys above the top row of letters. There are other similarities too: on a typewriter, there is a **space bar** running along the bottom of the keyboard, a single press of which moves the printing head a space to the right. On the computer keyboard, there is a similar bar, a press of which moves the **cursor**, a blinking image on the screen of the VDU, one space to the right, without any character appearing.

Some of the other features of a computer keyboard are shown in Figure 1. Like an ordinary typewriter, the PC keyboard has two **shift** keys, which are identically marked with wide upward-pointing arrows [⇧] (Figure 1). When a shift key is pressed and held down, pressing a double-character key will give the upper character. For example, if, while holding down the shift key, you press the key bearing the characters 8 and *, you will obtain the asterisk.

Figure 1. A typical computer keyboard.

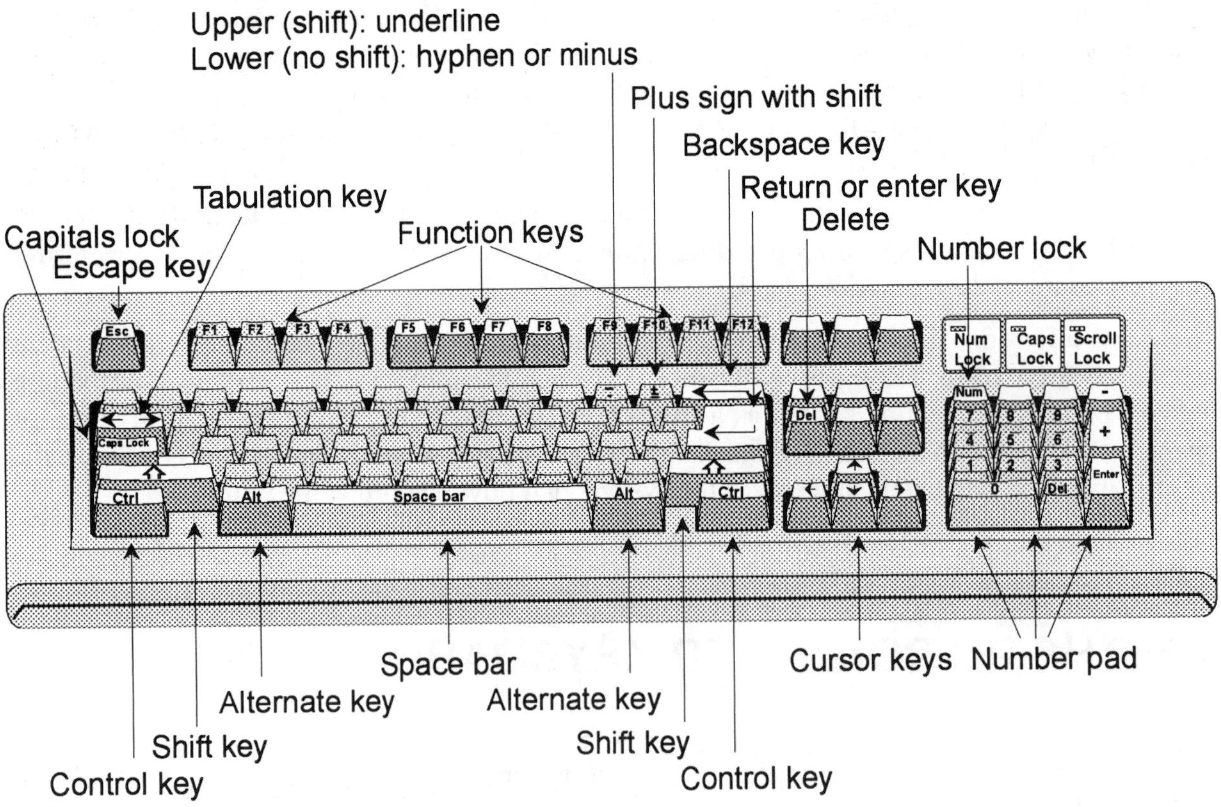

4

The shift keys also control whether letters are printed in **lower** or UPPER case. In the original, or **default**, set-up, pressing a letter key (say that marked E) will show that letter on the screen in lower case (e). But if the same letter key is pressed after a shift key has been pressed and held down, the same letter will appear in upper case (E). Should the user wish to type several letters in upper case, a single press of the **Capitals Lock** key (abbreviated to **Caps Lock** on the key - see below) will achieve this; lower case is restored by another press of Capitals Lock. The Capitals Lock key thus functions as a **toggle switch**: one press produces a change in state, which is reversed when the key is pressed again.

In this book, to make it clear that a key is to be pressed, rather than a sequence of letters typed, the key will be referred to by its name (or a shortened form of this) or its symbol enclosed in square brackets, as in the instruction: **Press** [⇧], meaning 'Press the shift key'.

The operation of pressing and holding down one key (such as [⇧]) and then pressing another will be represented by using the **slash character** (/) thus: [⇧]/E, which means 'Press and hold the Shift key, then press and release E'.

Sometimes, two or more keys are held down together. This will be indicated by separating the names of the keys by hyphens within a single set of square brackets: thus **[Ctrl-Alt-Del]** means that three keys are to be pressed and held down simultaneously.

Be sure to make a clear distinction between the **zero** (0) key (which is one of the number keys above the top row of letters) and the **letter O** (O) key, which is in the top row of letters. They may look similar on the keyboard, but a computer does not interpret the letter O as a zero.

On a computer keyboard, there are several additional keys with functions specific to computing (see Figure 1). For example, in a rectangular area to the right of the main keyboard, there is an extra set of number keys, known as the **number pad**, which is useful when one is typing in a succession of numerical values. Most of the keys on the number pad are labelled with a number plus another character. The numbers are obtained when the **Num Lock** function is active. (To ensure this, it may be necessary to press the **Num Lock** key - see below.)

1.3.2 A glossary of keys for future reference

The following, for your future reference as you work through this book, is a list of the keys on a PC keyboard. At this point, they will be described briefly, and you should try to identify them on a real computer keyboard at the earliest opportunity. With experience, the user may find alternative ways of carrying out some of the operations performed by these keys.

Alternate [Alt]

This, the bottom left key on the keyboard, is used like the **Shift** key: it works only in combination with other keys, being held down while the latter are pressed. For example, one might hold down the **Alternate** key while pressing E, an operation for which our notation is **[Alt]/E** .

Backspace [←]

The long horizontal key with the left-pointing arrow is the **Backspace [←]** key. When you are typing from a computer keyboard, the current entry point on the screen is indicated by the **cursor**, a small blinking image. Should the user type a letter or a number key, that character will appear at the cursor point. If you press **[←]**, the cursor will move one space to the left and delete any character that happens to be in that space.

Capitals Lock [Caps Lock]

As explained earlier, the **Capitals Lock [Caps Lock]** key is a **toggle switch**, determining whether letters are shown in upper or in lower case. The **[Caps Lock]** key affects only the letter keys.

The cursor keys (←, ↑, →, ↓)

The four keys with thin arrows pointing up, down, left and right are known as the **cursor** keys, because they move the cursor in the directions indicated.

Delete [Del]

A single press of the **Delete [Del]** key erases the character at the position of the cursor and replaces it with the next character on the right. The position of the cursor on the screen, however, is unchanged. The effect of continuing to press **[Del]** has the effect of 'sucking in' text from the right and deleting it, while the cursor remains stationary.

Escape [Esc]

The **Escape [Esc]** key is often used to change (or 'escape') from one activity to another.

Function keys [F1], [F2], ...

Along the top of the keyboard is a row of **function** keys, labelled **F1** to **F12**. Only keys **[F1]** to **[F10]** are used in SPSS for Windows. Their uses will be explained as they arise in the text.

Number Lock [Num Lock]

Like **[Caps Lock]**, this is a toggle switch: one press brings a change of state, which is reversed when the key is pressed again. It is located above the numerical keys on the right of the keyboard. When the **Num Lock** light is on, the number pad functions are disabled and numbers are typed; when the light is off, the functions are operative. Of course, numbers can be entered from the keys above the top row of letters independently of the state of the **Num Lock** facility.

Return [Rtn], [Enter] or [⏎]

On an electric typewriter keyboard, there is a **Return** key, the pressing of which enables the typist to begin a new line by rolling the platen to create a preset line space and moving the printing head to the left margin of the writing area of the paper. On the PC keyboard, to the right of the letter keys, is a large key, which is marked with a crooked arrow ⏎. Its main function is to **enter** (ie to transmit to the computer) the line that has just been typed by the user. It is therefore sometimes known as the **Enter** key. When one is typing material on the screen, however, the same key also returns the cursor to the start of the next line and so, in that context, the key is referred to as the **Return** key [Rtn]. In this book, we shall generally use the symbol ⏎ to refer to this dual-purpose, Enter/Return key.

The shift keys [⇧]

The two keys that are identically marked with wide, upward-pointing arrows are the **Shift** keys. Either key can be used. Their function was described at the beginning of this section.

Tabulation [| ← →|] or [Tab]

On the left of the keyboard, underneath [**Esc**], is the **tabulation** key [**Tab**].   As with an ordinary typewriter, pressing [**Tab**] moves the cursor directly to a predetermined position a set number of columns ahead. This is obviously invaluable to the typist who is producing tables of data. But [**Tab**] has other uses as well: for example, when in the Windows operating system (see below), the user can move from one application to another by pressing [**Alt**]/[**Tab**].

1.4 OPERATING SYSTEMS

An **operating system** is a sort of program-manager, or meta-program, which creates a computing **environment**, within which the user can access specific task-oriented programs, such as word processors and statistical packages. An operating system controls basic functions that are common to the use of **all** programs, and so acts as an interface between the computer's hardware and the software.

An operating system, however, also has several functions with which the user is directly concerned. These include disk formatting, file management and the running of programs. The **Windows** operating system was designed for PCs by the Microsoft company. Microsoft also devised the **Microsoft Disk Operating System (MS-DOS, or DOS** for short). While in this book the emphasis will be upon Windows, some consideration of DOS is also essential, especially the notation for storage units and the manner in which these are organised.

A PC system can be set up, or **configured**, so that the user works entirely in a Windows environment. It is also possible, however, to access Windows from DOS. A third possibility is that, especially if the user is on a PC network, a menu will appear which offers Windows as one of several possible choices.

1.4.1 Files and directories

The manner in which information is stored by a computing system may be clarified by analogy with an office filing system, in which an individual item (a document, such as a letter or a bill) is contained in a labelled folder which, in turn, is stored in one of the shelves of the cabinet which, in turn, may be just one of several such units in the office.

We have seen that, in a computing system, information is stored in units called **files**. Files can usefully be thought of as individual documents, like letters, or manuscripts. Files are stored in larger units called **directories**, which are like the labelled folders in a filing cabinet. Since there may be several directories on a disk, they correspond to the shelves in the cabinet. Finally, the files and directories can be located in different disk drives, that is, in different filing cabinets.

Each disk drive is labelled with a letter. Often the PC's own hard disk is known as **drive c** (it is immaterial whether upper or lower case is used), and the floppy disk drives as **drive a**, **drive b** and so on. If the PC is part of a network, the hard disk of the file server is usually labelled **f**. In **DOS notation** (which is used both in MS-DOS and in Windows), a drive's letter label is followed by a colon thus: **c:, a:, f:**.

1.4.2 The naming of files and directories

A **file name** (two words) can have two components:
    (1)   a **filename** (one word), which can be up to eight characters in length;
    (2)   an optional three-character **extension**.

For example, in the file name **ttest.sav**, the filename is **ttest** and the extension is **sav**.

The writing of file names is subject to strict rules. The filename component must not exceed eight characters and must have no spaces between its first and last characters. Also, a file name, whether or not there is an extension, **must not end with a full stop**. So **data** is a possible file name; but **data.** is not. The full stop, however, is the only acceptable separator of a filename from its extension: neither a semicolon nor a comma will do.   Like a file, a directory has a name of up to eight characters in length; but directory names rarely have extensions.

1.4.3 The organisation of files and directories

The information on a disk is organised hierarchically: files are contained within directories, which themselves can be organised at several levels. At the top of the hierarchy is the **root directory**, which is created by the system itself. In operating system notation, the root directory is denoted by the the **backslash character** (\): so the notation **a:** locates control in the root directory of the disk in drive **a**. If a file named **survey.sav** is stored on a floppy disk in drive **a**, in a directory named **research,** the **path name** of the file, that is, its position in the hierarchy, is **a:\research\survey.sav**, the second backslash indicating that the directory named **research** is a **subdirectory** of the root directory (which is represented by the first backslash).

Since subdirectories of the root directory can themselves contain directories, the path name of a file can be quite complex if it is buried deeply in the hierarchy. If a draft of a chapter (say Chapter 3) in a book has been stored on a floppy disk in drive **a**, in a file named **chapt3.doc**, in a directory named **section1**, within another directory called **book,** the file's path name would then be **a:\book\section1\chapt3.doc.**

1.5 GETTING STARTED: SOME PRELIMINARIES

To the reader who has the exclusive use of a PC which has been configured to operate in a Windows environment, there is little to say about the preliminaries: it is just a matter of turning on your machine and waiting for the first windows to appear. Many, however, will have access to Windows only as users of a PC network, in which case there are one or two formalities which must be observed before Windows can be accessed.

1.5.1 Booting up the machine

The first step, assuming that the user's machine has not been switched on, is to do so and wait for the computer to **boot up,** that is, load the operating system and run through certain routine checks and diagnostic procedures. The term **boot** is short for **bootstrap.** Bootstrapping is an operation by which some preliminary computer operating instructions are loaded into main memory in order to bring in further material from an external storage device. Nowadays, bootstrapping is carried out automatically when a computer is switched on.

Sometimes, during the course of a computing session, the system may suddenly freeze, or **hang:** that is, it will no longer respond to the user's instructions. When this happens, there is nothing for it but to 'start again', or **reboot** the machine. A complete rebooting process, which involves all the checking routines, is known as a **hard reboot.** To carry out a hard reboot, however, the user is advised not to switch off the machine's power, but to press the **reset** button, which is often (though by no means always) located somewhere on the front of the PC.

For many purposes, a limited rebooting process, which omits many of the routine checks in a hard reboot, is sufficient. This is known as a **soft reboot,** and is achieved by pressing, simultaneously, the **Control, Alternate** and **Delete** keys, that is, by pressing **[Ctrl-Alt-Delete].**

Even with a soft reboot, the user must accept the annoying fact that all the information in current memory that has not been saved to a file on disk will be lost. It is for this reason that you are advised to save frequently, so that if the machine hangs, or the whole system fails, or 'crashes', only the processing that took place since the last save will be lost. (Note, however, that SPSS for Windows offers the option of frequent automatic saving.)

Some machines require the user to insert a special disk before they will boot up; but with others, booting up will only take place if the floppy disk drive is empty. When the machine has been booted up, the user could be presented with any of several possible displays on the screen. It may be that the user first enters the DOS operating system, in which case the **DOS prompt**

C:\>

will appear. This means that the user is in drive **c** (the hard disk of the computer), at the level of the root directory. To access Windows, it will be necessary to type **win**.

When the user is on a PC network, it is usual for a menu to appear, offering a variety of choices, including access to Windows.

In the happiest scenario, the user accesses Windows directly on booting up the machine and works entirely within the Windows environment.

1.5.2 Logging in and logging out

For reasons of security and resource management, access to a communal computing system may require a procedure by which the user, having already made arrangements to use the system beforehand, presents proof of identification, in the form of a **user number** and a **password**. This is known as **logging in**, and has the effect of making some of the computer's processing capacity and storage available to the user for the duration of the session. It is therefore essential, at the end of the session, to inform the system that these resources will no longer be needed, a procedure known as **logging out**. (It is bad practice simply to switch off, because part of the system's capacity may continue to be monopolised; moreover, there is also the possibility that other users may be able to access your files!)

1.6 SUMMARY

1)   A computing system has 3 aspects:
        (1) **input**;
        (2) **central processing**;
        (3) **output**.

        Information is input either from the **keyboard** or from storage in **files**. The output appears on the screen of a **visual display unit (VDU)** and is printed to obtain a **hard copy**.

2)   Files are stored on **disks**, which are operated by **disk drives**. **Floppy disks** are portable; **hard disks** are not.

3) Since files are merely patterns of electromagnetic disturbance, they are peculiarly fragile and must be **backed up** on other disks or **tape**.

4) Although similar to that of a typewriter, the PC keyboard has a number of additional keys specific to computing, such as **[Alt]**, **[Ctrl]**, the **function** keys **F1, F2, . . .** and the **number pad.**

5) An **operating system** creates a computing **environment**, within which the user accesses and applies task-oriented **programs** and **packages.**

6) An operating system is loaded by a process known as **booting.**

7) In the **MS-DOS** operating system, commands are typed in from the keyboard; but in **Windows,** they are given by making selections of items from graphic displays.

8) For reasons of security and resource management, the user of a system will often be required to **log in** and **log out** of the system.

CHAPTER 2

SOME BASIC WINDOWS OPERATIONS FOR SPSS

2.1 INTRODUCTION

We can assume that the user with the exclusive use of a PC on which Windows has been loaded is already familiar with the system, at least to some extent. For the user of a network PC, however, Windows may be much less familiar, and it may be useful to outline those features that we have found particularly helpful when running SPSS.

We should also point out that there are already available several excellent, comprehensive texts on Windows (eg Microsoft, 1992). At this stage, however, just a few basic terms and techniques should be sufficient for the user who intends to work with SPSS.

2.1.1 Some characteristics of the Windows operating system

An operating system, such as MS-DOS or Windows, sets the scene, or creates an **environment**, within which the user accesses or runs programs and packages such as SPSS and word processors. (In Windows, the term **Application** is used to denote such items of software.) For example, in MS-DOS, the user, in response to **system prompts** that appear on the screen, gives commands by typing them in from the keyboard.

In contrast with MS-DOS, the Windows operating system creates a **graphics environment**, in which applications appear as graphical symbols known as **icons**. Commands are given by selecting from arrays or lists that appear on the screen. Selection is effected by controlling the position of an arrow (or other pointing symbol) on the screen.

Icons make their first appearance in a labelled rectangular area on the screen known as a **window**, which appears against a background known as the **desktop**. There are different kinds of windows, with different functions. Some contain arrays of icons; others invite the user either to adjust pre-set values or to enter further information. (The second type of window is known as a **dialog box**.)

2.1.2 Controlling the screen pointer in Windows

In Windows, the position of the screen pointer can be controlled by using a device called a **mouse**. In its most familiar form, the mouse is a small box, which sits on the top of the user's desk beside the computer and is moved around on the desk to control the pointer's position. (More recently, in some machines, the mouse has become a stationary structure, within which the screen pointer's position is controlled by manipulating a ball in a fixed socket.) On the upper side of the traditional mouse are two buttons, left and right. When the arrow has been positioned at the correct point on the screen, clicking (or sometimes double-clicking) the left button of the mouse transmits the user's choice to the computer. **Double-clicking** means pressing the left button down twice in very quick succession; otherwise the desired effect will not be obtained. In **click-and-drag** operations, the left button is held down, while the mouse is moved. This technique is useful for moving windows and icons about on the screen. It can also be used to change the size of a window. The right button of the mouse is used only occasionally.

It will soon be noticed that the screen pointer assumes a variety of forms. Its first shape is that of a small hour-glass, which indicates that 'something is going on', and the user should do nothing until the shape changes. The hour-glass will appear at the point when **Windows** is being accessed and whenever processing is taking place thereafter. Since PCs vary enormously in their capacity to process information, the user of smaller machines will be more aware of the hour-glass, because processing takes longer. In any case, the user should always bear in mind that *processing takes time*.

The other common screen pointer shapes are: a cross; a girder (cross-section); a diagonal arrow; a horizontal double-arrow; a vertical double-arrow; a diagonal double-arrow. Each of these has its significance and is a useful cue, but we shall consider the meaning of each pointer shape as it arises.

In Windows, it is also possible to give commands by pressing keys. In fact, as the user becomes accustomed to Windows, key pressing often becomes the preferred mode of operation, since it is faster than manipulating the mouse.

Some readers, with experience of Windows in other contexts where acronyms such as **WIMP** (Window Icons Mouse and Pointer) and **GUI** (Graphical User Interface) are used, may wonder whether the procedures we refer to here are similar. We would assure them that, in essence, they are: the difference is largely one of terminology.

2.1.3 Keeping more than one application open

One of the outstanding features of Windows is that the user can keep several applications open at the same time. This means that it is quite possible to be writing a report of an experiment in a word-processing application and (when SPSS is also active) to import computing output from SPSS into the same document file. This is an enormously useful capacity.

If more than one application has been opened, it will be found that pressing **[Alt]/[Tab]** repeatedly will bring each open application successively to the screen.

2.2 THE PROGRAM MANAGER

The first window to appear is the **Program Manager** window (Figure 1). (This caption appears in the coloured strip, or **title bar,** which runs across the top of the window. This bar is a feature of every window.)

Within the **Program Manager** Window, can be seen other open windows. The selection will vary depending on the applications and facilities that have been installed in the computer. The three most important ones shown in Figure 1 are **Main, Accessories,** and from the point of view of this book, **SPSS.** The applications within **Main** effectively 'set the scene' for the running of packages such as SPSS. Note that the layout of these windows can vary from one computer to another.

Figure 1. The Program Manager Window

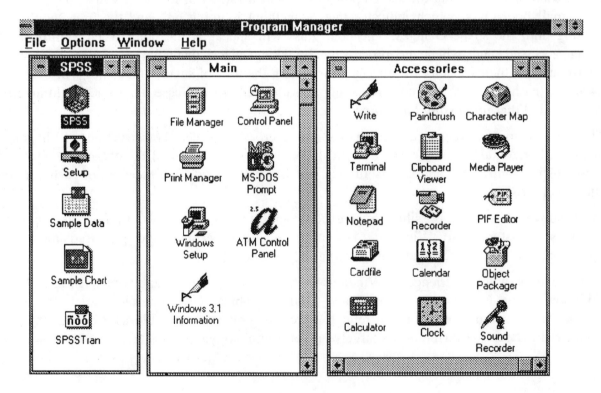

2.2.1 Opening and closing a window

The **Program Manager** window remains available throughout the Windows session. Other windows, however, must be opened before they can be used. Each of the icons that are visible in the Program Manager window can be opened into its own window by double-clicking on its icon. To confirm this, try double-clicking on the **Clipboard Viewer** icon, within the window of the **Accessories** group of applications.

There is more than one way of closing a window. On the left of the coloured title bar in any window is a small square containing a short horizontal bar. This is the **Control-menu** box. Double-clicking on its Control-menu box will close the window of any application. (The same effect is obtained by pressing [Alt]/[F4].) Clicking on the **Control-menu** box of the **Program Manager** quits Windows altogether, after the user has confirmed this instruction by clicking on the **OK** button in a display known as a **confirmation dialog**. (There is also a **Cancel** button, in case of a change of mind.)

2.2.2 Controlling the size and position of a window

On the right hand side of the title bar are two small squares: the left (the **Minimise** button) contains a downward-pointing arrow; the right (the **Maximise** button) has an upward-pointing arrow.

Clicking on the **Minimise** button reduces any window to an icon in the desktop. Try this with the **Program Manager** window. The effect is quite dramatic: the window is reduced to a tiny icon in the bottom left corner of the screen. Restore the window by double-clicking on the Program Manager icon. Clicking on the **Maximise** button expands the window to fill the entire screen, so that the desktop area previously outside the window now disappears. Restore the window to its original size by double-clicking on the **title bar** or by clicking on the outer of the two squares to the right of the title bar (see Figure 1).

Finer control of the position and size of a window can be achieved by two **click-and-drag** operations (see Section 2.1.2). The **position** of the entire window can be adjusted by clicking-and-dragging on the window's title bar. The **height or width** of a window can be adjusted by clicking-and-dragging on a border; to change **both height and width**, click-and-drag on the lower right corner. The success of a **click-and-drag** window-shaping operation depends upon the shape of the screen pointer, which must assume the double-arrow shape: horizontal for an adjustment of width; vertical for an adjustment of height; diagonal for an adjustment of both width and height.

2.2.3 Scrolling

Some lists of items are so long that the items cannot all be seen at once through a window. On the borders of some windows, there are grey bars with arrows at either end: at vertical borders, the upper and lower arrows point up and down, respectively; those on the left and right sides of horizontal borders point left and right. These are known as **scroll bars**. By clicking on the arrows, the view through the window can be changed at will. The reader can experiment with scroll bars when studying the **File Manager** window, which is described in the next section.

2.2.4 The menu bar

In the **Program Manager** window, just underneath the title bar, is a white bar on which is written the words: **File, Options, Windows** and **Help**. The first letter of each of these words is underlined. The white bar is known as a **menu bar**, and the words it contains are the title captions of its menus (these vary considerably from window to window).

When a menu's title caption is clicked on with the mouse, there appears a **drop-down menu,** a white rectangle obscuring part of the window. (The drop-down menu can also be obtained by pressing [Alt] and typing the underlined letter in the menu's title: e.g. [Alt]/f obtains the **File** menu.) On the drop-down menu is a list of items, each of which is a command. A command is run by clicking on its name in the menu or pressing the underlined letter. Among the items in the **File** menu, for example, is E**x**it. In the **Program Manager** window, clicking on **Exit** in the **File** menu quits Windows, as would pressing X.

We shall denote a choice from a menu by indenting an item label in relation to the name of the chosen menu thus:

File
      Exit

2.3 THE FILE MANAGER WINDOW

Within the **Main** window, the icon representing the **File Manager** appears as a drawing of a filing cabinet. Double-click on this filing cabinet to obtain the **File Manager** window, part of which is shown in Figure 2. The specific directories and file names will, of course, vary; moreover, the manner in which these are displayed depends upon the options selected.

The menu bar has seven captions, of which only **File** and **Disk** will be discussed here. **Tree** and **View** provide options that control how the directories and files are tabulated and viewed.

2.3.1 Viewing the organisation of directories and files

Inside the title bar of the **File Manager** window, is the caption **C:\SPSSWIN*.*** . This path name locates the directory called SPSSWIN in drive **c** (ie the computer's hard disk). In the expression *.*, the left and right asterisks are, respectively, a **generic filename** and a **generic extension**: that is, the names of all the files in the directory will be listed. (Because of its generic referent, the asterisk is known as a **wildcard character**.)

On the left of the window, is a list of directory icons, each icon having the form of a schematic folder. One of these, **spsswin**, is highlighted and its icon is a picture of an opened folder. By clicking on the arrows above and below the central vertical scroll bar, the icons of other directories can be seen. The icons in the right half of the window may consist of several types. They all represent files that are contained in the directory called **spsswin**. Most depict a dog-eared sheet of paper to represent **data files**; others may be rectangular in shape, with a dark upper border to represent **program files**. Notice that if the user clicks on another directory, say **gemapps**, the caption in the title bar will change to **C:\GEMAPPS*.***, and the names of the file icons that are visible through the right half of the window will also change. By clicking on the arrows at the left and right ends of the horizontal scroll bar, the icons of other files within the directory can be seen.

Figure 2. Part of the File Manager window

2.3.2 Floppy disks

It is quite possible to use SPSS for Windows without having a floppy disk at all; moreover, if the user has the exclusive use of a PC, any new files can be saved to the machine's hard disk. In practice, however, every PC user needs to use floppy disks at least occasionally. Since even a hard disk can become corrupted, valuable files should be backed up, and one way of doing that is by replicating them on floppy disks. There are other considerations also. It is now common for editors of journals to require a disk containing the 'manuscript' of a paper that has been accepted for publication. Moreover, most people have access to a PC only as users of a network, and are not permitted to store information on hard disk. For such users, floppy disks are the only means of storing important files. We assume, therefore, that the reader has available two floppy disks of the high density (1.44M) type. (The formatting of a smaller-capacity (720K), double-density disk, however, presents no problem.)

2.3.2.1 The purpose of formatting

For a floppy disk to be usable by an operating system, it must be given a set of magnetic markings that the system can recognise. This process is known as **formatting**. On a floppy disk, information is stored in thin annuli known as **tracks**. Each track, in turn, is divided into a number of smaller storage units known as **sectors**. The tracks and sectors are numbered and the information they receive is determined by the formatting procedure.

It is only necessary to format a floppy disk once: thereafter, it can be used in session after session immediately the machine has been booted up. (Note that formatting a disk again destroys any information that was previously on it.) The user is strongly advised to format a second floppy disk, as a back-up for storage of important files. Even this precaution can fail on occasion, as when a disk drive becomes damaged and destroys any disk inserted in it. Really important files should not be entrusted to floppy disks alone: they should also be stored on a hard disk. Moreover, as an extra precaution, the contents of a hard disk should occasionally be stored on magnetic tape.

2.3.2.2 Inserting a floppy disk into the computer

When inserting a floppy disk into the slit of a disk drive, keep the label uppermost and insert the side with the metal piece first. A floppy disk has a **write-protect notch**. When you can see through the notch, the write-protect mechanism is in operation: fresh information cannot be stored on the disk, and any attempt to do so will result in an error message. Before inserting your first floppy disk, therefore, make sure that its plastic tab has been drawn across, occluding the notch. This disables the write-protect mechanism.

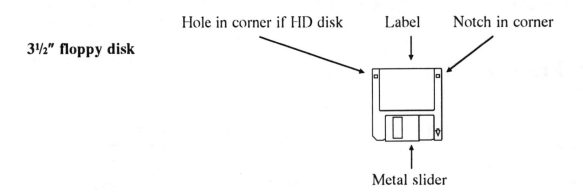

3½″ floppy disk

Hole in corner if HD disk   Label   Notch in corner

Metal slider

2.3.2.3 Formatting floppy disks

Before proceeding, check that a disk has already been inserted into the floppy disk drive.

From the menu bar of the **File Manager** window, choose
Disk

      Format Disk

This will bring to the screen the **Format Disk** dialog box (Figure 3).

A **dialog box** is a special kind of window which requests information from the user, who must then type in values or change the settings indicated. Within the **Format Disk** dialog box are five labelled boxes, three of which are contained within a larger box, labelled **Options**. The small oblong boxes are known as **text boxes**. There are three text boxes in the dialog box, **Disk In, Capacity,** and **Label**. The two small square boxes (**Make System Disk** and **Quick Format**) are **check boxes**. If a check box is clicked on with the mouse, an X shows, indicating that the function is active. The grey rectangles labelled **OK, Cancel,** and **Help** are known as **command push-buttons**, because they tell the Windows File Manager to act immediately. This is true for all Windows programs and applications, including SPSS.

Figure 3.

The Format Disk dialog box

Check that the **Disk In** box contains the label of the correct disk drive (usually **a**), and that the **Capacity** box shows the correct storage capacity (usually 1.44MB). If you are formatting a double-density disk, click on the scrolling arrow to the right of the **Capacity** box and select 720KB by clicking on that value when it appears. You will also be given the option of adding a label (your name, or that of the application). Click on the **OK** button to start the formatting procedure. Thereafter, all is plain sailing, with the system giving continuous information on the stage the formatting process has reached. When the formatting of the first floppy disk is complete, accept the offer to format another disk and repeat the process. When the second disk has been formatted, opt for **N** to terminate the process.

2.3.2.4 Copying files to and from a floppy disk

Copying files from a floppy disk to a hard disk or vice versa is a very simple operation in Windows. In the **File Manager** window, underneath the title bar, is another bar containing icons representing various disk drives: **a, b** and so on. Notice that in Figure 2 the icon for drive **c** has a box around it showing that it is the one presently selected and hence all the files on the right-hand side are files on the disk drive **c**. To copy one of these files on to a floppy disk in drive **a**, click-and-drag the file's icon to the drive icon **a**, and release the button.

To copy a file from a floppy disk in drive **a** to the hard disk **c**, it is necessary first to click on the disk drive icon **a** in order to get the filename icons listed on the right-hand side of the window. Then select the source file icon and drag it on to the disk drive icon **c**.

To copy a file from one floppy disk to another, place the source disk in drive **a**. In the **File Manager** window, click on the disk drive icon **a** to obtain the icons of the files on the disk. Click and drag the file's icon to the disk drive icon labelled **c**. This operation will duplicate the source file on the computer's hard disk, leaving the original on the source floppy disk. Now place the target floppy disk in drive **a**, click on the disk drive icon **c** to obtain the icons of the **c** disk files, and then click-and-drag the copy in **c** to the disk drive icon labelled **a**. This will transfer the file to the target disk.

An alternative method of copying a file is to select the file icon (eg **bank.sav**) of the file to be copied and then click on **Copy** within the **File** menu to open the **Copy** dialog box (Figure 4). The two small circles, one of which is marked, are known as **radio buttons**, and arise in situations where only one choice can be made from a list of items. In this case, we are given the choice between copying a file to a disk or placing it in a temporary store known as the **Clipboard**. Assuming that we want a permanent copy of the file, at a specified destination, the upper of the two buttons in Figure 4 is the one that should be marked. Enter the destination of the copied file in the **To** box and then click on **OK**.

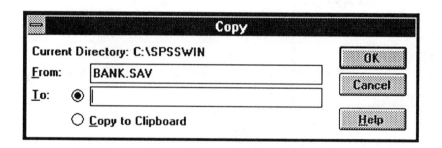

Figure 4.

The Copy dialog box

It should be noted that, when backing up an SPSS file, the foregoing procedures are unnecessary, because the user can save the file directly from SPSS to a floppy disk and repeat the procedure with a second disk.

2.3.2.5 Deleting a file

Select the file icon of the file to be deleted (eg **bank.sav**) and then click on **Delete** in the **File** menu to open the **Delete** dialog box (Figure 5). Click on **OK** if the file name is correct: you will be asked to confirm the delete decision in a subsequent box.

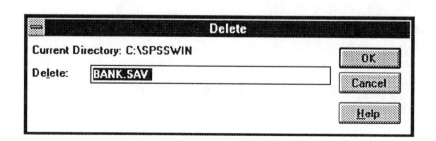

Figure 5.

The Delete dialog box

2.3.2.6 Copying the contents of an entire disk

If you want to copy the entire contents of a **source disk** into a **destination disk**, choose
Disk
     Copy Disk

This will open the **Confirm Copy Disk** dialog box, which will remind the user that the copying process will erase all data previously stored on the **destination** disk. To proceed, click on the **Yes** box. Then comes an instruction to insert the **source disk** (the disk that is being copied). Do so and click on **OK**. The copying process will then proceed, its progress being shown in an information box on the screen. Presently, the user will be prompted to insert the **destination** disk. Do so and click on **OK**. When the process has been completed, the **File Manager** window will be restored.

2.4 SUMMARY

1)   The first window to appear is the **Program Manager**, which contains the window of the **Main** group of **Applications**. A window can be opened by double-clicking on its icon. A window can be closed by double-clicking on its **Control-menu** box.

2)   A window can be **re-sized** by **clicking-and-dragging** on a border or corner, **maximised** by pressing the **Maximise** button and **reduced to an icon** by pressing the **Minimise** button. It can be **restored** by double-clicking on its icon. It can be **moved** by clicking-and-dragging on its title bar. Its size can be fine-tuned by clicking-and-dragging either on an edge (to widen or deepen it) or a corner (to do both). Often a complete list of items cannot be seen through a window, in which case **scroll bars** can be used to reposition the window.

3)   New floppy disks must be **formatted** by entering the **File Manager**, and choosing
Disk
    Format

    In the **Disk** menu is a command for **copying an entire disk** to a specified destination.

4)   The **File** menu includes **Copy** for copying a file and **Delete** for deleting a file. A file can also be copied by dragging a file icon on to a disk drive icon.

CHAPTER 3

INPUTTING AND EDITING DATA

3.1 INTRODUCTION

In this chapter, the operation of SPSS for Windows (hereafter, SPSS) will be illustrated by considering the first stages in the processing of the results of a simple psychological experiment.

In Section 3.2, a number of research terms are introduced. Since these translate readily into procedures for data analysis with SPSS, they serve as a useful conceptual interface between methodology and data analysis. While there can be no question that the availability of a package with the versatility and power of SPSS is of great assistance to the researcher, there are, nevertheless, a number of cautions and caveats that should be borne in mind. These are the substance of Section 3.3.

Section 3.4 shows how the results of a simple psychological experiment are recast into a form suitable for entry into SPSS. In Section 3.5, the inputting of data into SPSS is described and some of the capabilities of SPSS's Data Editor are explored. It will be seen that some of the editing functions in SPSS can be very useful for inputting certain kinds of data, as when an item (such as a code number or a string) must be repeated many times.

The saving and retrieval of a data set are described in Section 3.6. The procedure for calculating the means and standard deviations for the groups within the data set is illustrated in Section 3.7. The printing of SPSS items such as data, numerical output, plots, and charts is described in Section 3.8.

Finally, in Section 3.9, two special topics are considered:

(1)   the selection (or exclusion) of certain cases for statistical analysis;

(2)   the weighting of cases according to their frequencies.

3.2 SOME RESEARCH TERMS

3.2.1 Variables

Much research concerns supposed relationships among **variables**. A **variable** is a characteristic, or property, of a person, an object or a situation, which comprises a set of different values or categories. **Quantitative variables**, such as height, weight or extraversion, are possessed **in degree**; **qualitative** variables, such as sex, blood group or nationality, are possessed **in kind**. While one person can be taller, heavier or more extraverted than another, it makes no sense to say that a Chinese person has more (or less) of the attribute of nationality than, say, an American.

3.2.2 Hypotheses

A **hypothesis** is usually a provisional supposition that one variable, known as the **independent variable**, has a causal effect upon another, the **dependent variable**. It may be hypothesised, for example, that children's pre-school knowledge of phonology (the independent variable) affects their reading proficiency at a later stage (the dependent variable).

3.3 DATA ANALYSIS WITH A STATISTICAL COMPUTING PACKAGE: SOME CAUTIONS AND CAVEATS

At this point, it may be well to amplify some earlier statements. The availability of powerful computing packages such as SPSS has made it a simple matter to subject a data set to all manner of statistical analyses and tests of significance. To proceed immediately to such formal analysis, however, is a decidedly risky practice.

3.3.1 Transcription errors

In the first place, it is only too easy, particularly with a large data set, to make serious errors in transcribing the results of a study into a computer. Great care, therefore, is necessary at the stage of data entry. Fortunately, there are several precautions that can be taken to minimise the chances of transcription error. For example, the system can be alerted to the input of impossible values, such as a negative reaction time or an IQ of 1000.

3.3.2 The influence of outliers and asymmetrical distributions

But there are other, equally important, reasons for a thorough preliminary examination of the data set. Statistics such as the mean and standard deviation are intended to express, in a single number, some characteristic of the data set as a whole: the former is intended to express the **average**, that is, the general level, typical value, or **central tendency**, of a set of scores; the latter is a measure of their **spread**, or **dispersion**. There are circumstances, however, in which the mean and standard deviation are very poor measures of central tendency and dispersion, respectively, as when the distribution of scores is markedly skewed, or when extreme values, or **outliers**, exert undue **leverage** upon the values of these statistics.

3.3.3 Formal tests, statistical models and their assumptions

There is yet another potential problem. The ease of access to formal tests of significance that a modern computing package confers upon the user belies the risk involved in applying such tests before the properties of a data set (even one that has been entered without transcription error) have been fully investigated. The making of a formal statistical test of significance always presupposes the applicability of a statistical **model**, that is, an interpretation (usually in the form of an equation) of the data set as having been generated in a certain manner. The model underlying the one-sample t-test, for example, assumes that the data are from a normal population. To some extent, statistical tests have been shown to be robust to moderate violations of the models upon which they are predicated. But there are limits to this robustness, and there are circumstances in which a result, declared by an incautious user to be significant beyond, say, the 0.05 level, may actually have been much more probable under the null hypothesis than the given tail probability would indicate. There is no way of avoiding this pitfall, other than by thoroughly exploring the data first to ascertain their suitability for specified formal tests.

Several years ago, Tukey (1977) wrote a famous book on the description and depiction of data sets by means of a set of techniques known collectively as **exploratory data analysis (EDA)**. These useful methods have now found their way into all good modern computing packages.

The use of EDA in SPSS will be considered at a later point.

3.4 A SIMPLE EXPERIMENT

In this section, the results of a simple experiment are recast in a form suitable for entry as a data set into SPSS.

3.4.1 The experimental design

In an experiment on the relative efficacy of two mnemonic methods for the recall of verbal material, each individual in a pool of 30 participants is randomly assigned to one of three equal-sized groups:

(1)   A **control** group, which receives no training.
(2)   A group trained to use the **Galton's Walk** method (**Mnemonic A**).
(3)   A group trained to use the **Peg** method (**Mnemonic B**).

Each participant is presented with verbal material and asked (at a later stage) to reproduce it in free written recall. The dependent variable is the number of words recalled.

3.4.2 The results

The results of the experiment are shown in Table 1.

Table 1.
The numbers of words recalled by subjects with different mnemonic training histories

Control Group	3	5	3	2	4	6	9	3	8	10
Mnemonic A	10	8	15	9	11	16	17	15	7	10
Mnemonic B	29	15	14	15	17	10	8	11	18	19

3.4.3 Laying out the data in a form suitable for entry into SPSS

The layout of the data in Table 1 is unsuitable for input to SPSS. The application expects to receive values in the form of a rectangular array, or **matrix**, whose columns represent variables and whose rows represent subjects: **no row should contain data on more than one**

subject. Clearly, this is not the case with the arrangement in Table 1, where each row contains the data from ten different subjects.

In this experiment, the dependent variable (amount recalled) is **quantitative**. The independent variable (group membership, or the condition under which each subject was tested), however, is **qualitative**, since it comprises three categories. Each category, nevertheless, can be identified by assigning to it an arbitrary code number: for example, the code numbers *1*, *2* and *3* could be assigned to the Control, Mnemonic A, and Mnemonic B conditions, respectively. These values are entirely arbitrary: any three numbers will do, as long as they are different, because the numbers are to function as **labels**, rather than expressing the degree to which some property is possessed. The entire set of code numbers indicating the experimental conditions under which scores were obtained is known as a **grouping variable**. In an SPSS data sheet, each column must contain the values of one (and only one) variable: in the present case, the first column could contain the independent (grouping) variable, that is, the code numbers (*1*, *2* or *3*) that identify the condition under which each subject performed; the second column could contain the scores that all the subjects achieved in the experiment. In Table 2, the results in Table 1 have been recast, so that each row now contains two data per subject:

    (1)   A code number showing the group to which that person was assigned.

    (2)   The score that person achieved under the coded condition.

Table 2.

The data of Table 1, recast in a form suitable for entry into SPSS

(Note that the bracketed items have been included here for explanation only: they are not actually entered into SPSS. Only the values in the columns headed Group and Score are entered.)

	Group	Score	
(Subject 1)	1	3	
(Subject 2)	1	5	
.	.	.	(Group 1: The controls)
.	.	.	
(Subject 9)	1	8	
(Subject 10)	1	10	
(Subject 11)	2	10	
(Subject 12)	2	8	
.	.	.	(Group 2: Mnemonic A)
.	.	.	
(Subject 19)	2	7	
(Subject 20)	2	10	
(Subject 21)	3	20	
(Subject 22)	3	15	
.	.	.	(Group 3: Mnemonic B)
.	.	.	
(Subject 29)	3	18	
(Subject 30)	3	19	

3.5 INPUTTING AND EDITING THE DATA SET

3.5.1 Obtaining the Data Editor Window

In Chapter 2, we saw that when Windows is accessed, the first window to appear is the **Program Manager**, which itself contains several other open windows. Among these is a window labelled **SPSS**. This is the window of the **SPSS program group**. The SPSS icon depicts a coloured cube. Double-click on this icon to obtain three overlapping windows:

     (1)   The **SPSS application window** (captioned **SPSS for Windows**).

     (2)   The **Output window** (captioned **!output1**).

     (3)   The **Data Editor window** (captioned **Newdata**).

As the **Data Editor** window was forming on the screen, the reader may have noticed the appearance of the hour-glass, which always appears when 'something is happening', and also various messages in the bar that runs horizontally across the base of the SPSS Application window. The final message to appear there is: 'SPSS Processor is ready'. This bar is known as the **status bar**. Like the hour-glass, the status bar apprises the user of the stage of operations: for example, if a large data set is being read from a file, progress is continually monitored, case by case, in the status bar. This **case counter** is one of several useful types of message that appear in different parts of the status bar: there are also messages about the weighting of cases (**weight status**), the selection of specified portions of the data set (**filter status**) and whether the data set has been split into several separate groups for analysis (**split file status**).

The **Data Editor** window is shown in Figure 1.

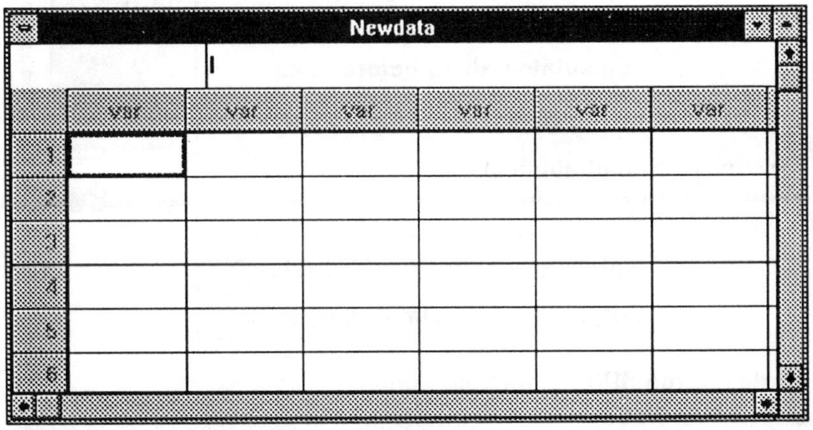

Figure 1.
The Data Editor window

Notice that in both the **Data Editor** and the **SPSS Application** windows, the title bars are coloured on the screen; whereas that in the **Output** window is grey. This indicates that, of the three windows, only the first two (in order of mention) are presently **active**, that is, the items therein can be accessed directly by clicking within the appropriate areas.

The **Data Editor** window is a grid, whose rows represent subjects (or **cases**) and whose columns will contain values of the variables whose labels will eventually appear at the tops of the columns. In such a grid, the intersection of a row and a column is known as a **cell**. Each cell of the grid, therefore, will usually contain the score of one particular subject on one particular variable. Initially, every column in the **Data Editor** window has the heading **var**, and all the cells are empty.

3.5.2 To how many decimal places should values be displayed? The Preferences dialog box

Since we are about to enter numbers into the **Data Editor**, we need to consider the form in which those values will be displayed in the grid. A convenient procedure is to specify a standard, or **default**, format for all values, which can then be over-ridden (if necessary) by subsequent choices of format for specified variables only.

In the menu bar of the **SPSS application** window are the headings of nine drop-down menus: **File, Edit, Data, Transform, Statistics, Graphs, Utilities, Window** and **Help**.

Choose
Edit
      Preferences

to obtain the **Preferences** dialog box (Figure 2).

Figure 2. The Preferences dialog box

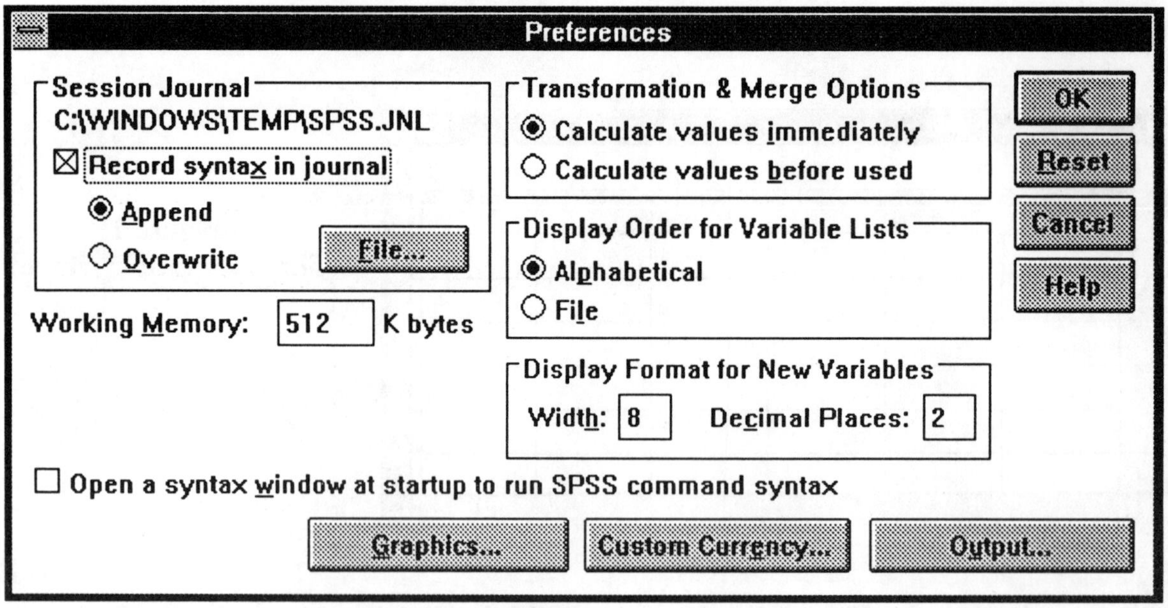

Within the **Display Format for New Variables** box are two text boxes, labelled **Width** and **Decimal Places**, in each of which a number is already entered. If those numbers are *8* and *2*, respectively, a total of eight spaces will be allocated to each value and all values will be displayed to two places of decimals, even if they are integers (ie *3* will appear as 3.00).

All the data in Table 2, however, are integers, so there is no need for values to be written as decimals at all. Click on the **Decimal Places** box, press [←] to erase the number and type in a zero. The effect of this change will be to show all values as integers, and the data display will be much easier to read. Leave the **Preferences** dialog box by clicking on **OK**. Note that the default preferences for your system may be different from those shown: Windows is a very flexible system which can be set up in many different ways.

3.5.3 Variable names and value labels

Having recast the results in Table 1 into the form shown in Table 2, we are now almost ready to begin entering the data into SPSS. Before doing that, however, we must first assign sensible names to our variables and (for the grouping variable) explanatory labels to the values. In Table 2, the first column contains the code numbers of the grouping variable, and the second contains the scores of the subjects tested under the conditions codified in the first column. We shall name the first and second columns *group* and *score,* respectively.

3.5.3.1 A notational convention

In this book, we shall use a **bold** typeface for the names of menus, the names of dialog boxes and the items therein. For variable names and values, *italics* will be used. Emboldening will also be used for emphasis and for technical terms.

3.5.3.2 Rules for assigning variable names

The choice of names for variables is governed by a set of six rules: A variable name...

(1)   must not exceed **eight characters**. (A **character** is a letter, a digit or a symbol.)
(2)   must **begin with a letter.**
(3)   must **not end with a full stop.**
(4)   **can** contain letters, digits or any of the characters @, #, _, or $.
(5)   must **not** contain any of the following:
    (i)   A blank.
    (ii)   Special characters, such as !, ?, and *, other than those listed in (4).
(6)   must **not be** one of the keywords (such as AND, NOT, EQ, BY and ALL) that SPSS uses as special computing terms.

The names we have chosen, *group* and *score,* clearly meet the requirements of all the above rules. Note, however, that while the name *group1* would also have been satisfactory, *group 1* would not, because it contains a space, violating rule 5. Watch out for length too (rule 1): *red_cube* is satisfactory; but *red_cubes* is not, because the total number of characters (including the underline symbol) exceeds the permitted limit of 8.

3.5.3.3 Assigning the chosen variable names

To assign the variable name *group* to the first column in the grid, proceed as follows:

Double-click on the grey area at the top of the first column. This will obtain the **Define Variable** dialog box (Figure 3). **The Variable Name** text box contains a default variable name, *var00001*. The **Variable Description** box contains the information that the **Type** (of variable) is **Numeric8.0**. These are the default specifications that were set in **Preferences** (see Section 3.5.2).

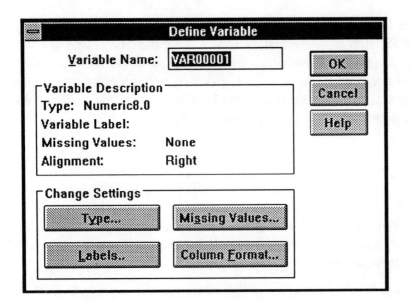

Figure 3.
The Define Variable dialog box

Notice that the **Change Settings** box contains four **subdialog command buttons: Type, Labels, Missing Values** and **Column Format**. These permit the user to make specifications that apply only to one particular variable. For example, although the variable type has been set at **Numeric8.0**, clicking on **Type** will bring to the screen the **Define Variable Type** dialog box (Figure 4).

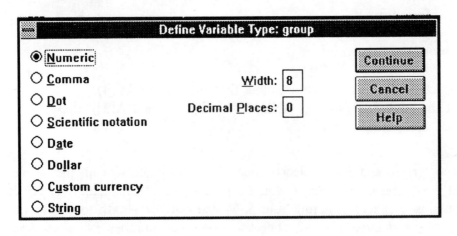

Figure 4.
The Define Variable
Type dialog box

By inserting new values in the **Width** and **Decimal places** text boxes, the user can alter the display format for the present variable only: the other variables will continue to have the default specifications **Numeric8.0** unless further amendments are made on an individual basis. Click on **Continue** to return to the **Define Variable** dialog box.

Within the **Define Variable** dialog box is the **Variable Name** text box: type *group* into it. There is no need to remove the default variable name (*var00001*) first: that will be overwritten when the chosen name is typed in. The chosen name, *group,* although reminding the reader that this is a grouping variable, conveys no further information. A longer, more meaningful, label is required. To assign one, click on the **Labels** subdialog button to obtain the **Define Labels** dialog box (Figure 5).

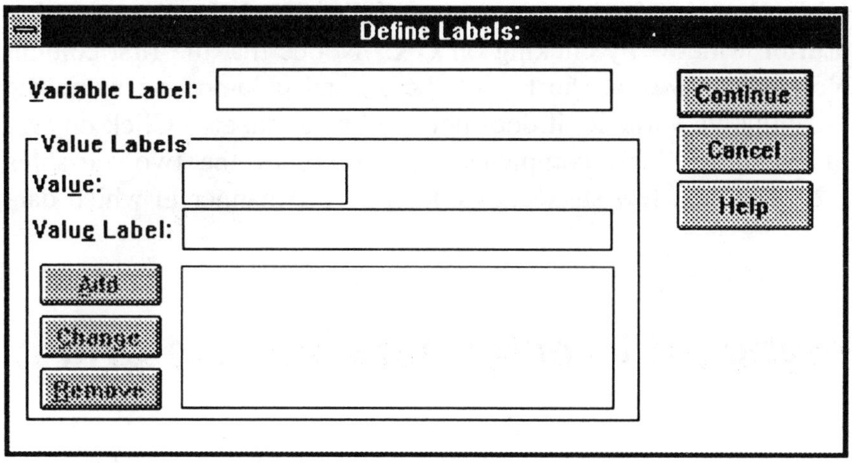

Figure 5.
The Define Labels dialog box

The **Variable Label** text box gives the user the opportunity to supply a fuller label for the grouping variable. This will make the statistical output easier to interpret. Type in an informative name such as *Mnemonic Training History.*

The rules governing the naming of variables (Section 3.5.3.2) do not apply to the assignment of labels in the **Define Labels** dialog box. Here, the name can be anything up to 120 characters in length and (as in *Mnemonic Training History)* can include spaces. Moreover, unlike the naming of variables, assigned variable labels are case sensitive and displayed exactly as they are entered. It should be borne in mind, however, that should a name with the maximum of 120 characters be chosen, fewer characters will actually be displayed in the output (though the precise number varies in different procedures).

3.5.3.4 Assigning value labels

With a grouping variable comprising a set of arbitrary code numbers, it is useful to assign **value labels** showing what these numbers represent.

With the **Define Labels** dialog box (Figure 5) on the screen, type the lowest code number *1* into the **Value** text box. In the **Value Label** text box, type *Control.* This will embolden the **Add** button below. When **Add** is clicked, the following will appear in the lowest box:
      1 = "Control".

In a similar manner, proceed to label the values *2* and *3,* so that in the lowest box can be seen:

    1 = "Control"
    2 = "Mnemonic A"
    3 = "Mnemonic B"

Value labelling, like variable labelling, is governed by much looser constraints than is variable naming. A value label can be up to 60 characters in length, is case sensitive and can contain spaces. As with variable labels, however, fewer than the maximum of 60 characters (usually only about 20) will actually be displayed in the output. Now that all three values of the grouping variable have been labelled, click on **Continue.**

We are now back in the **Define Variable** dialog box again (Figure 3). This time, however, it will be found that the **Variable Description** box contains a fuller label for the grouping variable. Return to the **Data Editor** window by clicking on **OK.** Notice that the first column is now headed *group.* Double click on **var** at the top of the second column and name the variable *score.* As *score* is a quantitative variable, it does not need value labels. Click on **OK** to return to the **Data Editor** window. This completes the naming of the two variables required for the data in Table 2. The next few subsections describe the manner in which data are entered into SPSS.

3.5.4 Using the keyboard to enter data into the grid

In the **Data Editor** window (Figure 1), just underneath the title bar, is a white bar. This is the **cell editor.** In the grid beneath can be seen a black rectangle, the **cell highlight,** formed by the thickened borders of one of the cells. (When the **Data Editor** is first accessed, the highlight will be located at the top cell of the leftmost column.)

In the cell editor, on the left, is an entry showing the current location of the cell highlight: for example, the entry **2:group** locates the highlight at the cell in the *second* row of the column headed *group.* A value typed in from the keyboard will appear in the cell editor. If a cursor key (or ↵) is pressed, this value is transferred to the highlighted cell.

The subsequent location of the highlight depends upon which key is pressed: if the ↑ or ↓ cursor key is pressed, the new location is a cell above or below the original position; if the ← or → cursor key is pressed, the highlight moves to the left or the right, respectively. The position of the cell highlight can also be controlled by using the mouse. Clicking on any cell will highlight it and its row and column coordinates will appear in the cell editor.

3.5.5 Editing

The **Data Editor** offers a range of functions, some of which are extremely useful not only for amending data that are already in the grid but also for inputting data values that are repeated many times.

3.5.5.1 Changing isolated values in the grid

Enter a few numbers in the grid. Any of these can be changed at will by targeting the cell concerned with the black rectangle, typing a new value and pressing a cursor key or ↵.

3.5.5.2 More complex editing: blocking, copying and pasting

Initially, only one cell in the grid is highlighted. It is possible, however, to highlight a whole block of cells. This **blocking** operation is achieved very simply, either by clicking-and-dragging with the mouse or by proceeding as follows:

Press and hold [⇧] and press the ↓ cursor a few (say four) times. It will be seen that five cells are now highlighted: the original cell and four new ones below, whose entries now appear in **inverse video** (that is, in white against a black background).

The blocking operation can be used to copy, say, the values in one column into another column. Highlight a column of values that you wish to copy. Now, choose
Edit
> **Copy**

Next, highlight the cells of the target column and choose
Edit
> **Paste**

The values in the source column will now appear in the target column.

3.5.5.3 Making multiple copies

The block-and-paste technique can be used to make repeated entries of the same value into **as many of the other grid cells as required.** Enter a value (say *100*) into a cell in the grid. Choose
Edit
> **Copy**

Now highlight a column of cells underneath the original value and choose
Edit
> **Paste**

This will enter the original value (*100*) into all the other highlighted cells. This operation is very useful when entering multiple copies of code numbers or strings (see below) into the grid.

3.5.5.4 Deletion of values from the grid

To delete the values in a cell (or block), highlight the area concerned and press [⇧]/ **[Delete]**.

To delete a whole row of values, click on the grey box containing the row number (see Figure 1). This will highlight every cell in the row. Pressing **[Delete]** will remove the whole row from the grid. (Press firmly and look for the hour-glass screen pointer: this means that the **Delete** procedure has been successfully activated.) Similarly, clicking the grey box containing the name of a column will highlight all the cells in the column, and pressing **[Delete]** will remove the entire column of values from the grid.

3.5.6 Entering the data of Table 2 into the grid

When inputting the data of Table 2 into the grid, good use can be made of the editing operations described in Section 3.5.5. To enter the first (unbracketed) column of values of Table 2 into the grid, place the value *1* in the first (topmost) cell of the first column *group*. Choose

Edit

> **Copy**

Using the [⇧] and downward cursor keys, highlight the first 10 cells in the first column. It will be found that on choosing

Edit

> **Paste**

the value *1* will appear in each of the highlighted cells. Target the 11th cell in the first column and enter the value *2* in that cell. Proceed as above to enter the value *2* in all of the cells from 11 to 20, inclusive. In similar fashion, enter the value *3* in each of the cells from 21 to 30, inclusive.

The values in the second column (*score*) of Table 2 are entered as described in Section 3.5.4, since each cell contains a different value.

3.5.7 Entering string variables into the data grid

A **string** is a sequence of characters (digits, letters, symbols, blanks) which is treated as a unit by the system. A **string variable** is a qualitative variable whose categories (or **values**) are entered into the grid as strings, rather than arbitrary code numbers, as in a grouping variable. Thus a string can be simple words such as *French* or people's names such as *Abraham Lincoln*.

A **short string variable** has string values of up to eight characters in length; a **long string variable** has values exceeding eight characters in length. The distinction is important, because some SPSS procedures only work with short string variables.

Suppose we want to record the names of all the subjects taking part in the learning experiment and that the longest name does not exceed 20 characters in length. In the **Data Editor** (Figure 1), double-click on the grey area at the top of the third column to obtain the **Define Variable** dialog box (Figure 3). In the **Variable Name** text box, type the name of the string variable *name*. Notice, however, that in the **Variable Description** box is the entry **Type: Numeric8.0**. In fact, until it receives information to the contrary, SPSS for Windows always assumes that variables will be of the numeric type.

To specify a string variable, click on **Type**, to obtain the **Define Variable Type** dialog box (Figure 4). In the box is a list of eight variable types, each with a radio button. SPSS initially marks the **Numeric** button. Click on the **String** button at the foot of the list. The **Decimal Places** text box immediately disappears, leaving only the **Width** box, with the value *8* that was set in **Preferences**. Delete *8* in the **Width** box and type in *20*. Click on **Continue** and then on **OK**. The variable *name* will now appear at the head of the third column, which is now much wider than before. The names of the subjects can now be typed into each row of this column.

3.5.8 The treatment of missing values

When the user enters a value into a previously empty grid, a default variable name (such as *var00001*) will appear at the head of the column concerned. Enter, say, five such values into the first column of the grid. Now enter a single value into the first cell of the second column. You will see that a period (.) appears in each of the four cells beneath. In SPSS, there are no empty cells within the data file, which is assumed to be rectangular. If no value has been entered, the system supplies the **system-missing** value, which is indicated in the data grid by a full stop. SPSS will exclude system-missing values from its calculations of means, standard deviations and other statistics.

It may be, however, that the user wishes SPSS to treat, for some purposes, certain responses actually present in the data set as missing. For example, suppose that, in a survey of political opinion, five categories are used (A, B, C, D & E), but category E was recorded when the person refused to answer and D was a category that indicated a failure to understand the question. The user wants SPSS to treat responses in both categories as missing, but retain information about the relative frequencies of such responses in categories D and E in output listings. In SPSS terminology, the user wants certain responses to be treated as **user-missing** values.

To define user-missing values, obtain the **Define Variable** dialog box and click on **Missing Values**. This will obtain the **Define Missing Values** dialog box (Figure 6).

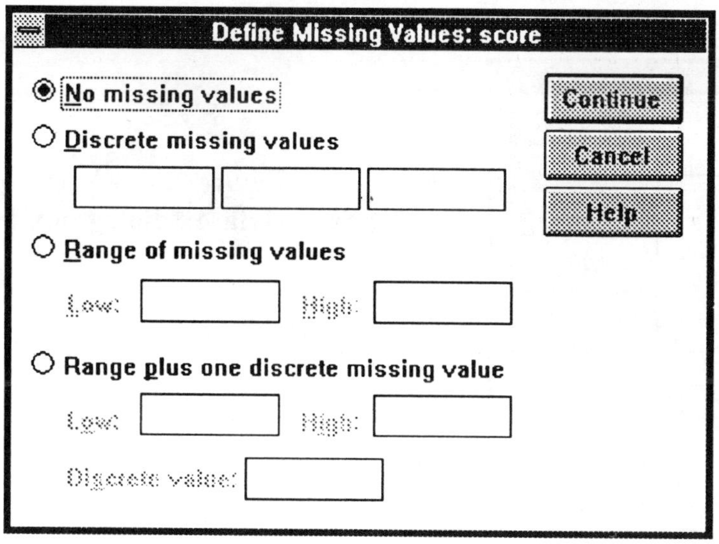

Figure 6.
The Define Missing Values dialog box

Initially, the **No missing values** radio button is marked. The three text boxes underneath give the user the opportunity to specify up to three **Discrete Missing Values**, referred to in SPSS as *missing (1)*, *missing (2)*, and *missing (3)*. These may either be numerical, as with a grouping variable, or short string variables. The other options in the dialog box are for quantitative variables: the user may define a missing value as one falling within a specified range, or one that falls either within a specified range or within a specified category.

In analysing a set of exam results, for instance, the user might wish SPSS to treat as missing:

     (1)   Any marks between, say, 0 and 20.

     (2)   Cases where the candidate walked out without giving any written response. (A walk-out could be coded as an arbitrary, but salient, number, such as -9: the negative sign helps it stand out).

This coding can be achieved by clicking on the **Range plus one discrete missing value** button, entering the values *0* and *20* into the **Low** and **High** boxes, respectively, and *-9* into the **Discrete value** box. Click on **Continue** to return to the **Define Variable** dialog box.

3.6 SAVING THE DATA SET

3.6.1 Saving a set of data which has just been typed into the grid

Having gone to considerable trouble to enter the data into the Data Editor, the user will wish to save them in a form that can be called up instantly at the next session, rather than having to type in all the values again. To save the data to a file, proceed as follows. In the **SPSS application** window, choose

File

     Save As

This obtains the **Save Data As** dialog box (Figure 7)

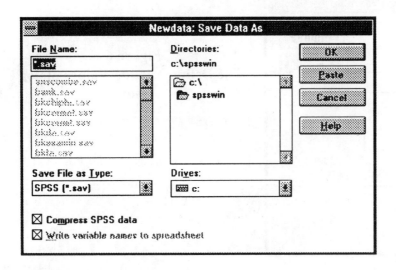

Figure 7.
The Save Data As dialog box

In the **File Name** text box, is * with the extension **.sav**, reminding the user that data files are saved with the extension **.sav**. Notice also that, in the **Save File as Type** text box, is already entered **SPSS{*.sav}**. This is the format used by SPSS. The user can type into the **File Name:** box any name with the extension **.sav** and it will be saved as a file of the type displayed in the **Save File as Type** box. (Note, however, that the file name assigned must conform to the rules for naming variables (Section 3.5.3.2).) In the present example, a suitable file name would be **firstset.sav**. The faint names in the box beneath the **File Name:** box are the names of data files already saved.

Notice that under the caption **Directories:** is the entry **c:\spsswin**. We have seen that a directory can be thought of as a folder containing documents (files). The entry **c:\spsswin** means that, unless instructed otherwise, SPSS will save the data to the file **firstset.sav**, located on the PC's hard disk (drive **c**) in the directory **spsswin**. The path name for the file will be **c:\spsswin\firstset.sav**. The saving is effected by pressing **OK**. {In some network configurations, this may be disallowed because the **spsswin** directory is 'read only'.}

Generally it is better to avoid placing files in program directories: if files are to be saved to the same hard disk as the program directory, create another directory for this purpose, such as **data**, by choosing in the **Windows File Manager**
File
>   **Create Directory**

The path name would be **c:\data\firstset.sav**.

It is often better to save to a floppy disk, especially when using a computer in a network. In that case, the entry in the **Drives** box (Figure 7, bottom right) must be changed to **a**, by scrolling the arrow in the grey area to the right, and selecting **a**. Clicking on **OK** will now save the file **firstset.sav** to the disk in drive **a**.

3.6.2 Reading data into the grid from storage in a file

Suppose that, prior to ending a Windows session, the user has saved the data in the grid to a file named **firstset.sav** on floppy disk **a**. Later, the data can be restored to the Data Editor window by proceeding as follows:

Choose
File
>   **Open**
>   **Data**

This will produce the **Open Data File** dialog box (Figure 8).

In appearance, this box is very similar to the **Save Data As** box. There are the same **File Name**, **File Type** and **Drives** boxes, and the directory is specified as **c:\spsswin**.

If the data set has been saved to the file **a:\firstset.sav**, drive **a** (not drive **c**, as shown in the dialog box) must be specified by clicking on the grey area to the right of the **Drives** text box. The **File Type** specification should already be correct (SPSS{*.sav}), so that to enter the correct name in the **File Name** text box, it should only be necessary to type in ***.sav** to obtain a list of all files with the extension **.sav** on the floppy disk in drive **a**. Place the file name into the **File Name** text box by highlighting the appropriate filename in the list.

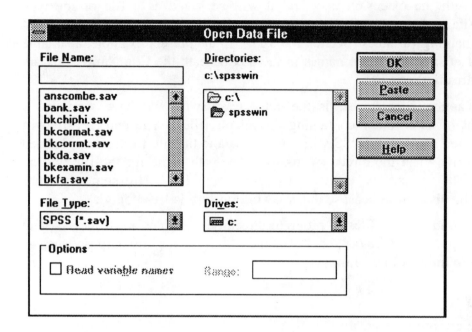

Figure 8.
The Open Data File
dialog box

Click on **OK** to restore the **Data Editor** window (Figure 1), which will now contain the data in its cells. While data are being read into the Data Editor from a file, the hour-glass will appear and messages will appear in the Status Bar at various stages in the operation. The message **'SPSS Processor is ready'** signals the end of the procedure.

3.6.3 Transferring an SPSS/PC+ data set to SPSS for Windows

Users who already have data command files existing within the DOS environment of SPSS/PC+ may wish to transfer them to the Windows environment in order to gain more convenient access to graphics and to Windows cross-linking facilities. This is easily done in the following steps:

1)   Within SPSS/PC+, execute the usual data commands (DATA LIST, VARIABLE LABELS and so on, to which has been added a new command, such as

SAVE OUTFILE **'a:mydata.sys'.**

which creates a **system file** (see ***Kinnear & Gray: SPSS/PC+ Made Simple, 1992***, section 2.7.1). Notice carefully the obligatory extension **.sys** to the filename and the period concluding the command.

2)   Within SPSS for Windows, choose
Data
   Open
    Data
to open the **Open Data File** dialog box (Figure 8).
Within the **File Type** box, click on the arrow to its right to open the choice of file types. Select **SPSS/PC+ [*.sys]**. Select also drive **a** within the **Drives** box. The dialog box will now appear as in Figure 9.

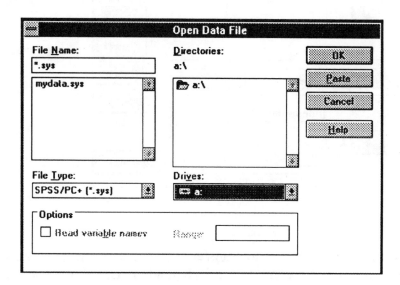

Figure 9.
The Open Data File dialog box after selecting SPSS/PC+ [*.sys] file type and a: drive

3)   Click on the file name (eg **mydata.sys**) and then on **OK** to load it into SPSS for Windows. The **Data Editor** window will then appear and after a few moments will show the variable names and data as previously specified in SPSS/PC+. Any extended variable labels, value labels and missing values information will also be transferred.

4)   Save the data set in the usual manner to a **.sav** file.

Note that SPSS is able to read files of different formats as the list of file types shows. Use the Help system to find out more about the method of doing this.

3.7   OBTAINING A LISTING OF MEANS AND STANDARD DEVIATIONS

Now that the data have been entered into the Data Editor and saved safely to a file, it is time to calculate some statistics. A full treatment of the description and exploration of a data set is given in Chapter 4; at this point, however, we shall content ourselves with finding the means and standard deviations of the scores in the three treatment groups.

Choose
Statistics
    Compare Means

and then click on **Means** to obtain the **Means** dialog box (Figure 10).

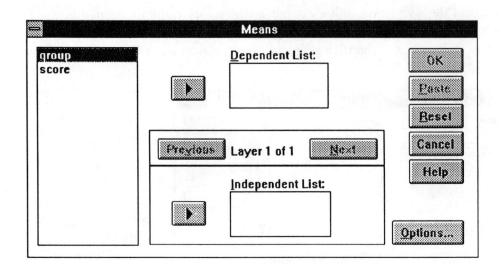

**Figure 10.
The Means dialog
box**

Click on the variable name *score* and > to transfer that name to the **Dependent List** box. Click on *group* and > to transfer that name to the **Independent List** box. The dialog box will now appear as in Figure 11.

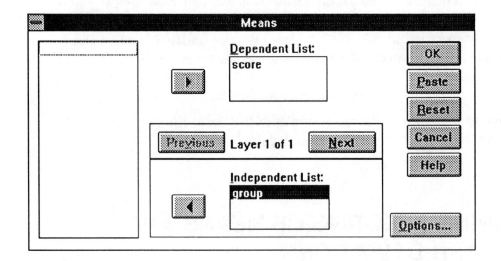

**Figure 11.
The completed
Means dialog box**

Click on **OK** to run the procedure. A table of means, standard deviations and numbers of cases (Output Listing 1) will be produced in the **Output** window.

Detailed instructions on the printing of the data set and output listing will be given in the next section.

Output Listing 1. The Means and Standard Deviations

```
        - - Description of Subpopulations - -

Summaries of     SCORE      Number of Words Recalled
By levels of     GROUP      Mnemonic Training History


Variable       Value  Label               Mean    Std Dev   Cases

For Entire Population                    10.6000   5.2431      30

GROUP            1    Control             5.3000   2.8304      10
GROUP            2    Mnemonic A         11.8000   3.6148      10
GROUP            3    Mnemonic B         14.7000   4.0014      10

    Total Cases = 30
```

3.8 PRINTING IN SPSS

It is always reassuring to have in one's possession a hard copy of important computer output. For example, after a series of complicated editing operations, the user may wish to print out the contents of the Data Editor to have a permanent record of the perfected data set.

It may be necessary to check that a suitable printer is connected to the computer (or to the network) by inspecting the information within the **Printer Setup** item in the **File** drop-down menu. Local advice may be required.

When the **Print** item in the **File** drop-down menu is selected, the **Print** dialog box will appear. Bear in mind that only the contents of the **active** window will be printed: thus if the data set is to be printed out, the **Data Editor** window must be active (a window is activated by clicking anywhere on it or by selecting the appropriate window name from the list of windows at the foot of the **Windows** drop-down menu). Similarly, if it is the output listing that is to be printed, the **Output** window must be active. Charts and graphs are in the **Chart Carousel** window.

3.8.1 Printing out the entire data set

To print out the entire contents of the Data Editor, ensure that the **Data Editor** window is active as described above and choose
File
> **Print...**

This obtains the **Print** dialog box, which has the caption **a:\firstset.sav** in its title bar (see Figure 12).

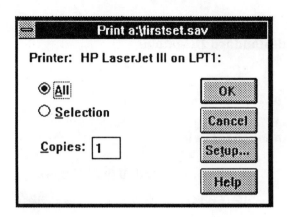

Figure 12.
The Print dialog box

If the **All** button is marked, the entire data set will be printed out. (If the **Selection** button is marked, only a selected part of the data set will be printed out - see below.) The user can also amend the entry in the **Copies** text box to obtain multiple hard copies.

Click on **OK** to start the printing (which may take some time).

3.8.2 Printing out a selection from the data set

To print out only selected parts of the data set, use the click-and-drag method to define the target sections by blackening them. This requires a little practice: it will be found that when the mouse arrow touches the lower border of the window, the latter will scroll down to extend the blackened area to the desired extent.

When the **Print** dialog box (Figure 12) appears, the marker will now be on **Selection**. Click on **OK** to obtain a hard copy of the selected areas.

3.8.3 Printing other items

To print items such as listings of tables and results, graphs, scatterplots, and diagrams, ensure that the correct window is active before following the procedures that have just been described.

3.9 SOME SPECIAL OPERATIONS

So far, the emphasis has been upon the construction of a complete data set, the saving of that set to a file on disk, and its retrieval from storage. There has also been consideration of a number of widely applicable editing functions.

There are occasions, however, on which the user will want to operate selectively on the data. It may be, for instance, that only some of the rows comprising a data set are of interest (those contributed by the subjects in one category alone, perhaps); or the user may wish to exclude subjects with outlying values on specified variables. In this section, some of these more specialised manoeuvres will be described.

Transformations and recoding of data will be discussed in Chapter 4.

3.9.1 Case selection

Let us assume that we have the data of our running example in the grid: there are two variables, *group* and *score*.

Suppose, for example, that we want to analyse only the data from the two mnemonic groups (ie exclude the control group).

Choose
Data
      Select Cases

This will produce the **Select Cases** dialog box (see Figure 13).

Figure 13. The Select Cases dialog box

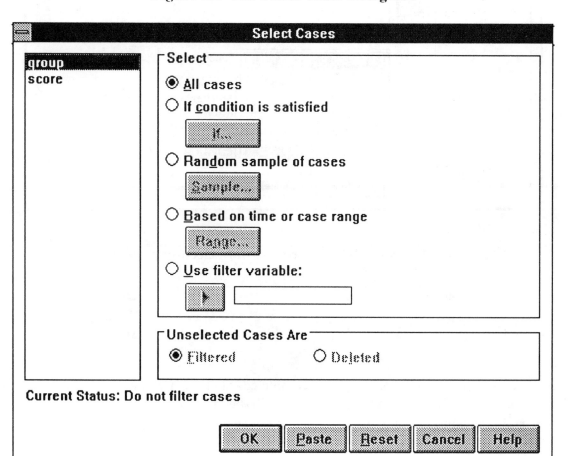

On the left in Figure 13 is a list of the variables in the data set: *group* and *score*. We want to include a case in the data if the row contains the values *2* or *3* for the variable *group*. To do this, we must make what is known as a **conditional** instruction (of the form **Select cases if ...**), which will only be carried out if the condition is met.

Notice that in Figure 13, the **All cases** radio button is marked, a default setting telling SPSS that there is to be no selection. Use the mouse to mark the button labelled **If condition is satisfied**. Clicking on **If...** will select the **Select Cases If** dialog box (Figure 14).

On the left in Figure 14 is the same list of the variables. Highlight *group* and click on > to transfer it to the upper box on the right. The conditional expression can be typed directly into this box or it can be assembled by clicking on buttons in the lower box. Click on = to transfer it to the box above, and then on *2* in order to select the cases in group 2. Click on | (this is the logical operator OR and is located beside the logical operator AND, which is represented by the symbol **&**). Highlight the variable name *group* within the variable name box and click on > to transfer it again to the conditional expression box. Finally select = and *3* to complete the expression shown in Figure 15 which means 'select cases if group = 2 OR group = 3'. Note that the expression must be in the form shown: SPSS will not understand *group = 2 | 3*.

Figure 14. The Select Cases If dialog box

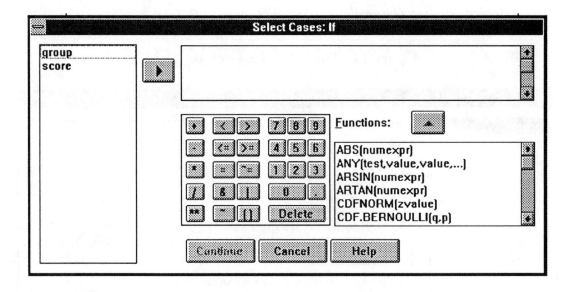

Figure 15. The conditional expression for selecting groups 2 and 3

When the conditional expression has been completed, click on **Continue** and then on **OK** to return to the **Data Editor** window, where it will be noticed that a new column labelled **filter_$**, and containing 1s and 0s, has appeared. The 1s and 0s represent the selected and unselected cases, respectively. The row numbers of the unselected cases have also been marked with an oblique bar. This is a useful indicator of **case selection status.**

{The reader will have noted that the selection could equally have been made with the expression **group ~= 1** (the symbol ~= means *not equal to*).}

Any further analyses of the data set will exclude the cases within group 1. The case selection can be cancelled by returning to the **Select Cases** dialog box, clicking on **All cases**, and then on **OK**.

3.9.2 The weighting of cases by their frequencies of occurrence

Suppose that fifty women and fifty men are asked whether they disapprove of a popular, but violent, television programme. Their responses can be summarised in what is known as a **contingency table** (Table 3).

Table 3. A contingency table

| | | Disapprove? | |
		Yes	No
Sex	Female	30	20
	Male	10	40

The purpose of constructing a contingency table is to bring out whatever relationship there may be between two qualitative or nominal variables (see Section 3.2). In the present example, the qualitative variables are *Sex of Respondent* and *Answer to Question*. The former comprises the categories *Male* and *Female;* the latter's categories are *Yes* and *No.* It is clear from Table 3 that there is indeed a relationship between the two variables: a markedly higher proportion of the female respondents disapproved of the programme.

As with the data in Table 1, a contingency table must be recast to make it suitable for entry into SPSS. Earlier, it was said that SPSS expects a data set in the form of a matrix whose rows are subjects and whose columns are variables. Clearly, the arrangement of the data in Table 3 does not conform to this requirement: the two columns represent values of the same variable; and a row represents the responses of several subjects.

In part, the solution is to carry the variables in columns of code numbers, as we did with the data from the mnemonics experiment (see Table 2). This meets the requirement that each column in the grid relates to a single variable. In the present case, however, it remains to be made clear that each cell entry represents the response not of one person but of several. This is achieved by entering the cell frequencies into the third column in the **Data Editor** window. In Table 4, the categories of the *sex* variable have been assigned the code numbers *1* and *2* for *female* and *male*, respectively; and the response categories *Yes* and *No* have been coded as *1* and *0*, respectively. SPSS can then be instructed to weight the category combinations by multiplying them by the corresponding frequencies in the third column.

Name the variables as described in Section 3.5.3.3, and assign labels as described in Section 3.5.3.4. Enter the data in Table 4 into the **Data Editor** window.

It is now necessary to inform SPSS that each row of entries under *sex* and *disapp* is to be weighted by the corresponding entry in *freq*.

**Table 4. A recasting of the data in Table 3, to make the data
suitable for entry into SPSS**

Sex	Disapp	Freq
1	1	30
1	0	20
2	1	10
2	0	40

Choose
Data
    Weight Cases

to open the **Weight Cases** dialog box (Figure 16).

Figure 16. The Weight Cases dialog box

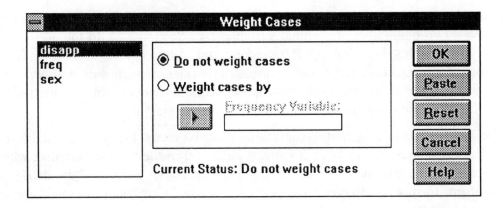

On the left is a list of the variables in the data set: *sex, disapp, freq*. We want to weight each row (case) by the corresponding frequency in the third column. Click on the **Weight cases by** button. Next, highlight the variable *freq*. This will embolden the arrow button which, when clicked, will transfer the name *freq* to the **Frequency Variable** text box. Click on **OK** to run the procedure.

The weighting of cases is an essential preliminary to the analysis of nominal data in the form of contingency tables, as described in Chapter 11.

3.10 SUMMARY

1) **Quantitative variables** are possessed in **degree**; **qualitative variables** are possessed in **kind**.

2) A **hypothesis** is a provisional supposition that a specified **independent variable** has a causal effect upon a specified **dependent** variable.

3) Where possible, statistics should always be interpreted in the light of a thorough **exploration** of the data set. **Formal statistical analysis** should follow, not precede, the exploratory phase.

4) SPSS expects to receive a data set in which each row represents one (and only one) subject, or **case**, and whose columns represent the variables on which the subjects have been measured.

5) Data are entered into the **cells** of the **Data Editor** window.

6) Individual values are easily replaced by entering their substitutes in the same cells. More complex operations can be carried out by the **block-and-paste** method.

7) Among the features of a **dialog box** are **command buttons, subdialog command buttons, radio buttons, check boxes** and **text boxes**.

8) The format in which values will appear in the **Data Editor** window can be predetermined by choosing
Edit
   Preferences

9) **Variable-naming** is achieved by double-clicking on the head of the column. With a grouping variable, assign **value labels** by clicking on the **Labels** subdialog button in the **Define Variable** dialog box.

10)   The choice of a **variable name** is governed by strict rules.

11)   When entering string values, make sure that the **Variable Type** has been set to **String**. This is achieved by pressing the **Type** subdialog button in the **Define Variable** dialog box and marking the **String** radio button in the **Define Variable Type** dialog box.

12)   On the assumption that the data set is rectangular, SPSS assigns a **system-missing value** to any cell in which no entry has been made. This assignment is indicated by a point in each of the cells concerned. The user, however, may wish to designate certain values that are actually in the data set as missing by assigning **user-missing values**.

13)   To save a data set that has been entered into the **Data Editor** window, ensure that this is the active window by clicking anywhere within it or selecting it from the list of windows at the foot of the **Windows** pull-down menu. Then choose
File
   Save As
and type in a suitable file name with the extension **.sav** after selecting the appropriate disk drive.

14)   To retrieve a data set from a file, choose
File
   Open
     Data
and highlight the required file name after selecting the appropriate disk drive.

15)   If the data set exists in SPSS/PC+, it is possible to transfer it together with all the variable and value labels to SPSS for Windows provided it is in the form of a **system file** (ie. a file with the extension **.sys**). Within SPSS/PC+, execute all the data commands, together with a SAVE OUTFILE command specifying the file name, to create the system file on a floppy disk. Then within SPSS for Windows, choose
File
   Open
     Data
and select **SPSS/PC+ [*.sys]** from the **File Type** box and drive **a:** from the **Drives** box. Click on the file name and then on **OK** to effect the transfer.

16) Print out items or selected items from any window by ensuring that it is active. (Click anywhere within it or select it from the list of windows at the foot of the **Windows** drop-down menu.)
Then choose
File
  Print
A selected part of a window can be printed by highlighting the selection.

17) To **select cases**, choose
Data
  Select Cases
and prepare a suitable conditional expression within the **Select Cases: If** dialog box.

18) When a variable contains counts, or frequencies, **weight cases** by choosing
Data
  Weight Cases
taking care to identify the variable that contains the frequencies or counts.

CHAPTER 4

LISTING AND EXPLORING DATA

4.1 INTRODUCTION

The SPSS package has been designed to carry out a wide range of statistical tests with ease and rapidity. Before the user can proceed with any data analysis, however, certain preparatory steps must first be taken.

First of all, it is essential to check whether the data have been correctly entered into the computer: a chain is no stronger than its weakest link and it is of paramount importance to ensure that all subsequent inferences rest upon a firm factual foundation. Having checked that the data have been correctly entered, one might be tempted to proceed immediately to command SPSS to perform various formal statistical tests. The user is strongly warned against this, however.

The process of data analysis should be thought of as taking place in two phases:
  (1)   Exploration and description of the data.
  (2)   Confirmation of data characteristics.

It is to the second phase of analysis that formal statistical testing belongs: the performance of a **t-test** or an **analysis of variance** should be seen as the end-point of a careful consideration of the features of your own data set, rather than an automatic first step.

There are two main reasons for taking such a cautious approach. Firstly, the user who proceeds immediately to carry out various tests may miss the most illuminating features of the data.

Secondly, the performance of a statistical test always presupposes that certain assumptions about the data are correct. Should these assumptions be false, the results of statistical tests may be quite misleading.

The researcher who explores a data set thoroughly may find therein characteristics of great significance. There is always the possibility, however, that these patterns are chance occurrences and that, were the research to be repeated with fresh subjects, they might not reappear. The purpose of a statistical test is to **confirm** the characteristics of a data set, in the sense that the researcher wants to be able to say, with a high degree of confidence, that a characteristic of the data has not arisen through chance and is **robust**.

The researcher works with several kinds of data:

(a) **Interval data** (measurements on an independent scale with units).
(b) **Ordinal data** (ranks or assignments to ordered categories).
(c) **Nominal data**, which are merely statements of qualitative category membership.

Of the three kinds of data, types (a) and (b) relate to **quantitative** variables; whereas (c) refers to **qualitative** variables. The term *categorial* is sometimes used to include qualitative data and quantitative data in the form of assignments to ordered categories. This term thus straddles the distinction between types (b) and (c).

Suppose we have a set of measurements, say the heights in inches of a group of women. There are usually three things we want to know about such a data set:

(1) The general **level**, or **average value**, of their heights.
(2) The **dispersion** of height, ie the degree to which the individual scores tend to **vary** around or **deviate** from the average, as opposed to clustering closely around it.
(3) The **distribution shape**, ie the relative frequencies with which heights are to be found within various regions of the total range of the variable.

In this book, we must assume that you already have some knowledge of the statistics that measure the level and dispersion of a set of scores. The most well-known measures of level are the **mean**, the **median** and the **mode**; and dispersion is measured by the **standard deviation** and **quantile range** statistics. We also assume that you understand some terms relating to the distribution of the data set, such as **skewness, bimodality** and so on. Should you be a little rusty on these matters, we strongly recommend that you read the relevant chapters of a good text on the topic, such as Gravetter & Wallnau (1992), chapters 1 to 4, Howell (1992), chapters 1 and 2, or Anderson (1989), chapters 1 to 3. Hartwig & Dearing (1979) provide a readable account of a set of more recent statistical measures known collectively as **exploratory data analysis (EDA)**.

Before considering the various exploratory statistical measures available on SPSS, it might be useful to remind the reader how to find the various menus, how to complete the dialog boxes, and how to amend information in dialog boxes.

4.2 FINDING MENUS

In the menu bar of the **SPSS Application** window are nine drop-down menus (Figure 1):

Figure 1. The nine drop-down menus

SPSS for Windows
File Edit Data Transform Statistics Graphs Utilities Window Help

Some items in the **Data Menu** (**Define Variable, Select Cases, Weight Cases**) have already been considered in Chapter 3. For this chapter, the relevant menus are **Statistics, Graphs**, and **Transform**. Within the **Statistics** menu, the relevant items are **Summarize** and **Compare Means**. The **Summarize** menu (Figure 2) includes **Frequencies, Descriptives, Explore, Crosstabs**, and **List Cases**; the **Compare Means** menu includes **Means**.

Statistics	Graphs	Utilities	Window	Help
Summarize	**Frequencies...**			
Compare Means	Descriptives...			
ANOVA Models	Explore...			
Correlate	Crosstabs...			
Regression				
Loglinear	List Cases...			
Classify	Report Summaries in Rows...			
Data Reduction	Report Summaries in Columns...			

Figure 2.
The Summarize menu

Within the **Graphs** menu (Figure 3) are various types of graph such as **Bar, Line**, and **Boxplot**, as well as **Scatter** (for a bivariate scatterplot). Since, however, some of these graphs are available in other procedures in the **Summarize** menu, we shall consider them later. Finally, within the **Transform** menu (Figure 4) are **Compute** and **Recode**. The meanings of these items will be explained later.

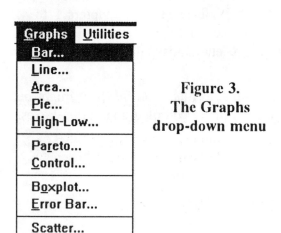

Figure 3.
The Graphs
drop-down menu

Figure 4. The Transform drop-down menu

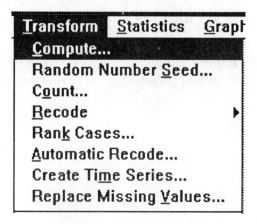

4.3 LISTING AND DESCRIBING DATA

Before illustrating the use of various menu items, it is necessary to have a suitable data set. Let us assume that a set consisting of two quantitative variables *weight* and *height*, and two qualitative variables *gender* and *bloodtyp*, has already been set up in the **Data Editor** window (see the first seven of thirty cases in Figure 5).

	gender	weight	height	bloodtyp
1	M	75	178	O
2	M	100	196	O
3	M	60	145	A
4	M	71	170	O
5	M	80	180	B
6	M	69	175	O
7	M	78	185	AB

Figure 5.
The first 7 cases of the data set in the Data Editor window

4.3.1 Listing data

It is sometimes convenient to be able to list the data for a particular variable (or perhaps a few variables) rather than having to scan a particular column (or columns) in the **Data Editor** window. For example, the user might wish to see two variables side-by-side which in the **Data Editor** window are several columns apart.

Choose:

Statistics
>   **Summarize**
>>   **List Cases**

and then complete the **List Cases** dialog box (Figure 6) to indicate which variables are to be listed.

Select the variables of interest (for example, *gender* and *bloodtyp*) by clicking on the variable name and then on > to enter it into the **Variable(s)** box. It is also useful to click on the **Number cases** box in order to have the data listed with case numbers. {Although there is not a variable in the **Data Editor** window for case numbers, SPSS automatically registers each row in a system variable *$casenum*.}

Finally click on **OK**. Part of the output is shown in Output Listing 1.

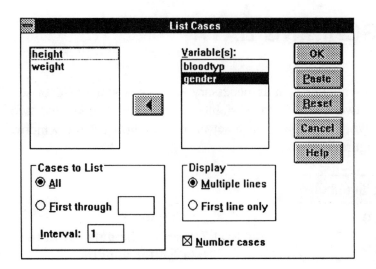

Figure 6.
The List Cases dialog box

```
BLOODTYP GENDER

 1  O        M
 2  O        M
 3  A        M
 4  O        M
 5  B        M
 6  O        M
 7  AB       M
 8  A        M
 9  O        M
10  B        M
```

Output Listing 1.
Output from List Cases

4.3.2 Describing categorial data

The **summarize** item within the **statistics** drop-down menu contains procedures for describing qualitative and categorial data, namely **Frequencies** and **Crosstabs**. Items from the **Graphs** drop-down menu can also be used; but these will not be described in this section, since some of them are also available within **Frequencies**.

Frequencies gives frequency distributions for all types of data (nominal, ordinal, and interval). There are options for additional statistics, and for plots such as barcharts and histograms (see also **Explore** below for other ways of displaying barcharts and histograms).

Crosstabs generates contingency tables, which list cell frequencies for categorial data classified by at least two variables. The tables also show row and column frequencies and percentages. Various statistics computed from contingency tables, such as **chi-square**, the **phi coefficient**, the **contingency coefficient**, **lambda**, **Kendall's tau-b** and **tau-c**, **Pearson's correlation coefficient r**, and **gamma**, are available in the **Options** box in Crosstabs.

4.3.2.1 Frequencies

The following example demonstrates the use of the descriptive statistics procedures for the two qualitative variables *gender* and *bloodtyp*.

Click on
Statistics
    Summarize
        Frequencies

to open the **Frequencies** dialog box (Figure 7).

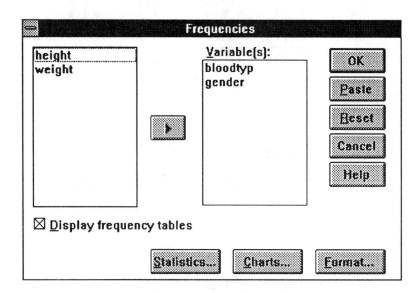

Figure 7.
The Frequencies dialog box

Highlight the variables *bloodtyp* and *gender* and then click on > to transfer them into the **Variable(s)** box. Click on **Charts** to obtain the **Frequencies: Charts** dialog box (Figure 8) and then on the **Bar Chart(s)** button. There is also the choice of frequencies or percentages for the y axis in the **Axis Label Display** box. Click on **Continue** and then on **OK**.

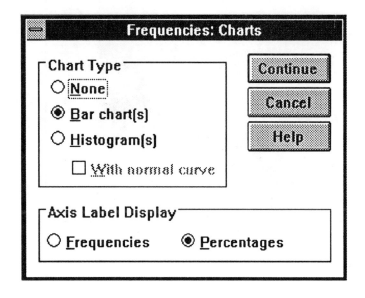

Figure 8.
The Frequencies: Charts dialog box

The output consists of a table and bar chart for each variable. The tables are listed in Output Listing 2 and the bar chart for *bloodtype* is shown in Figure 9 (the bar chart for *gender* is not reproduced). Note that the bar chart can also be requested directly from the **Bar** option within the **Graphs** drop-down menu.

Output Listing 2. Frequency listings

BLOODTYP

Value Label	Value	Frequency	Percent	Valid Percent	Cum Percent
Group A	A	6	18.8	18.8	18.8
Group AB	AB	3	9.4	9.4	28.1
Group B	B	6	18.8	18.8	46.9
Group O	O	17	53.1	53.1	100.0
	Total	32	100.0	100.0	

- -

GENDER

Value Label	Value	Frequency	Percent	Valid Percent	Cum Percent
Female	F	16	50.0	50.0	50.0
Male	M	16	50.0	50.0	100.0
	Total	32	100.0	100.0	

Figure 9. Bar Chart for Bloodtyp

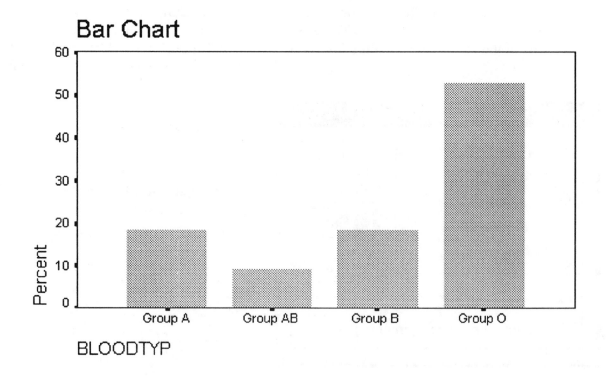

56

4.3.2.2 Crosstabs

Crosstabs generates contingency tables from nominal or ordinal categorial data. Here we illustrate the procedure with *bloodtyp* and *gender*.

Choose
Statistics
    Summarize
        Crosstabs

to open the **Crosstabs** dialog box (Figure 10).

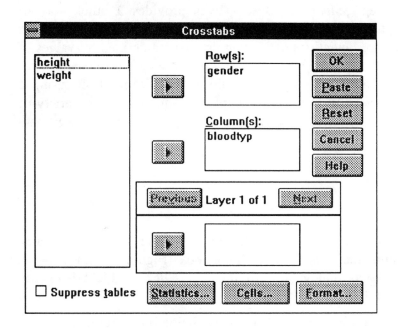

Figure 10.
The Crosstabs dialog box

Enter one of the variables into the **Row(s)** box by clicking on its name and then on >. Enter the other variable into the **Column(s)** box. Click on **OK**. The output is shown in Output Listing 3.

Output Listing 3. Contingency table from Crosstabs

```
GENDER   by   BLOODTYP
```

		BLOODTYP				Page 1 of 1
	Count	Group A	Group AB	Group B	Group O	
		A	AB	B	O	Row Total
GENDER						
Female	F	3	1	3	9	16 50.0
Male	M	3	2	3	8	16 50.0
	Column Total	6 18.8	3 9.4	6 18.8	17 53.1	32 100.0

```
Number of Missing Observations:   0
```

It is important to be clear that **Crosstabs** is only applicable to contingency tables as described in Chapter 3: it should be requested only for **categorial data** (ie nominal data or those that are assignments to ordered categories). Crosstabs should not be requested for interval data or ranks.

4.3.3 Describing interval data

Frequencies, Descriptives, Means and **Explore** are the principal procedures for describing and exploring interval data, the last two also allowing quantitative variables to be classified by categories of a qualitative variable (eg *gender*). **Descriptives** provides a quick way of obtaining a range of common descriptive statistics, both of central tendency and of dispersion. **Means** calculates the means and standard deviations of subpopulations (as defined by values of a grouping or coding variable). The procedure has an option for a one-way analysis of variance. Note especially that **Means** cannot be used for variables that have not been grouped by another variable; **Descriptives** must be used instead. **Explore** contains a large variety of graphs and diagrams (also available directly from the **Graphs** drop-down menu) as well as a variety of statistics.

4.3.3.1 Frequencies

The first example is the use of **Frequencies** with the variable *height*. Enter the variable name *height* into the **Variable(s)** box within the **Frequencies** dialog box (Figure 7) and click on **Charts** to open the **Frequencies: Charts** dialog box (Figure 8). Click on the **Histogram** button within the **Chart Type** box and then on **Continue**.

Click on the **Statistics** button to open the **Frequencies: Statistics** dialog box (Figure 11).

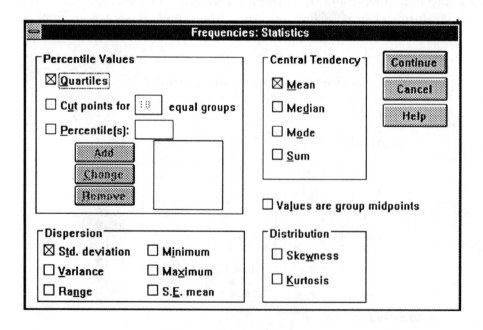

Figure 11.
The Frequencies:
Statistics dialog box

Click on the **Mean** check box within the **Central Tendency** box, and on the **Std. deviation** check box within the **Dispersion** box. Click on the **Quartiles** check box within the **Percentile Values** box: this will print the 25th, 50th and 75th percentile values. Other percentiles can be specified if desired by clicking on the **Percentile(s)** box and filling in whatever values are wanted (eg 90, 95). Click on **Continue** and then on **OK** to run the procedure.

{A histogram can also be requested by selecting **Histogram** from the **Graphs** drop-down menu instead of using **Frequencies**.}

The statistical output is shown in Output Listing 4 and the histogram in Figure 12.

Output Listing 4. The mean, standard deviation, and quartiles for height

```
HEIGHT      Height in Centimetres
Mean           170.281      Std dev        13.679


Percentile      Value      Percentile      Value      Percentile      Value
  25.00        162.250       50.00        170.500       75.00        181.500

Valid cases        32      Missing cases        0
```

Figure 12. The Histogram as requested from Frequencies

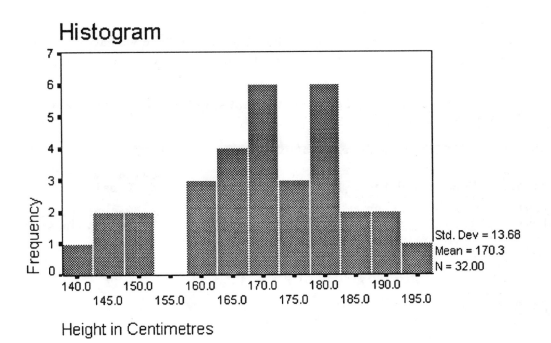

4.3.3.2 Descriptives

Descriptives provides a quick way of generating several well-known statistics such as the mean, standard deviation, variance, maximum and minimum values, range and sum.

Choose
Statistics
    Summarize
        Descriptives

and open the **Descriptives** dialog box. Transfer the variables names *height* and *weight* into the **Variable(s)** box and then click on **Options** to open the **Descriptives: Options** dialog box (part of which is shown in Figure 13).

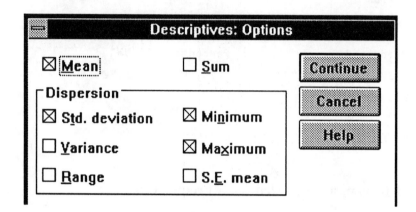

Figure 13.
The upper part of the Descriptives: Options dialog box

Select the statistics of interest by clicking on the check boxes (here we have selected just a few of them). Click on **Continue** and then on **OK**. The output is shown in Output Listing 5.

Output Listing 5. The descriptive statistics for weight and height

```
Number of valid observations (listwise) =         32.00

                                                  Valid
Variable    Mean    Std Dev    Minimum    Maximum  N  Label

WEIGHT     70.22     15.93         48        120   32  Weight in Kilograms
HEIGHT    170.28     13.68        142        196   32  Height in Centimetres
```

4.3.3.3 Means

When statistics such as the mean and standard deviation are required for one variable that has been grouped by categories of another (eg *height* grouped by *gender*), the appropriate procedure is **Means**.

Choose
Statistics
    Compare Means
        Means

to open the **Means** dialog box.

Click on *height* and on > to transfer the name into the **Dependent List** box. Click on *gender* and on > to transfer the name into the **Independent List** box. The completed dialog box is shown in Figure 14. Click on **OK** to run the procedure. The output is listed in Output Listing 6.

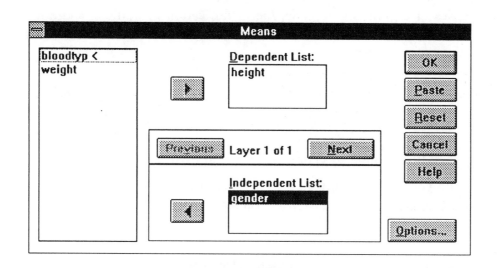

**Figure 14.
The Means dialog
box**

Output Listing 6. The mean height for each level of gender requested with Means

```
        - - Description of Subpopulations - -

Summaries of      HEIGHT      Height in Centimetres
By levels of      GENDER


Variable        Value  Label              Mean    Std Dev    Cases

For Entire Population                  170.2813   13.6789       32

GENDER      F        Female           163.9375   12.0635       16
GENDER      M        Male             176.6250   12.4626       16

   Total Cases = 32
```

In Figure 14, notice the centrally located box containing two subdialog buttons **Previous** and **Next,** as well as the caption **Layer 1 of 1.** Here a **layer** is an independent variable, such as *gender*. If you click on **Next,** you can add another independent variable such as *nationality,* so that the data are classified thus:

1st Layer	*Gender*	Male		Female	
2nd Layer	*Nationality*	French	German	French	German

SPSS will give the mean and standard deviation of each of the four combinations of gender and nationality. Layering is very useful when one is calculating the means and standard deviations for data from a factorial analysis of variance (see Chapters 8-10).

4.3.3.4 Explore

The **Explore** procedure offers many of the facilities already illustrated with the other procedures and allows quantitative variables to be subdivided by categories of a qualitative variable (eg *gender*). Its special features include the plotting of **boxplots** side-by-side for each variable in different categories of a grouping variable, the identification of outliers, and other displays such as the **stem-and-leaf** and **histogram**. Boxplots provide a valuable visual comparison of the distributions of variables.

Choose
Statistics
    Summarize
        Explore
to open the **Explore** dialog box (the completed version is shown in Figure 15).

To see how height varies with gender, click on the variable name *height* and on > to transfer it to the **Dependent List** box, and then click on *gender* and on > to transfer it to the **Factor List** box.

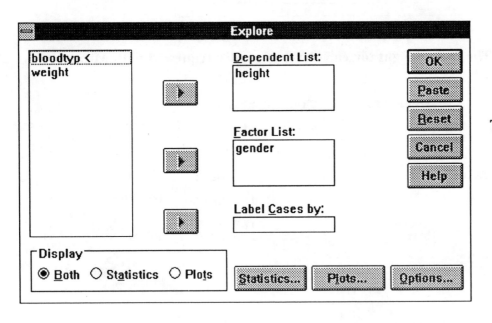

**Figure 15.
The Explore dialog box for height categorised by gender**

Click on **Plots** to open the **Explore: Plots** dialog box (part of which is shown in Figure 16) and select the **Stem-and-leaf** check box in the **Descriptive** box.

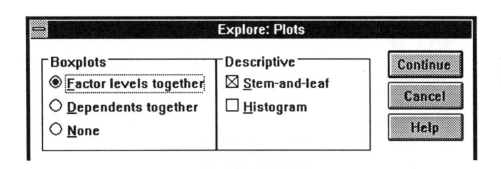

Figure 16.
The upper part of
the Explore: Plots
dialog box

{The default setting for the boxplots is a side-by-side plot for each factor; if, however, we had wished to plot height and weight side-by-side at each level of gender, it would have been necessary to enter both *height* and *weight* in the **Dependent List** box and to mark the **Dependents together** radio button within the **Boxplots** box.}

Click on **Continue** and then on **OK** to run the procedure. The descriptive statistics and the stem-and-leaf display for *heights* on Males (one of the levels of *gender*) is shown in Output Listing 7; the output for Females is not reproduced here.

Output Listing 7.
Descriptive statistics, and stem-and-leaf display for height categorised by gender (only Males shown here)

```
    HEIGHT      Height in Centimetres
By  GENDER      M           Male

Valid cases:        16.0   Missing cases:        .0   Percent missing:

Mean        176.6250  Std Err      3.1157  Min    145.0000  Skewness     -.9470
Median      179.0000  Variance   155.3167  Max    196.0000  S E Skew      .5643
5% Trim     177.3056  Std Dev     12.4626  Range   51.0000  Kurtosis     1.6419
95% CI for Mean <169.9841, 183.2659>      IQR     14.5000  S E Kurt     1.0908

Frequency      Stem & Leaf

     1.00  Extremes       (145)
     1.00        16  *  0
      .00        16  .
     4.00        17  *  0002
     2.00        17  .  58
     4.00        18  *  0023
     1.00        18  .  5
     2.00        19  *  00
     1.00        19  .  6

Stem width:        10
Each leaf:      1 case(s)
```

The boxplots for *height* subdivided by *gender* are shown in Figure 17.

Figure 17. Boxplots of height categorised by gender

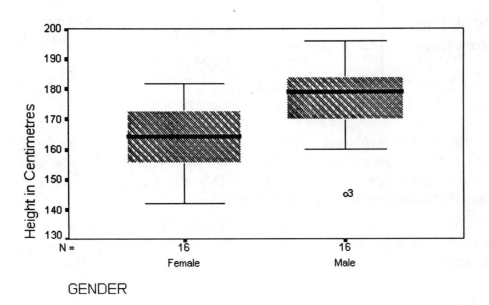

The line across the box represents the median value. The box itself embraces the middle 50% of the cases (ie from the 25th percentile to the 75th percentile) while the extensions (known as whiskers) connect the largest and smallest values that are not categorised as outliers or extreme values. An **outlier** (O) is defined as a value more than 1.5 box-lengths away from the box, and an extreme value (*) as more than 3 box-lengths away from the box. The number(s) alongside O and * are the case number(s). Skewness is indicated by an eccentric location of the median within the box.

Notice that the distribution of heights for females is much more symmetric than that for males. The **o³** under the Male boxplot indicates the existence of an outlier and that it is the value for case 3. This value (145cm) is much lower than the average height for males and its presence is also noted in the stem-and-leaf display in Output Listing 7. Boxplots are especially useful for identifying outliers and extreme values in data sets, and can be requested directly by choosing the **Boxplot** item within the **Graphs** drop-down menu.

4.3.4 Other graphical procedures

The final exploratory procedures to be described here are some of those included in the **Graphs** pull-down menu. Several of the items (eg boxplot, histogram) have already been encountered in other procedures: here we shall concentrate on the pie-chart and the scatterplot. The pie-chart provides a picturesque display of the frequency distribution of a qualitative variable; the scatterplot depicts the bivariate distribution of two quantitative variables and should always be examined before calculating a correlation coefficient or conducting a regression analysis.

4.3.4.1 Pie Chart

To draw a pie chart of the categories within *bloodtyp*, choose
Graphs
    Pie

to open the first of the **Pie Charts** dialog boxes (not reproduced here).

Click on **Define** to open the **Define Pie: Summaries for Groups of Cases** dialog box (the completed version is shown in Figure 18). Click on *bloodtyp* and on > to paste the name into the **Define Slices by** box. Click on **% of cases** so that the slices represent percentages rather than the values of N. Finally, it is desirable to have a title: click on **Titles** and type the desired title into the box (eg BLOOD GROUPS) and click on **Continue**.

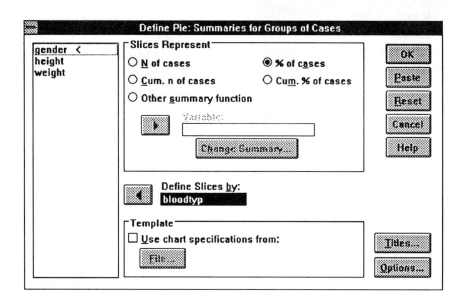

Figure 18.
The Define Pie:
Summaries for Groups
of Cases dialog box

Click on **OK** to draw the pie-chart, which is reproduced in Figure 19.

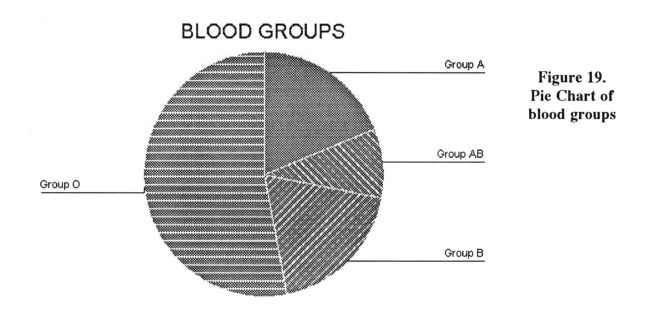

Figure 19.
Pie Chart of
blood groups

4.3.4.2 Scatterplot

To plot the scatterplot of *height* against *weight*, choose
Graphs
    Scatter

to open the **Scatterplot** dialog box (not reproduced here).

Click on **Define** to open the **Simple Scatterplot** dialog box (the completed version is shown in Figure 20).

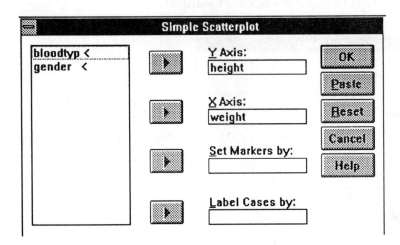

Figure 20.
The upper part of the Simple Scatterplot dialog box

Enter *height* into the **Y Axis** box and *weight* into the **X Axis** box by clicking on each variable name and then on the corresponding > button. Click on **OK** to execute the plot, which is shown in Figure 21.

Figure 21. The Scatterplot of height against weight

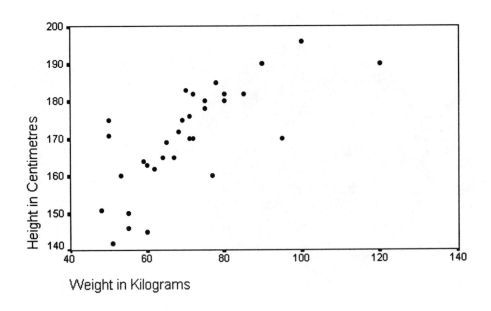

4.4 MANIPULATION OF THE DATA SET

4.4.1 The need to reduce or transform the data set

After a data set has been entered into SPSS, it may be necessary to modify it in certain ways. For example, an exploratory data analysis may have revealed that atypical scores, or **outliers**, have exerted undue influence, or **leverage**, upon the values of statistics such as the mean and standard deviation (for a discussion of outliers, see Hartwig & Dearing, 1979). One approach to this problem is to remove the outliers and repeat the analysis with the remaining scores, on the grounds that it is better to have statistics that describe 95% of the data well than 100% of it badly. Cases can be dropped from the analysis by using **Select Cases** (Chapter 3).

Sometimes it is necessary to **transform** the values of a variable in order to satisfy the distribution requirements for the use of a particular statistic. Transformations such as the square root, or the logarithm, are easily made with **Compute**.

Finally, it is sometimes convenient to combine or alter the categories of a variable. This is achieved with the **Recode** procedure, which can construct a new variable containing the new category assignments.

4.4.2 The COMPUTE procedure

The **Compute** procedure can be used either to transform the values of one or more variables into a new variable (say their square roots, or logarithms), or to change the values within an existing variable (not recommended). For example, suppose that from the variable *score,* the user wishes to create another variable *sqrtval,* whose values are the square roots of those in the original variable.

Click on
Transform
    Compute

to open the **Compute Variable** dialog box (Figure 22). Assuming there is a variable *score* already in the **Data Editor** window, the box will appear as shown, with the existing variable names printed in the lower left-hand box, a blank space for the name of the target variable in the upper left-hand box, and a menu of operators and functions in the middle.

Type in the name of the target variable *sqrtval,* and click on the arrow on the right of the **Functions** box to scroll down through the functions to **SQRT[numexpr]**. Click on this and then ^ to paste it into the **Numeric Expression** box where it will appear as **SQRT[?]**. Click on *score* and > to make this variable the argument of the square root function. The expression **SQRT[score]** will now appear in the **Numeric Expression** box. The final pattern of the dialog box is shown in Figure 23.

The most commonly used transformation functions are

LG10	**logarithm to the base 10**
SQRT	**square root**
LN	**natural logarithm**
ABS	**absolute value**

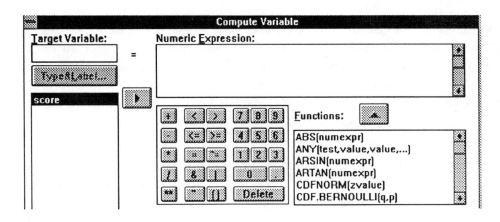

**Figure 22.
The upper part of
the Compute
Variable dialog
box**

Click on **OK** to run the procedure. A new column *sqrtval*, containing the square roots of the values of *score*, will appear in the **Data Editor** window. (It may be necessary to change **Variable Type** to show decimals - see Chapter 3.)

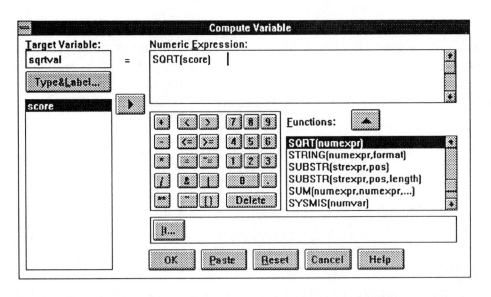

**Figure 23.
The completed
Compute Variable
dialog box**

Compute can also be used to combine values of variables. For example, the procedure can compute a new variable *meanval* from the equation *meanval = (french + german + spanish)/3*, which sums the three scores and divides by three; if any value is missing, a system-missing result is recorded. Alternatively, the function *mean* can be used (eg *meanval = mean (french, german, spanish)*). *Mean* computes the mean of the valid values; the result is recorded as missing only if all three scores are absent.

Finally, conditional computations can be commanded by clicking on the **If** button in the **Compute Variable** dialog box and then clicking on **Include if case satisfies the condition**. A conditional statement, such as the one in Figure 24, can then be compiled within the box.

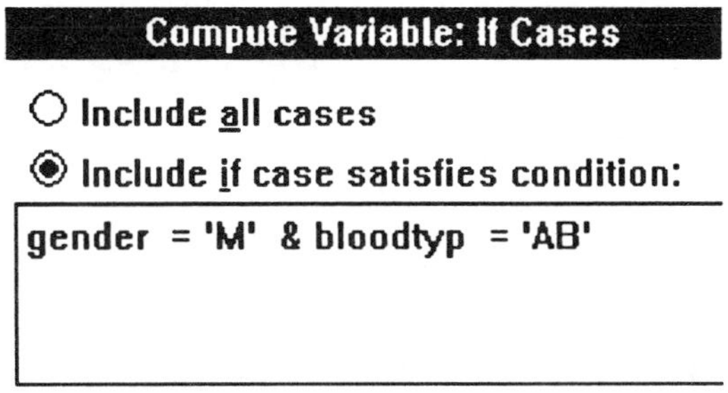

Figure 24.
A conditional statement in the Compute Variable: If Cases dialog box.

Click on **Continue** to return to the **Compute Variable** dialog box where, for example, the **Target Variable** might be nominated as *group* and the **Numeric Expression** as *1*. This would then have the effect of categorising all males with bloodgroup AB into value *1* of the variable *group*. Other values for *group* could be assigned by specifying other combinations of *gender* and *bloodtyp*.

4.4.3   The RECODE procedure

We have seen that the **Compute** procedure operates upon one or more of the variables in the data set, so that there will be as many values in the transformed variable as there were in the original variable. Sometimes, however, the user, rather than wanting a transformation that will convert all the values of one or more variables systematically, may want to alter only some of the values. Having defined a variable such as social class (*socclass*) as comprising five categories, for example, the researcher may subsequently wish to combine two or more of the original categories into a single category. Suppose that categories *3*, *4* and *5* are now to be given the single value of *3*. This can be achieved by using the **Recode** procedure.

Choose
Transform
   Recode

and click on **Into Different Variables** to open the **Recode into Different Variables** dialog box (the completed version is shown in Figure 25). Just as in the case of **Compute**, it is possible to change the values to the recoded values within the same variable; but we recommend storing the recoded values in a new variable, perhaps *newsclas*. The procedure for recoding categories *3*, *4*, and *5* into the single category *3* (while keeping the existing values *1*, *2* and *3* as they are) is as follows:

Click on *socclass* and on > to paste the name into the **Numeric Variable -> Output Variable** box. Type the name of the output variable (*newsclas*) into the **Name** box and click **Change** to insert the name into the **Numeric Variable -> Output Variable** box, which will now appear as shown in Figure 25.

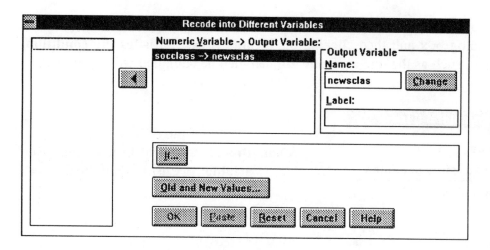

**Figure 25.
The completed
Recode into
Different Variables
dialog box**

Click on the **Old and New Values** box to open the **Recode into Different Variables: Old and New Values** dialog box (the completed version is shown in Figure 26). Since values 1-3 are to remain unchanged, click on **Range** option and type *1* in the first box and *3* in the second. Click on **Copy old value(s)** in the **New Value** box and then on **Add**. Return to the **Old Value** box, click on **Value** and enter *4* in the box. Click on **Value** in the **New Value** box and type in *3*. Click on the **Add** button again. Do the same for *5* by entering *5* in the **Old Value** box, *3* in the **New Value** box and clicking on **Add**. The final result is shown in Figure 26.

Figure 26. The completed Recode into Different Variables: Old and New Values dialog box showing values 4 and 5 being recoded into 3 but the rest remaining as before

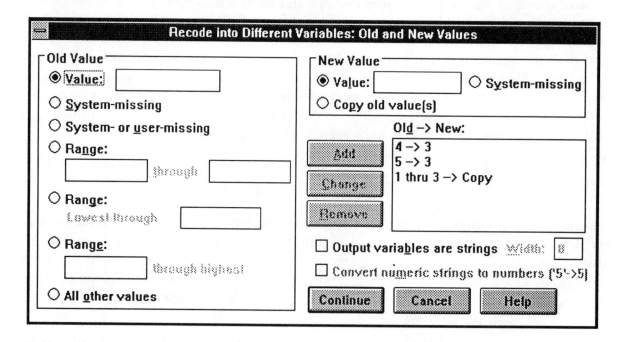

Click on **Continue** and then on **OK** to run the procedure. A new column, headed *newsclas* and containing the recoded values, will appear in the **Data Editor** window.

The **Recode** procedure can also be used to recode ordinal or interval data into coded categories. For example, a set of examination marks in the variable *score* (all falling within the range from 0 to 100) can be recoded into two categories *Pass* and *Fail* in a new variable *passfail* by entering the information shown in the dialog box in Figure 27.

Figure 27. Recoding values into two categories Pass and Fail

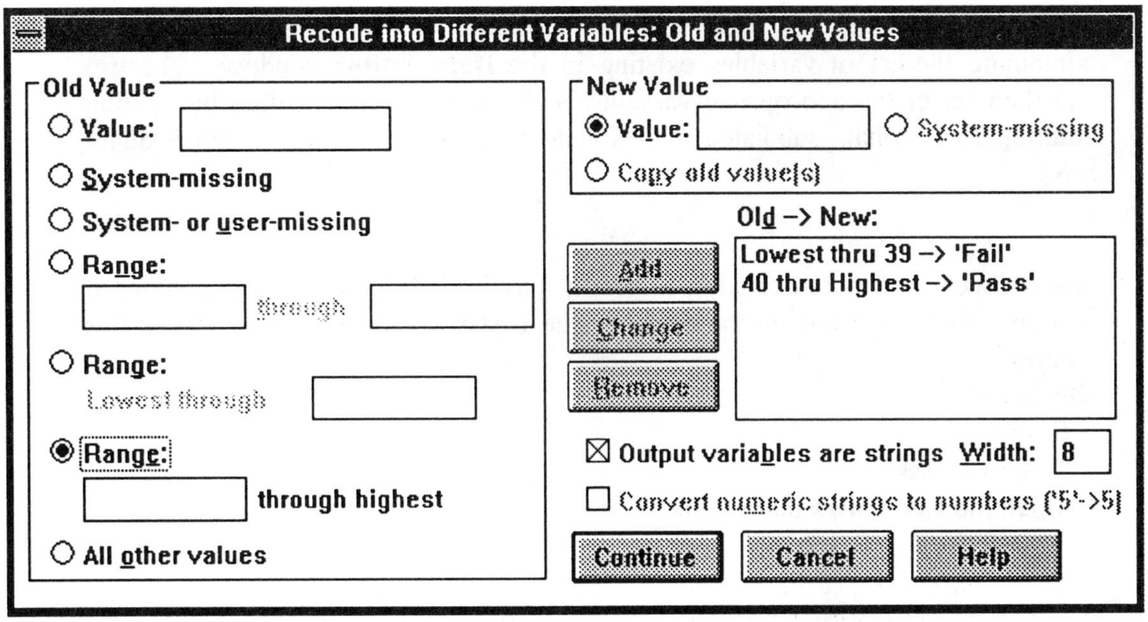

The first range of scores *Lowest thru 39* is prepared by clicking on the fifth radio button and entering the value *39* in the box. Then click on the check box **Output variables are strings**. Type *Fail* into the **New Value** box and click on **Add**. The second range of scores *40 thru Highest* is prepared in a similar manner after clicking on the sixth radio button, entering the value *40* in the box, and then *Pass* in the **New Value** box. Notice that the word **thru** includes the specified value either before or after the word. Thus this procedure will categorise all exam marks less than 40 as *Fail* and all those of 40 and above as *Pass*.

A section of the **Data Editor** window showing the new variable *passfail*, together with its categories of Pass or Fail, is shown in Figure 28.

	score	passfail
1	34	Fail
2	45	Pass
3	76	Pass
4	87	Pass
5	34	Fail

Figure 28.
Part of the new variable *passfail* created by Recode

4.5 SUMMARY

1) Before carrying out formal statistical tests, a set of data should always be explored to check for possible transcription errors, to ascertain whether there are outliers, and to examine distribution shape. The drop-down menus **Transform**, **Statistics** and **Graphs** contain several procedures for listing and exploring data. Once a menu item has been selected, a dialog box appears on the screen containing the list of variables existing in the **Data Editor** window. The user can then select the appropriate variables and various options (often by opening additional, optional, subdialog boxes before returning to the original dialog box).

2) When checking for transcription errors, it may be helpful to have the values of selected variables listed on the screen. The **List Cases** procedure achieves this. Choose
Statistics
  Summarize
    List Cases
to open the **List Cases** dialog box.

3) The procedures **Frequencies** and **Crosstabs** are suitable for exploring categorial data. **Frequencies** lists frequency distributions, and draws plots such as bar charts and histograms. **Crosstabs** generates contingency tables for data classified by at least two categorial variables. The plots can also be requested from the **Graphs** drop-down menu.

4) The procedures **Frequencies, Descriptives, Means** and **Explore** are suitable for exploring interval data, the last two being especially useful if it is desired to subdivide a quantitative variable by levels of a qualitative variable. **Explore** contains a range of descriptive statistics, graphs and plots. The graphs and plots can also be requested from the **Graphs** drop-down menu.

5) Pie-charts for depicting the distributions of qualitative variables and scatterplots for showing bivariate distributions are available within the **Graphs** drop-down menu.

6) The **Compute** procedure can be used to modify variables by transforming them or combining them. The **Recode** procedure changes the categories of a variable.

72

CHAPTER 5

CHOOSING A STATISTICAL TEST

5.1 INTRODUCTION

In this chapter, we consider the second phase of data analysis mentioned at the beginning of Chapter 4: the use of formal statistical tests to confirm that the patterns we have observed in the data were not merely chance occurrences and are 'robust', in the sense that they would be replicated were the research project to be repeated.

While this is not a statistics textbook as such, it was felt that in view of the great variety of tests offered to the user by SPSS, at least some guidance for making selections among these should be offered.

It may be helpful, if simplistic, to suggest that the choice of a statistical test depends upon 3 considerations:
- (1) **The question** you are asking.
- (2) The **level of measurement** of your data.
- (3) The plan, or **design**, of your research.

5.1.1 Studying one variable: goodness of fit

In Chapter 3 (Section 3.2.1), it was said that much psychological research concerned supposed relationships between (or among) **variables**, defined as characteristics of persons, objects or situations comprising sets of values or categories. This is by no means always true, however.

73

Sometimes the researcher draws a single sample of observations in order to study a single population comprising all possible values (or categories) of *one* variable.

A question about a single population is usually one of **goodness of fit**: has the sample been drawn from a population with certain specified characteristics? For example, suppose a researcher wants to know whether 5-year-old children of a certain age, when leaving a room, show a preference for one of two doors, A and B. One hundred 5-year-olds are observed leaving the room and their choices are noted. Here the population comprises the choices (A or B) of 5-year-olds in general. Of the hundred children in our study, 60 leave by door A and 40 by door B. The null hypothesis states that the probability of choosing A (or B) is 0.5 : more formally, it states that we have sampled 100 times from a Bernoulli population with $p = 0.5$. Does this theoretical distribution fit our data?

With a sample of nominal data such as the children's choices in the present example, the **binomial test** is appropriate. With interval data, as when we ask whether the performance, on a standardised test, of a group of schoolchildren is typical of those in their age group, a **one-sample t-test** could be used to test the null hypothesis that the population mean has the putative 'population' value (ie the mean performance of the test's standardisation sample).

5.1.2 Studies yielding two or more samples of data: comparing averages

Now suppose we carry out an experiment comparing the memory performance of two groups of students: one group has been trained in the use of a mnemonic method; the other has not. This experiment will result in **two samples of data**, on the basis of which the *comparison* is made between the two corresponding populations of mnemonically trained and untrained people.

In this study, there are actually *two* variables:
  (1)   *Recall.*
  (2)   The *training method* used (*mnemonic*, *none*).

The independent variable, *training method*, is manipulated by the experimenter to study its effect upon the dependent variable, *recall*.

There is available a set of **two-sample tests** designed to permit inferences about the averages of the two corresponding populations. In choosing among these tests, the user must consider:
  (1)   The level of measurement of the data.
  (2)   Whether the two samples are independent or related.

Two samples can be regarded as **independent** if there is no basis for pairing the values in any way; whereas if there is such a basis, as when the same subject is tested under both conditions, they are **related** samples. *This distinction is absolutely crucial in the correct choice of a statistical test*.

For interval data, there are available the **independent samples** and **paired samples t-tests**. (Note that SPSS uses the term **paired samples** rather than **related samples** in the case of t tests.)   For ordinal data, there are the **Mann-Whitney** (independent samples) and the **Wilcoxon matched pairs** (related samples) tests. For nominal data, there are the **chi-square** (independent samples) and **McNemar** (related samples) tests.

In more complex experiments, as when an untrained group is compared with two other groups trained in different mnemonic methods, **three or more samples** of data may be gathered, with a view to comparing the averages of three or more populations.

Again, there are statistical methods tailor-made for the making of such inferences. For interval data, (independent samples) there is available the **one-way analysis of variance (ANOVA)** and (for related samples) the **one-factor within-subjects ANOVA**. For ordinal data (independent samples), there is the **Kruskal-Wallis k-sample test** and (for related samples) the **Friedman** test. For nominal data, (independent samples) there is the **chi-square** test for association and (for related samples of dichotomous nominal data) the **Cochran Q** test.

This information is summarised in Table 1.

Table 1

Choosing a test for comparing averages of two or more samples of scores.

	Dependence of samples	
Type of data	**Independent**	**Related**
TWO SAMPLES		
Interval	Independent samples t-test	Paired samples t-test
Ordinal	Mann-Whitney	Wilcoxon test, Sign test
Nominal	Chi-square	McNemar
THREE OR MORE SAMPLES		
Interval	One-way ANOVA	Within subjects ANOVA
Ordinal	Kruskal-Wallis k-sample	Friedman
Nominal	Chi-square	Cochran's Q (dichotomous nominal data only)

5.1.3 Making comparisons in more complex experiments: factorial analysis of variance

In the examples considered so far, there has been only *one* independent variable. It is quite possible, however, in a single experiment, to study the effects of two or more independent variables, by using one of a set of methods known as **factorial analysis of variance.** (Some of the commonest ANOVA designs and statistical analyses are described in Chapters 7, 8, 9 and 10).

5.1.4 Measuring degree of association: two variables

Consider the following research question: do tall fathers tend to have tall sons? You select 200 fathers who have sons and measure the height of each father and that of his eldest (or only) son. Your question is whether there is a statistical association between the two variables *father's height* and *son's height*: are these two variables **correlated**?

Table 2 shows some of the correlation coefficients and other measures of strength of association that are available for the different kinds of psychological data.

Table 2. Measures of association between two variables

Type of data	Statistic
Interval	Pearson correlation (r)
Ordinal	Spearman's rho, Kendall's tau-a, tau-b, tau-c
Nominal	Phi Cramer's V

5.1.5 Predicting one variable from knowledge of another: simple regression

If there exists an association between two variables, this can be exploited to predict the values of one variable from knowledge of those of the other. For example, if there is an association between the heights of fathers and their sons (which there certainly is), what is the height of a son whose father is, say, five feet ten inches in height? This is a problem in **simple regression,** which is described in Chapter 12.

5.1.6 Predicting one variable from knowledge of several others: multiple regression

It may be that a young man's height is associated not only with that of his father but also the latter's financial circumstances. In **multiple regression** (Chapter 12), knowledge of a person's scores on two or more variables (the independent variables, or **regressors**) is used to estimate that person's score on a target variable (the dependent variable, or **criterion**). We can expect that if height and father's income are indeed correlated (they are), multiple regression will produce a more accurate prediction of a young man's height than a simple regression with either of the two independent variables considered on its own.

5.2 MORE THAN ONE DEPENDENT VARIABLE: MULTIVARIATE STATISTICS

In all the examples so far considered, there was just one dependent variable. In factorial ANOVA, for example, there may be several independent variables; but there is only one dependent variable. The ANOVA, therefore, is an example of a **univariate** statistical method. There is, however, available a set of methods designed for situations in which there are two or more dependent variables. These methods are known as **multivariate statistics**.

5.2.1 Multivariate analysis of variance (MANOVA)

Returning to the memory experiment (Section 5.1.2), suppose that two measures of recall were used:
- (1)   Number of items.
- (2)   Number of errors.

In **multivariate analysis of variance (MANOVA),** these dependent measures are combined into a single variable in such a way that the mean scores of the different groups on this new variable are spread out, or dispersed, to the greatest possible extent. The differences among the group means on the new dependent variable are then tested by methods similar in rationale to univariate analysis of variance. We shall not consider MANOVA in any detail in this book.

5.2.2 Discriminant analysis

If, in an experimental study with two or more dependent variables, those dependent variables can be combined to produce a new dependent variable which can separate the groups, it is to be expected that this new combination variable might itself become a useful **independent** variable, from the point of view of predicting group membership. **Discriminant analysis (DA)** is the obverse of MANOVA: the same composite variable is computed with a view to predicting group membership. In fact, in many ways, discriminant analysis is mathematically equivalent to MANOVA. Discriminant analysis is the subject of Chapter 14.

5.2.3 Factor analysis

In all the situations so far described, the independent variables, whether measured during the course of the study, or manipulated by the experimenter, have been *overt*, in the sense of being directly observable. Suppose, however, that people are tested on a number of variables and the correlations among those variables are calculated. Among the correlations, certain patterns may emerge suggesting that subgroups of the original set of variables are manifestations of underlying, or **latent**, psychological variables, which may, in this sense, be regarded as independent variables.

Factor analysis (see Chapter 15) is a set of methods designed to identify the latent psychological independent variables thought to underlie the correlations among a set of tests.

5.3 THE ANALYSIS OF MULTIWAY CONTINGENCY TABLES: USING LOGLINEAR MODELS

In the past two decades, there have been dramatic developments in the analysis of nominal data in the form of multiway contingency tables. In particular, the application of loglinear models of the cell frequencies in such tables has made it possible to tease out the relationships among the attributes in the classification in a way that was not possible before.

Loglinear analysis is the subject of Chapter 13.

5.4 GETTING HELP

In a book of this sort, which is primarily concerned with the use of a computing package, it is not possible to offer more than a few signposts to the reader wishing to select and use a statistical test correctly. In the following sections we offer two suggestions.

5.4.1 Further reading

Of the many textbooks that offer advice on the selection of statistical tests, we have found Howell (1992) to be among the most consistently helpful. Like several other authors (Siegel, 1956; Greene & D'Oliveira, 1982; Tabachnik & Fidell, 1989), Howell offers a decision tree to help the reader make the correct selection. The trees vary considerably in appearance, a fact reflecting the different approaches advocated by their authors (Siegel was an advocate of nonparametric statistics; Howell emphasises parametric univariate ANOVA methods; Tabachnik & Fidell are more concerned with multivariate statistics). From the point of view of the experimental psychologist, Howell's is perhaps the most helpful.

While such decision trees are very helpful in the early stages of study, one invariably finds situations to which none of the proposed schemes really applies convincingly. For example, are counts (the number times a target is hit by the subject over 20 trials, the number of errors per page of print and so on) interval or ordinal data? Are ratings to be regarded as interval data or ordinal? Decisions about which, among a set of variables, are dependent and which are independent can also be difficult. Some situations require the construction of a special statistical model, rather than the application of a standard test.

5.4.2 Getting help in SPSS

SPSS offers a very useful Help facility. By entering the Help drop-down menu and selecting the Search option, one can, by typing in key phrases, obtain useful information about how to find and run procedures. For example, for a one-sample t-test, the user is directed to the dialog box for a related-samples t-test and given clear instructions on how to modify the data set for the one-sample test.

5.5 A GENERAL SCHEME FOR DATA ANALYSIS WITH SPSS

The analysis of a set of data takes place in two phases:
(1)   **Data entry and exploration** at a general level.
(2)   Formal **statistical analysis**.

5.5.1 Phase 1 - Data Entry and Exploration

Prepare data file

Within the **Statistics** drop-down menu, explore data with procedures from the **Summarize** submenu such as **Frequencies, Descriptives, Explore, Crosstabs**

Inspect listings on the screen, check for outliers, study the distributions, and so on.

If necessary, deselect outliers or transform distributions with procedures from the **Data** or **Transform** drop-down menus.

5.5.2 Phase 2 - Statistical Analysis

Select an appropriate SPSS statistical procedure as shown in Table 3.

Table 3. General scheme for selecting statistical tests in SPSS

Degree of relation-ship among variables	Significance of differences in level between/among variables	Prediction of group membership	Finding latent variables

Correlation
Regression
Crosstabs
Loglinear Analysis
Nonparametric
  Tests
	T-Test
	One-way ANOVA
	ANOVA
	Nonparametric
	  Tests
		Discriminant
		  Analysis
			Factor Analysis

If necessary, amend dialog boxes and re-execute

Print listing file (optional)

This completes Phase 2. Inspection of the output may lead to the identification of more outliers and the need to repeat the analysis with a reduced data set. Further refinements may be added: additional statistics can be commanded; tables of residuals can be requested; and plots of the results obtained.

5.6 BASIC TERMS IN EXPERIMENTAL DESIGN

The most common statistical procedures that psychologists use are for testing differences between (or among) the means of different samples. The next chapter examines the case of two means and the subsequent four chapters extend the discussion to comparisons among three or more means. At this point, we shall introduce some basic terms in experimental design.

Variables: the dependent and independent variables

We have seen that a **variable** is a property or characteristic of a person, an object, or a situation. Height and weight are possessed in degree, and so are examples of **quantitative variables**. Gender, on the other hand, is not possessed in degree: it is a set of two mutually exclusive categories {male, female }. Gender is a **qualitative variable**.

In research, the object is often to show that some variables, known as **independent variables**, influence (or have a causal effect upon) others, which are known as **dependent variables**. In a true experiment, the independent variable is manipulated by the experimenter, either by assigning different samples of subjects to different levels, or by testing the same subjects under the various conditions making up the variable. **Experimental research**, which is characterised by the presence of one or more manipulated variables, is contrasted with **correlational research**, where all variables are recorded as they occur in the subjects during the investigation.

Factors and levels

Some experiments are of complex design, having two or more independent variables. In the context of analysis of variance (the set of statistical techniques for analysing data from such experiments), the independent variables are known as **factors** and the experiments as **factorial experiments**. A factor, then, is a set of related conditions or categories. Strictly, we should distinguish between true treatment factors, which are manipulated by the experimenter, and **subject variables**, such as sex. For example, we might test for a sex difference in performance by sampling 100 men and 100 women. This is **quasi-experimentation**, rather than true experimentation, and it is only too easy to give a false interpretation to any difference that may emerge. Nevertheless, the statistical analysis is the same whether a variable is truly manipulated or a subject variable.

The various conditions or categories that make up a factor are known as the **levels** of that factor, even though, in the case of the gender categories, one is no 'higher' or 'better' than another.

Completely randomised experiment

If an experiment has just one treatment factor, and each subject is tested once, at one level of the factor, the experiment is said to be of **completely randomised design.**

Factorial experiment

When an experiment has two or more factors, it is said to be a **factorial experiment.**

Repeated measures

A factor is said to have **repeated measures** on a factor if subjects are tested at all levels of the factor.

Between subjects and within subjects factors

A factor with no repeated measures is a **between subjects** factor; one with repeated measures is a **within subjects** factor.

Completely randomised factorial experiment (between subjects experiment)

An experiment with two or more factors, none of which has repeated measures, is known as a **completely randomised factorial** experiment. Such experiments are also known as **between subjects** experiments.

Repeated measures experiment (within subjects experiment)

Experiments in which there are repeated measures on **all** factors are known as **repeated measures** or **within subjects** experiments.

Experiments of mixed design

An experiment is said to be of **mixed design** if **some** (but not all) of its factors are within subjects (ie have repeated measures).

ANOVA and MANOVA

When only one **dependent variable** is measured, one of the set of statistical procedures known as **analysis of variance** (usually abbreviated to **ANOVA**) may be appropriate (there are nonparametric alternatives). When more than one dependent variable is measured, the appropriate procedure is **multivariate analysis of variance** (usually abbreviated to **MANOVA**).

5.7 SUMMARY

1) A typical SPSS session consists of two phases. The first comprises the preparation and exploration of data, using procedures such as **frequencies, descriptives, explore,** and **crosstabs.**

2) The second phase involves formal statistical testing, with procedures such as **correlation, regression, t-test, one-way ANOVA, ANOVA, loglinear analysis, discriminant analysis, factor analysis,** and **nonparametric tests.**

3) The following terms are defined:

    Independent and **dependent** variables, **factor, level, completely randomised** design, **factorial** design, **completely randomised factorial (between subjects)** design, **repeated measures (within subjects)** design, **mixed (between subjects and within subjects** factors) design, **ANOVA, MANOVA.**

CHAPTER 6

COMPARING THE AVERAGES OF TWO SAMPLES

6.1 INTRODUCTION

Suppose that a psychological experiment has been carried out, in which the performance of two groups of people has been measured under two conditions, an experimental condition and a control. For example, the task could be the memorisation of the content of a written passage, and the purpose of the experiment might be to compare the recall performance of a group of subjects who have been given special training in a mnemonic technique with that of an untrained control group. We may find that the mean performance of the experimental (trained) group is higher than that of the untrained (control) group. If this experiment were to be repeated, however, the averages for the two groups would almost certainly take different values. In statistical terms, this is because the scores actually obtained from each group are merely a **sample** from an infinite pool, or **population**, of possible values. Can we be confident that if the experiment were to be repeated, we would get the same result? To answer this question we need to run a formal statistical test.

Possibly the best known statistical test for comparing the average levels of two samples of interval data is the **t-test**, which is designed to test the difference between two **means** for **significance**. Our hypothesis is that the mnemonic technique enhances recall. This is the **experimental hypothesis**. In traditional significance testing, however, it is not the experimental hypothesis that is directly tested but its **negation**, which is known as the **null hypothesis** (H_0). In this example, H_0 states that, in the population, there is no difference between performance under the mnemonic and control conditions. If H_0 fails the test, we shall conclude that our experimental hypothesis, which in statistical terms is known as the

alternative hypothesis, is correct.

The performance of a statistical test requires a knowledge of the **sampling distribution** of the test statistic. The **p-value** of a statistic such as t or F (or some other test statistic) is the probability, assuming that H_0 is true, of obtaining a value **at least as extreme as the one actually obtained**. Should the p-value be small, this is taken as evidence against H_0, because a value that extreme is unlikely (though possible) under H_0. Traditionally, H_0 is rejected if the p-value is no more than 0.05; but in many areas, an even lower p-value, say 0.01, is now the conventional criterion for rejection. When the p-value of a statistic is at least as small as the conventional value, the value of the statistic is said to be **significant**.

Should the p-value be larger than the conventional small value, H_0 is **accepted**. This does not mean that it is actually true: it means only that the evidence is insufficient to justify rejection.

To sum up:

1) If the p-value is greater than 0.05, H_0 is accepted and the result is **not significant**.

2) If the p-value is less than 0.05 but greater than 0.01, H_0 is rejected and the result is **significant beyond the 5 per cent level**.

3) If the p-value is smaller than 0.01, H_0 is rejected and the result is **significant beyond the 1 per cent level**.

In this book, we assume that you are familiar with the t-test, at least to some extent. If you are not, we strongly recommend that you read the relevant sections of a good statistical text: eg Gravetter & Wallnau (1992; chapters 9-11) give a lucid account. With independent samples, the t statistic is calculated by dividing the difference between the sample means by an estimate of the standard deviation of the distribution of differences, which is known as the **standard error of the difference**. Should the sample variances have similar values, it is common practice to work with a pooled estimate of the supposedly constant population variance; but if they do not, the pooled estimate is not used and a **separate variance** test is made. The null hypothesis is rejected if the obtained value of t lies in either tail of the sampling distribution. The precise value of t needed for significance depends upon the **degrees of freedom** of the distribution, which in turn depends upon the sizes of the samples in the experiment; but an absolute value of t greater than or equal to 2 is usually significant, unless the samples are very small indeed. Very small samples should be avoided in any case, because the test would have insufficient power to reject H_0. (The **power** of a statistical test is the probability that H_0 will be rejected given that it is false.)

Table 1 shows the SPSS menus (in upper case letters) for the various two-sample situations. The left half deals with parametric tests (ie those making assumptions about population parameters), the right half with nonparametric tests (ie those making no assumptions about population parameters). Each half is subdivided according to whether the samples are independent or related (SPSS refers to related samples as **paired samples** in the case of the t-test but as **related samples** for nonparametric tests).

Table 1. SPSS Menus (upper case words) within the STATISTICS pull-down menu for various two-sample situations

Data derived from populations assumed to have normal distributions and equal variances		No specific assumptions about the population distributions	
Independent samples	**Paired samples**	**Independent samples**	**Related samples**
COMPARE MEANS	COMPARE MEANS	NON-PARAMETRIC TESTS	NON-PARAMETRIC TESTS
⇩	⇩	⇩	⇩
INDEPENDENT-SAMPLES T-TEST	PAIRED-SAMPLES T-TEST	2 INDEPENDENT SAMPLES	2 RELATED SAMPLES

6.2 PARAMETRIC METHODS: THE T-TESTS

6.2.1 Assumptions underlying the use of the t-test

The model underlying a t-test assumes that the data have been derived from normal distributions with equal variance. Computer simulations have shown that even with moderate violations of these assumptions, one may still safely proceed with a t-test, provided the samples are not too small, do not contain outliers (atypical scores), and are of equal (or nearly equal) size. Should a preliminary exploration of the data (as recommended in Chapter 4) indicate that the assumptions of a t-test model have been seriously violated, an alternative test should be chosen from the portfolio of **nonparametric** tests in the **Nonparametric Tests** menu. Nonparametric tests do not carry specific assumptions about population distributions and variance.

6.2.2 Paired and independent samples

In an experiment on lateralisation of cortical functioning, a subject looks at a central spot on a computer screen and is told to press a key on recognition of a word which may appear on either side of the spot. As a check on whether the word has been truly recognised, the subject is also asked to type the word just identified. The experimental hypothesis is that words presented in the right visual field will be more quickly recognised than those in the left visual field, because the former are processed by the left cerebral hemisphere, which is thought to be more proficient with verbal information. For each subject, the median response time to forty words in each of the right and left visual fields is recorded, as indicated in Table 2:

Table 2. Paired data: Median word recognition times in milliseconds for words in the left and right visual fields

Subject	Left Field	Right Field
s1	323	304
s2	512	493
s3	502	491
s4	385	365
s5	453	426
s6	343	320
s7	543	523
s8	440	442
s9	682	580
s10	590	564

This experiment is said to be of **repeated measures**, or **within-subjects**, design, because the performance of the same subjects has been measured under both conditions (word in right field, word in left field).

Now suppose that **different** subjects had been tested with words in the right and left visual fields. The data table might appear as in Table 3:

Table 3. Independent samples: Median word recognition times in milliseconds for words in the left and right visual fields

Subject	Left Field	Subject	Right Field
s1	500	s11	392
s2	513	s12	445
s3	300	s13	271
s4	561	s14	523
s5	483	s15	421
s6	502	s16	489
s7	539	s17	501
s8	467	s18	388
s9	420	s19	411
s10	480	s20	467

This variant of the experiment is said to have **no repeated measures**, or to be of **between subjects** design: each subject is tested under only one condition. Notice that there is no basis on which the subjects in the two conditions can meaningfully be paired; indeed, with no repeated measures, the samples can be of different sizes. It is recommended, however, that samples should always be the same size wherever possible.

With suitable paired data, the **paired samples t-test** can be used to test the difference between the means of the two sets of scores for significance. With suitable independent data, the **independent samples t-test** is used. These tests are available in the **Compare Means** section of the **Statistics** menu. Note that the data are entered differently in the two cases, as explained below.

6.2.3 The paired samples t-test

Prepare the data file from the data in Table 2 as follows:

Using the techniques described in Chapter 3 (Section 3.5), define the variables *leftfld* and *rightfld* (fuller names, such as *Left Visual Field* and *Right Visual Field* can be assigned by using the **Define Labels** procedure). Type the data into the two columns and save the data set to a file such as **a:pairt.sav**.

The t-test is selected by choosing
Statistics (see Figure 1)
    Compare Means
        Paired-Samples T Test ...

to open the **Paired-Samples T Test** dialog box (the completed version is shown in Figure 2).

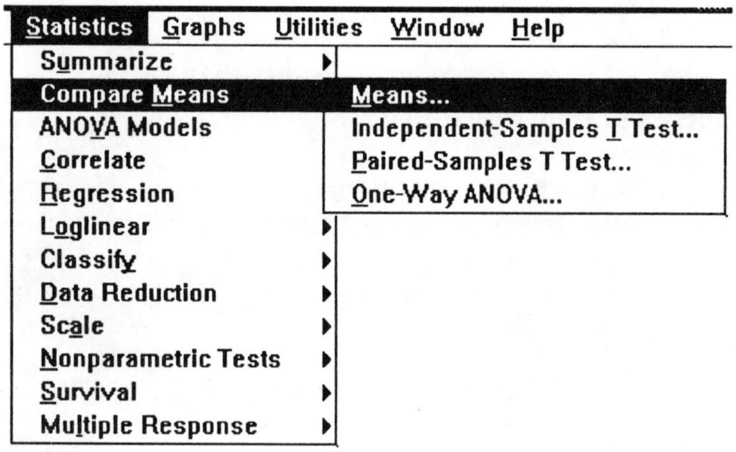

Figure 1.

The Compare Means menu

Highlight the two variable names in the left-hand box (by clicking on them with the mouse), and then click on the > box to transfer the names into the **Paired Variables** box. Click on **OK** to run the t-test, the output for which is shown in Output Listing 1.

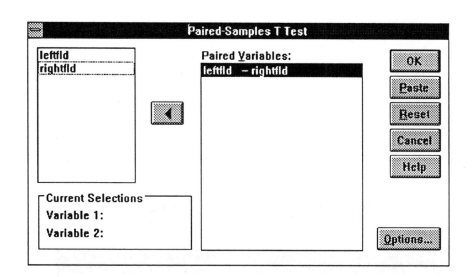

Figure 2.

The completed Paired-Samples T Test dialog box

Output Listing 1. t-test output for paired samples

```
- - - t-tests for paired samples - - -
```

Variable	Number of pairs	Corr	2-tail Sig	Mean	SD	SE of Mean
LEFTFLD Left Visual Field				477.3000	112.091	35.446
	10	.975	.000			
RIGHTFLD Right Visual Field				450.8000	97.085	30.701

	Paired Differences			t-value	df	2-tail Sig
Mean	SD	SE of Mean				
26.5000	27.814	8.796		3.01	9	.015
95% CI ⟨6.598, 46.402⟩						

The listing begins with some statistics for each of the two variables considered separately, followed by statistics of the distribution of differences between the paired scores (Paired Differences). The correlation coefficient for the two variables (0.975), the t-value (3.01) with its associated degrees of freedom (9), and the 2-tail p-value (0.015) are also given. Finally the 95% confidence interval (CI) is (6.598 to 46.402).

The listing shows that the null hypothesis can be rejected, since the tail probability (.015, or 1.5%) is less than .05 (5%). The difference between the means is significant.

To check for anomalies in the data, it is recommended that a scatterplot of the data points be constructed. Use the **Graphs** pull-down menu (Figure 3).

Choose
Graphs
    Scatter

to open the **Scatterplot** dialog box (Figure 4).

Figure 3.

The Graphs pull-down menu

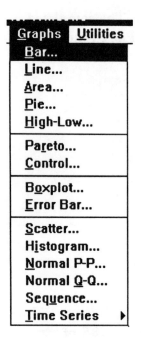

Figure 4. The Scatterplot dialog box

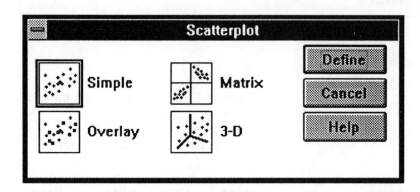

Notice that, as the default selection, the **Simple** version is already highlighted with a thick black box. That will be quite satisfactory, so click on **Define** to obtain the **Define** dialog box (Figure 5). Enter the variable names into the **y-axis** box and the **x-axis** box (in this example, it does not matter which name goes in which axis).

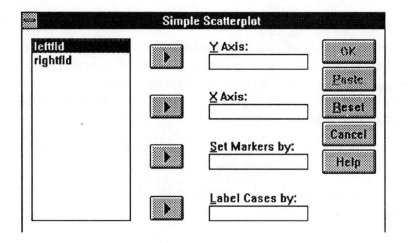

Figure 5.

The upper part of the Simple Scatterplot dialog box

Click on **OK** to obtain the scatterplot (Figure 6) in the **Chart Carousel** window.

Figure 6. The scatterplot of Left Visual Field against Right Visual Field

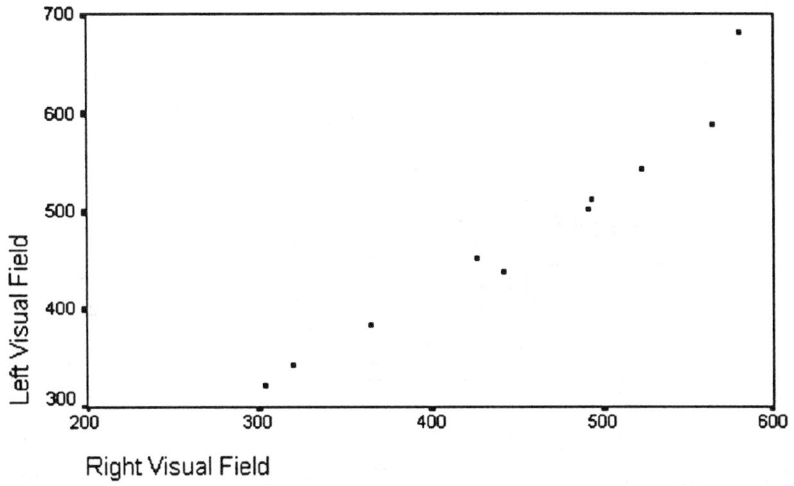

No marked outlier appears in the scatterplot. It should be noted that the presence of an outlying pair of scores, even one showing a difference in the same direction as the others, can have the effect of increasing the denominator of the t statistic more than the numerator and so reduce the value of t to insignificance. This effect is illustrated in Exercise 4. The vulnerability of the standard deviation to the leverage exerted by outliers derives from the fact that the elements of the variance are the **squares** of deviations from the mean, and large deviations continue to have a disproportionate influence, even after the square root operation by which the standard deviation is derived from the variance has been carried out.

When outliers are present, the user can either consider removing them or choose a nonparametric method such as the **Sign test** or the **Wilcoxon matched pairs test**. The former is completely immune to the influence of outliers; the latter is much more resistant than the t-test.

6.2.4 The independent samples t-test

In this analysis, each score is identified by a code number indicating the condition under which the score was obtained. The code numbers are carried in a grouping variable. Using the techniques described in Chapter 3 (Section 3.5), define the grouping (independent) variable as *field* and the dependent variable as *rectime*. Fuller names (eg *Visual Field* and *Word Recognition Time*) and value labels (eg *Left Field* and *Right Field*) can be assigned by using the **Define Labels** procedure. Type in the data and save to a file such as **a:indept.sav**.

The t-test is selected by choosing
Statistics
    Compare Means
        Independent-Samples T Test ...

to open the **Independent-Samples T Test** dialog box (Figure 7).

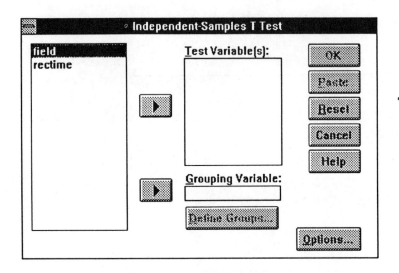

Figure 7.

The Independent-Samples T Test dialog box

Highlight the variable *rectime* in the left-hand box. Transfer *rectime* to the **Test Variable(s)** box by clicking on >. Similarly, highlight the grouping variable *field* and transfer it to the **Grouping Variable**. At this point the **Grouping Variable** box will appear with ? ? as shown in Figure 8.

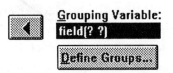

Figure 8.

The Grouping Variable part of the Independent-Samples t-test dialog box before defining the groups

It remains to define the values of the groups by clicking on **Define Groups** (Figure 7), typing the value *1* into the **Group 1** box and the value *2* into the **Group 2** box, and clicking on **Continue**. The values 1, 2 will then appear in brackets after *field* in the Grouping Variable box. Click on **OK** to run the t-test, the output for which is shown in Output Listing 2.

Output Listing 2. t-test output for Independent Samples

```
t-tests for independent samples of  FIELD   Visual Field
```

Variable	Number of Cases	Mean	SD	SE of Mean
RECTIME Word Recognition Time				
Left Field	10	476.5000	73.083	23.111
Right Field	10	430.8000	72.793	23.019

```
Mean Difference = 45.7000

Levene's Test for Equality of Variances: F= .068   P= .797
```

	t-test for Equality of Means				95%
Variances	t-value	df	2-Tail Sig	SE of Diff	CI for Diff
Equal	1.40	18	.178	32.619	(-22.847, 114.247)
Unequal	1.40	18.00	.178	32.619	(-22.847, 114.247)

The output starts with statistics of the two groups, followed by the value of the difference between means (Mean Difference). Since one of the assumptions for a valid t-test is homogeneity of variance, the **Levene test** for homogeneity of variance is included. Provided the F value is **not significant** ($p > 0.05$), the variances can be assumed to be homogeneous and the **Equal Variances** line of values for the t-test can be used. If $p < 0.05$, then the homogeneity of variance assumption has been violated and the t-test based on separate variance estimates (**Unequal Variances**) should be used.

In this example, the Levene test is not significant, so the t value calculated with the pooled variance estimate (Equal Variances) is appropriate. With a **2-Tail Sig** (ie p-value) of 0.178 (i.e. 17.8%), the difference between means is not significant.

6.3 NONPARAMETRIC METHODS

When there are serious violations of the assumptions of the t-test, nonparametric tests can be used instead. They should not be used as a matter of course, however, because should the data meet the requirements of the t-test, the comparable nonparametric test may lack the **power** to reject the null hypothesis, should that be false. It is best, therefore, to consider the parametric test first, resorting to the nonparametric alternative only if the data seriously violate the requirements.

SPSS has a wide selection of nonparametric tests in the **Nonparametric Tests** submenu of **Statistics**. The **Sign** and **Wilcoxon** tests are nonparametric counterparts of the paired samples t-test; the **Mann-Whitney** test is an alternative to the independent samples t-test.

Most nonparametric methods use measures, such as the median, that are resistant to outliers and skewness. In the tests described here, H_0 states that, in the population, the two **medians** are equal.

6.3.1 Related samples: the Wilcoxon, Sign & McNemar tests

Choose
Statistics
    Nonparametric Tests
        2 Related Samples ...

to obtain the **Two-Related-Samples** dialog box (Figure 9). Highlight the variable names and transfer them to the **Test Pair(s) List** box. Click on **OK** to run the test. The results are shown in Output Listing 3.

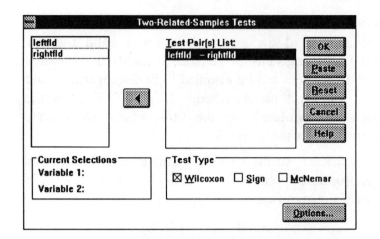

Figure 9.

Two-Related-Samples Tests dialog box

Although the Wilcoxon test assumes neither normality nor homogeneity of variance, it does assume that the two samples are from populations with the same distribution shape. It is also vulnerable to the influences of outliers - though not to nearly the same extent as the t-test. The **Sign test,** which is even more robust than the Wilcoxon, can be requested by clicking on its check box. The **McNemar test** is applicable to paired data relating to dichotomous qualitative variables.

Output Listing 3. The output for the Wilcoxon test

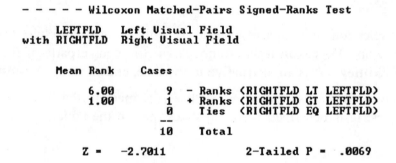

```
- - - - - Wilcoxon Matched-Pairs Signed-Ranks Test

         LEFTFLD    Left Visual Field
with RIGHTFLD  Right Visual Field


    Mean Rank    Cases

         6.00         9  - Ranks (RIGHTFLD LT LEFTFLD)
         1.00         1  + Ranks (RIGHTFLD GT LEFTFLD)
                      0    Ties  (RIGHTFLD EQ LEFTFLD)
                     --
                     10    Total

       Z =  -2.7011            2-Tailed P =  .0069
```

6.3.2 Independent Samples: the Mann-Whitney test

Choose
Statistics
   Nonparametric Tests
      2 Independent Samples ...

to obtain the **Two-Independent-Samples** dialog box (Figure 10). Highlight the test variable name *rectime* and transfer it to the **Test Variable List** box. Highlight the grouping variable name *field* and transfer it to the **Grouping Variable** box; click on **Define Groups** and add the group numbers *1* and *2* in the usual way. Click on **Continue** and then on **OK** to run the test. The results are shown in Output Listing 4.

Figure 10. The Two-Independent-Samples dialog box

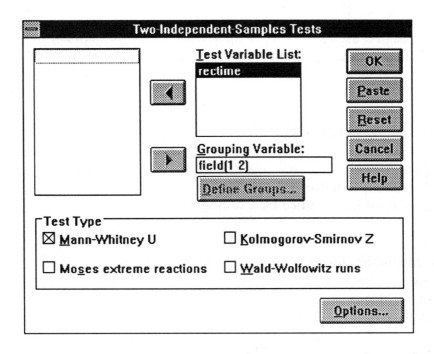

Output Listing 4. The output for the Mann-Whitney test

```
- - - - - Mann-Whitney U - Wilcoxon Rank Sum W Test

    RECTIME     Word Recognition Time
 by FIELD       Visual Field

  Mean Rank     Cases

     12.65         10   FIELD = 1   Left Field
      8.35         10   FIELD = 2   Right Field
                   --
                   20   Total

                              Exact          Corrected for ties
      U             W       2-Tailed P        Z      2-Tailed P
    28.5         126.5        .1051        -1.6259      .1040
```

6.4 SUMMARY

1) The **t-test** can be used to test for a significant difference between the means of two samples of interval data, provided the data are normally-distributed, and the samples have similar variances.

2) For independent samples, use
   Statistics
     Compare Means
       Independent-Samples T Test ...
   Each datum must be identified by a coding variable.

3) For paired samples, use
   Statistics
     Compare Means
       Paired-Samples T Test ...

   A **scatterplot** is recommended. Use
   Graphs
     Scatter
       Simple
   and define the variables for each axis.

4) If the assumptions for the t-test are violated, a **nonparametric** test can be used. Nonparametric tests do not assume normality and homogeneity of variance; though they may require that the two distributions have the same shape. These tests are available in
   Statistics
     Nonparametric Tests
       2 Independent Samples ... or **2 Related Samples ...**

CHAPTER 7

THE ONE-FACTOR EXPERIMENT WITH NO REPEATED MEASURES

7.1 INTRODUCTION

Suppose that an experiment has been carried out to compare the performance of two groups of subjects: an **experimental** group and a **control** group. Provided the data have certain characteristics (ie the samples have approximately normal distributions and comparable variances), an independent samples t-test can be used to test the null hypothesis (H_0) of equality of the two population means. If the test shows significance, we reject H_0: we conclude that there is a difference between the two population means, which is equivalent to the conclusion that the experimental manipulation does have an effect.

The same null hypothesis, however, can also be tested by using one of the set of techniques known as **analysis of variance** (**ANOVA** for short). Despite its name, the ANOVA, like the t-test, is concerned with the testing of hypotheses about **means**. In fact, if the ANOVA and the (pooled variance) t-test are applied to the data from a simple, two-group experiment, the tests will give the same result: if the t-test shows the difference between the means to be significant, then so will the ANOVA and vice versa.

The ANOVA, however, is more versatile than the t-test. Suppose that in an investigation of the effects of mnemonic strategies upon recall, three groups of subjects were tested:
- (a)   A group who had been trained in mnemonic method A.
- (b)   A group who had been trained in mnemonic method B.
- (c)   A control group, who were merely asked to memorise the material as well as possible.

This type of experiment, in which each subject performs under only one of the conditions making up a single independent variable, is said to have **one treatment factor** with **no repeated measures**. It is also known as the **completely randomised experiment**. From such an experiment, we would obtain three samples of scores, one for each of the three groups. The ANOVA can test the null hypothesis that all three population means are equal, ie neither mnemonic technique improves recall (in comparison with the control group). Note that, unlike ANOVA, the t-test cannot be used to evaluate a hypothesis about three or more population means: it can substitute for ANOVA only if there are two groups in the experiment.

Why couldn't a series of t-tests be used to make comparisons among the three group means? Couldn't we simply use three t-tests to compare the control group with the mnemonic A and mnemonic B groups, and mnemonic A with mnemonic B? The problem with that approach is that when multiple comparisons are made among a set of treatment means, the probability of at least one test showing significance **even when the null hypothesis is true** is higher than the conventional significance level (ie critical p-value) of 0.05 or 0.01; in fact, if there is a large array of treatment group means, the probability of at least one test showing significance is close to 1 (certainty)! This point is explained in greater detail in Gravetter & Wallnau (1992). It is sometimes asserted that an unplanned multiple comparisons procedure can only be carried out if the ANOVA F test has shown significance. That is not necessarily true: it depends on which comparisons one wishes to make (see Myers, 1979).

A lucid account of the rationale of the ANOVA is given in Gravetter & Wallnau (1992), Chapter 13. Basically, the ANOVA works like this. A group mean is taken to be an estimate of people's typical level of performance under that particular condition. But individual performance can vary widely and at times deviates markedly from the group mean. Think of this **within group** variability as background noise, or **error**. It may be, however, that mnemonic groups A and B achieved much higher average levels of performance than did the control group: in other words, there is high variability **between (ie among) groups**. The **ANOVA F statistic** is calculated by dividing an estimate of the **variability between groups** by the **within groups** variability:

$$F = (\text{variance between})/(\text{variance within}).$$

If there are large differences among the treatment means, the numerator of F (and therefore F itself) will be inflated and the null hypothesis is likely to be rejected; but if there is no effect, the numerator and denominator of F should have similar values, giving F close to unity. A high value of F, therefore, is evidence against the null hypothesis of equality of all population means.

There remains a problem, however. If H_0 is that all the means are equal, the alternative hypothesis is that they are not. If the ANOVA F test gives significance, we know there is a difference **somewhere** among the means, but that does not justify us in saying that any **particular comparison** is significant. The ANOVA F test, in fact, is an **omnibus test**, and further analysis is necessary to localise whatever differences there may be among the individual treatment means.

The question of exactly how one should proceed to further analysis after making the omnibus F test in ANOVA is not a simple one, and an adequate treatment of it earns an extensive chapter in many statistical texts: eg Kirk (1982, Chapter 3); and Howell (1992, Chapter 12). It is important to distinguish between those comparisons that were **planned** before the data were actually gathered, and those that are made as part of the inevitable process of unplanned data-snooping that takes place after the results have been obtained. Planned comparisons are often known as **a priori** comparisons. Unplanned comparisons should be termed **a posteriori** comparisons, but unfortunately the misnomer **post hoc** is more often used.

SPSS offers the user both planned comparisons and an assortment of unplanned data-snooping tests, such as **Tukey's Honestly Significant Difference (HSD) test, Scheffé's test** and so on. If these are unfamiliar to you, we urge you to read the relevant chapters in the books we have cited.

7.2 THE ONE-WAY ANOVA (NO REPEATED MEASURES)

7.2.1 The mnemonics experiment revisited

In Chapter 3 (Section 3.4.1), an experiment was described in which the performance of two groups of subjects, each trained in a different mnemonic technique (Mnemonic A or Mnemonic B), was compared with a group of untrained controls. The results are shown in Table 1, which is a reproduction of Table 1 in Chapter 3.

Table 1. Results of a memory experiment

No Mnemonic	3	5	3	2	4	6	9	3	8	10
Mnemonic A	10	8	15	9	11	16	17	15	7	10
Mnemonic B	20	15	14	15	17	10	8	11	18	19

In Chapter 3, Sections 3.4 and 3.5 describe how this set of results is recast into a form suitable for entry into SPSS. The SPSS data set (shown in Table 2, Chapter 3) comprises two columns: the first, headed *group*, contains the code numbers *1*, *2* and *3*, identifying the Control, Mnemonic A and Mnemonic B, respectively. The second column, headed *score*, contains each subject's score, which was achieved under the condition coded by the *group* variable on the same line.

The **Data Editor** was used to assign to the independent (grouping) variable the more informative variable label *Mnemonic Training History*, and to assign the value labels *Control*, *Mnemonic A* and *Mnemonic B* to the values *1*, *2* and *3*, respectively.

We shall assume that the data set was saved to the file **firstset.sav** on floppy disk, and can therefore be recalled immediately to the **Data Editor** by using the procedure in Section 3.6.2.

7.2.2 Procedure for the one-way ANOVA

The following instructions assume that the data set shown in Table 2, Chapter 3, has been restored to the **Data Editor**.

The one-way analysis of variance is selected by choosing (Figure 1)
Statistics
    Compare Means
        One-Way ANOVA

to open the **One-Way ANOVA** dialog box (the completed version is shown in Figure 2).

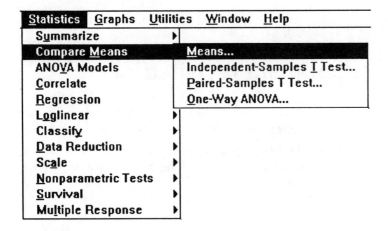

Figure 1.

The Compare Means menu

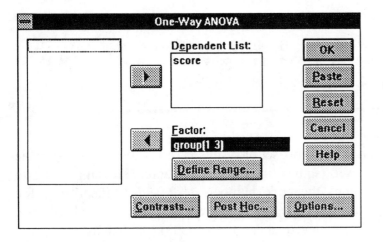

Figure 2.

The completed One-Way ANOVA dialog box

Click on *group* and then on > to transfer it to the **Factor** box. Click on the **Define Range** box and type *1* into **Minimum** box and *3* into the **Maximum** box. Click on **Continue**. Return to the variable names, click on *score* and then on > to transfer it to the **Dependent List** box.

Unplanned multiple pairwise comparisons among the means can be obtained by clicking **Post Hoc** and then clicking on the check box opposite **Tukey's honestly significant difference**. If descriptive statistics are desired, they can be obtained by clicking on **Options** and then on the check box opposite **Descriptive**.

Click on **Continue** and then on **OK** to run the ANOVA.

7.2.3 Output listing for the one-way ANOVA

7.2.3.1 The ANOVA summary table

Output Listing 1 shows the summary table for the **ONEWAY** analysis.

Note the **F Prob** value (ie the p-value) for the F ratio in the Analysis of Variance table. If it is less than 0.05, F is statistically significant. The smaller the value of F Prob, the stronger the evidence against the null hypothesis. In this example, H_0 can be rejected, since F Prob is very small indeed (it is shown as *.0000* in the listing, which means that it is less than *0.00005*).

Output Listing 1. The Summary Table for One-Way ANOVA

```
- - - - -  O N E W A Y  - - - - -


      Variable  SCORE
   By Variable  GROUP        Mnemonic Training History

                            Analysis of Variance

                          Sum of        Mean         F      F
         Source    D.F.    Squares      Squares     Ratio  Prob.
Between Groups      2     463.4000     231.7000    18.7415  .0000
Within Groups      27     333.8000      12.3630
Total              29     797.2000
```

7.2.3.2 Descriptive statistics for a one-way ANOVA

The listing continues with the descriptive statistics; these include the standard deviations and extreme values (see Output Listing 2).

Output Listing 2. Descriptive statistics for One-Way ANOVA

Group	Count	Mean	Standard Deviation	Standard Error	95 Pct Conf Int for Mean		
Grp 1	10	5.3000	2.8304	.8950	3.2753	TO	7.3247
Grp 2	10	11.8000	3.6148	1.1431	9.2141	TO	14.3859
Grp 3	10	14.7000	4.0014	1.2654	11.8376	TO	17.5624
Total	30	10.6000	5.2431	.9572	8.6422	TO	12.5578

GROUP	MINIMUM	MAXIMUM
Grp 1	2.0000	10.0000
Grp 2	7.0000	17.0000
Grp 3	8.0000	20.0000
TOTAL	2.0000	20.0000

7.2.3.3 Unplanned multiple comparisons with Tukey's HSD test

In Output Listing 3, details of Tukey's HSD test are tabulated. The table uses the specified range to show which pairs of groups differ at the 5% level. (This is the **per family** error rate: the probability that at least one comparison in the set will show significance.) The means are ordered and displayed from smallest to largest in the rows, and the asterisks in the lower part of the matrix indicate which pairs of groups differ significantly at the 5% level. We can see that groups 2 and 3 each differ from group 1, but they do not differ from each other. Finally, in Output Listing 4, the groups are divided into subsets, the members of each set differing insignificantly from one another.

Output Listing 3. The Tukey-HSD test output

```
      - - - - -   O N E W A Y   - - - - -

    Variable   SCORE
   By Variable GROUP       Mnemonic Training History

Multiple Range Tests:  Tukey-HSD test with significance level .050

The difference between two means is significant if
  MEAN(J)-MEAN(I)  >= 2.4863 * RANGE * SQRT(1/N(I) + 1/N(J))
  with the following value(s) for RANGE: 3.50

 (*) Indicates significant differences which are shown in the lower triangle

                         G G G
                         r r r
                         p p p

                         1 2 3
      Mean       GROUP

      5.3000     Grp 1
     11.8000     Grp 2     *
     14.7000     Grp 3     *
```

Output Listing 4. The homogeneous subsets from Tukey's HSD test

```
Homogeneous Subsets (highest and lowest means are not significantly different
Subset 1
Group        Grp 1
Mean         5.3000
- - - - - - - - -

Subset 2
Group        Grp 2          Grp 3
Mean         11.8000        14.7000
- - - - - - - - - - - - - - - - -
```

The rationale of Tukey's HSD is this: if the treatment means are arranged in order of magnitude, and the smallest is subtracted from the largest, the probability of obtaining a large difference increases with the size of the array of means. **The Studentized Range Statistic (q)** expresses the difference between a pair of means in any array as so-many standard errors of the mean, the latter being estimated with $\sqrt{(MS_{error}/n)}$, where n is the number of subjects in each treatment condition and MS_{error} is the ANOVA error mean square. The **Tukey HSD** test requires that, to achieve significance, any pairwise difference must exceed a critical value which depends partly upon a critical value of q, the latter being fixed by the values of two parameters:

    (1)   The number of means in the array.
    (2)   The degrees of freedom of MS_{error}.
            {If there are k treatment means and n subjects in each treatment group, the degrees of freedom of the error term is k(n - 1)}.

The critical difference (CD) is given by the formula

$$CD = q_{critical} \sqrt{(MS_{error}/n)}$$

Note that in **Tukey's HSD** test, the critical value for the significance of any of the pairwise comparisons is determined partly by the size of the *entire array* of means. There are other tests, such as the **Newman-Keuls**, which adjust the critical value according to whether the two means are close together or far apart in the left-to-right order of magnitude: in the Newman-Keuls test, the critical value for q is less for a pair of means that are close together in the ordering than for, say, the greatest and smallest means, which are at opposite ends of the ordered array. **Tukey's HSD** test, therefore, is more conservative than the **Newman-Keuls** test: that is, it gives fewer significant differences.

7.3 NONPARAMETRIC TESTS FOR ONE-FACTOR EXPERIMENTS

Should the data be unsuitable for ANOVA (as when there is marked heterogeneity of variance, or the data are highly skewed), one should consider using **nonparametric** tests, which require neither homogeneity of variance nor that the data be normally distributed. With ordinal data, the parametric ANOVA cannot be used in any case.

7.3.1 The Kruskal-Wallis test

In the **K Independent Samples ...** item of the **Nonparametric Tests** menu (Figure 3) is the **Kruskal-Wallis one-way ANOVA.**

Choose
Statistics
    Nonparametric Tests
        K Independent Samples

to open the **Tests for Several Independent Samples** dialog box (Figure 4).

Statistics	Graphs	Utilities	Window	Help
Summarize ▶				
Compare Means ▶				
ANOVA Models ▶				
Correlate ▶				
Regression ▶				
Loglinear ▶				
Classify ▶				
Data Reduction ▶				
Scale ▶				
Nonparametric Tests	Chi-Square...			
Survival	Binomial...			
Multiple Response	Runs...			
	1-Sample K-S...			
	2 Independent Samples...			
	K Independent Samples...			
	2 Related Samples...			
	K Related Samples...			

Figure 3.

The Nonparametric Tests menu

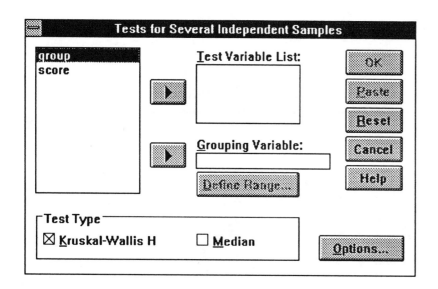

Figure 4.

The Tests for Several Independent Samples dialog box

Complete the dialog box as for one-way ANOVA and click on **OK**. The result of the test is shown in Output Listing 5.

Output Listing 5. The Kruskal-Wallis 1-Way ANOVA output

```
- - - - - Kruskal-Wallis 1-Way Anova

      SCORE
  by GROUP      Mnemonic Training History

     Mean Rank    Cases

          6.60      10      GROUP = 1    Control
         17.65      10      GROUP = 2    Mnemonic A
         22.25      10      GROUP = 3    Mnemonic B

                    --
                    30      Total

                                            Corrected for ties
    Chi-Square    D.F.  Significance    Chi-Square      D.F.  Significance
     16.6961       2       .0002         16.8121         2      .0002
```

For this example, the conclusion from both the parametric and the nonparametric tests is the same: in the population, performance is not at the same level in all three groups.

7.3.2 The chi-square test

Consider a one-factor experiment with three conditions, in which the dependent variable was whether or not the participants could solve a criterion puzzle ($1 = yes$, $0 = no$). A different sample of subjects was tested under each condition. The results are shown in Table 2.

Table 2. Results of a one-way experiment with a dichotomous dependent variable

Condition 1	Condition 2	Condition 3
0	0	1
0	1	1
0	0	1
0	0	1
1	1	0
0	1	1
0	0	1
0	0	1
0	0	1
0	1	1

These results can readily be recast in the form of a contingency table showing the number of participants who could (*Yes*), and could not (*No*), solve the puzzle for the various conditions (Table 3).

Table 3. Contingency table constructed from the data in Table 2

	Condition 1	Condition 2	Condition 3
Yes	1	4	9
No	9	6	1

From inspection of Table 3, it is clear that the group tested under Condition 3 outperformed the other groups. This pattern, however, can be confirmed by running a chi-square test of association, as described in Chapter 11.

7.4 SUMMARY

1) The one-way analysis of variance (ANOVA) is used for analysing data from an experiment of one-factor design with no repeated measures. The test assumes that the data are normally distributed and that there is **homogeneity of variance**. Should these assumptions be violated (the homogeneity assumption is especially important), other methods are available, such as the **Kruskal-Wallis** test.

2) The procedure for **one-way ANOVA** is
Statistics
  Compare Means
    One-Way ANOVA

3) Options include unplanned multiple pairwise comparisons, such as **Tukey's honestly significant difference (HSD)** test, and descriptive statistics.

4) If the assumptions for ANOVA are violated, a **nonparametric test** such as the **Kruskal-Wallis one-way ANOVA** can be used instead.
Select
Statistics
  Nonparametric Tests
    K Independent Samples

CHAPTER 8

FACTORIAL EXPERIMENTS WITH NO REPEATED MEASURES

8.1 INTRODUCTION

Chapter 7 was concerned with the type of experiment in which there is a single independent variable, or factor. The experimental design is shown in Table 1. In order to to see whether training in the use of a mnemonic method improved recall, three groups of subjects were tested:

(1)   A **control** group, untrained in the use of any mnemonic.
(2)   Another group trained in the use of **Mnemonic A**.
(3)   A third group trained in **Mnemonic B**.

Since the three conditions all relate to the type of mnemonic training the subjects receive, they can all be regarded as values or **levels** of a single treatment factor, *Mnemonic Training History* (or *Mnemonic Method*, for short).

Table 1. Design of the Mnemonics experiment

| | MNEMONIC METHOD | | |
	Control	Mnem A	Mnem B
SUBJECTS	group 1	group 2	group 3

An important feature of the mnemonics experiment is that each subject performed under only one condition: that is, there were **no repeated measures**. As a result, the experiment yielded three independent samples of scores. The one-factor experiment with no repeated measures on its single factor is also known as the **completely randomised** experiment.

Suppose, however, that the experimenter, having divided the subjects into the three groups, splits each group into two subgroups. Both subgroups perform under the same mnemonic condition; but one subgroup is tested first thing in the morning and the other last thing at night. If there are equal numbers of subjects in all subgroups, half the subjects in the entire experiment perform while fresh and the other half while tired. This version of the experiment now has **two factors**:

(1)   **Mnemonic method**, whose levels are **Control, Mnemonic A and Mnemonic B.**

(2)   **Alertness**, whose levels are **Fresh** and **Tired.**

Notice that in this design, each level of either factor is to be found in combination with every level of the other factor: the two factors are said to **cross**. The design can be represented as a table in which each row or column represents a particular level of one of the treatment factors, and a **cell** of the table represents one particular treatment **combination** (Table 2). The cell on the bottom right represents the combination *Tired, Mnemonic B*. The participants in group 6 were tested under that treatment combination.

Table 2. Design of a completely randomised, two-factor factorial experiment

		MNEMONIC METHOD		
		Control	Mnem. A	Mnem. B
	Fresh	group 1	group 2	group 3
ALERTNESS	**Tired**	group 4	group 5	group 6

Experiments with two or more crossed treatment factors are called **factorial** experiments. The experiment just described is a **two-factor** factorial experiment. Note also that each subject is tested under only one treatment combination: for example, a subject, having been trained in mnemonic A and tested first thing in the morning, is not tested again in the evening. In other words, **neither factor in the experiment has repeated measures**. Factorial experiments with no repeated measures on any of their treatment factors are also termed **completely randomised factorial** experiments. Since the levels of a factor can be said to vary **between** subjects, factors with no repeated measures are called **between subjects** factors. A factorial experiment in which all factors are between subjects (ie have no repeated measures) is known as a **between subjects experiment.**

Table 3 shows the mean scores of the subjects tested under the six treatment combinations. The row and column means, which are known as **marginal means**, are the mean scores at each level of either factor considered separately, ignoring the other factor in the classification.

Table 3. Summary of the results of the two-factor mnemonics experiment

		MNEMONIC METHOD			
		Control	Mnem. A	Mnem. B	row
ALERT-NESS	fresh	15	15	15	15
	tired	5	14	14	11
	column	10	14.5	14.5	

In a two-factor experiment, there are two kinds of possible treatment effects:

  (1)   **Main effects.**
  (2)   An **interaction.**

If the performance level is not the same at all levels of either treatment factor (ignoring the other factor in the classification), that factor is said to have a **main effect.** For example, should the scores of those subjects tested first thing in the morning be higher than those tested at night, there would be a main effect of the *Alertness* factor. Looking at the marginal row means, it is clear that this is indeed the case: the *Fresh* subjects performed better. Turning now to the marginal column means, it is clear that performance under either mnemonic training condition was superior than under the control condition: there is a main effect of the *Mnemonic Method* factor.

So far, it has been seen that by looking at the marginal means alone, possible main effects can be discerned. Turning now to the cell means, however, it is clear that the data show another striking feature. If we look at the *Fresh* subjects only, the performance means show a flat profile: the use of a mnemonic technique failed to produce any improvement with *Fresh* subjects. It was quite different with the *Tired* subjects: without the mnemonic training, their performance was markedly lower than that of the *Fresh* subjects; whereas, when trained, they performed nearly as well as did the *Fresh* subjects. The performance means of the *Tired* subjects thus show a very uneven profile, which does not parallel that of the *Fresh* subjects. The factor *Mnemonic Method* has different effects at different levels of the *Alertness* factor: it works strongly with *Tired* subjects; but it does not work at all with *Fresh* subjects. When one treatment factor does not have the same effect at all levels of another, the two factors are said to **interact.** The analysis of variance of data from a factorial experiment offers tests for the presence not only of main effects of each factor considered separately but also of interactions between (or among) the factors.

The interaction we have just described can be pictured graphically, as plots of the cell means against mnemonic method for each of *Fresh* and *Tired* groups (see Figure 1). There is thus a **fresh subjects** 'curve', which is horizontal, and a **tired subjects** 'curve' below it, with a different shape. The possible presence of an interaction is always indicated by profile heterogeneity across the levels of one of the factors.

Figure 1. A pattern of cell means suggestive of an interaction

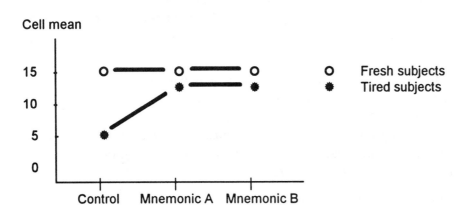

Algebraically, main effects and interactions are defined as independent: it is quite possible to obtain main effects without any interaction between the factors; and it is also possible to have an interaction without any main effects. Usually, however, the presence of an interaction requires the re-interpretation of a main effect. For example, a main effect may arise because one factor has a marked effect at one level of another factor but no effect at other levels, in which case there may be both a significant interaction and a significant main effect. This is what happened in the present example: there is a main effect of the *Mnemonic Method* factor; but that factor really only has an effect with *Tired* subjects, a fact which is brought out by consideration of the interaction between the two factors.

The manner in which the ANOVA tests for the presence of main effects and an interaction is lucidly described in Gravetter & Wallnau (1992, Chapter 15). If you are unfamiliar with such ANOVA terms as **sum of squares, mean square** and **degrees of freedom**, we urge you to read their chapter.

8.2 THE TWO-WAY ANOVA

Consider the fact that in recent years, developments in computer graphics have given an enormous fillip to the study of **human-machine interaction**. In **driving simulation,** for example, the participant sits in a car whose controls are linked to computer-generated images of an imaginary road to create a realistic driving experience. It is thus possible to test a person's performance in heavy traffic, icy conditions, or in emergencies requiring evasive action. A researcher plans to investigate the effects upon driving performance of two new anti-hay fever drugs, A and B. It is suspected that at least one of the drugs may have different effects upon fresh and tired subjects.

The researcher decides to carry out a two-factor experiment, in which the factors are:
 (1)   **Drug,** with levels **Placebo, A,** and **B.**
 (2)   **Alertness,** with levels **Fresh** and **Tired.**

There is already some reason to believe that both drugs may increase the level of arousal in tired subjects, in which case their driving should improve after ingestion of either drug. With fresh subjects, however, the effects of the drugs may be rather different: it is suspected that, with Drug A at least, their performance may deteriorate. In other words, the factors of *Drug* and subject *Alertness* may interact, so that at least one of the drugs may be dangerous to drivers.

In the experiment, all subjects take a flavoured drink which contains either (in the *A* or *B* conditions) a small dosage of one of the drugs or (in the control, *placebo* condition) no drug. Half the subjects are tested after reading for twenty minutes (the *fresh* condition); the other half are tested after cycling vigorously for the same time (the *tired* condition). A different sample of ten subjects is tested under each of the six treatment combinations *(fresh, control); (fresh, A); (fresh, B); (tired, control); (tired, A); (tired, B)*.

The results of the experiment are shown in Table 4.

Table 4. Results of the two-factor experiment

		DRUG		
		Placebo	**A**	**B**
ALERT-NESS	**Fresh**	24 25 13 22 16 23 18 19 24 26	18 8 9 14 16 15 6 9 8 17	27 14 19 29 27 23 19 17 20 25
	Tired	13 12 14 16 17 13 4 3 2 6	21 24 22 23 20 13 11 17 13 16	21 11 14 22 19 9 14 11 21 18

8.2.1 Preparing the data for the two-way ANOVA

SPSS uses a program called **ANOVA** for analysing data from factorial experiments that have no repeated measures. Prepare the data file as follows:

It will be necessary to use two coding (grouping) variables to indicate the treatment combination under which each score was achieved. If the coding variables are *alert* and *drug*, (a variable name must not exceed eight characters in length), and performance in the driving simulator is named *drivperf*, the data file will consist of three columns, the first two containing the coding variables, the third the dependent variable.

Define the three variables as described in Chapter 3, Section 3.5. Use the **Define Labels** dialog box to assign more meaningful names to the three variables: *Alertness, Drug Treatment,* and *Driving Performance* will be suitable. The **Value Labels** dialog box can be used to provide keys to the code numbers that make up the grouping variables *alert* and *drug*: in the *alert* column, the values *1* and *2* can be assigned the value labels *Fresh* and *Tired*, respectively; in the *drug* column, the values *1*, *2*, and *3* can be assigned the value labels *Placebo*, *Drug A*, and *Drug B*, respectively.

Use the cell editor to enter the data into the **Data Editor** grid (Figure 2). The three values in row 1 indicate that subject 1 achieved a score of *24* while still fresh and without ingesting any drug; row 12 indicates that subject 12 achieved a score of *8* while still fresh, but having ingested a dose of Drug A.

Save the data to a file with a path name such as **a:factor.sav** by choosing
File
    Save as.

	alert	drug	drivperf
1	1	1	24
2	1	1	25
3	1	1	13
4	1	1	22
5	1	1	16
6	1	1	23
7	1	1	18
8	1	1	19
9	1	1	24
10	1	1	26
11	1	2	18
12	1	2	8

Figure 2.

Section of the Data Editor grid showing some of the data from Table 4

(Each row represents one subject's score and the conditions under which it was achieved.)

8.2.2 Choosing a two-way ANOVA

The factorial analysis of variance is executed by choosing (Figure 3)
Statistics
    ANOVA models
        Simple Factorial

to open the **Simple Factorial ANOVA** dialog box (the completed version is shown in Figure 4).

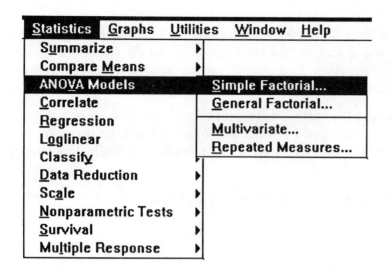

Figure 3.

The ANOVA menu

Complete the box in the same manner as for the Independent Samples T Test (see Chapter 6) by clicking the grouping variables into the **Factors** box and adding the minimum and maximum values of their levels using the **Define Range** box. The dependent variable is *drivperf*.

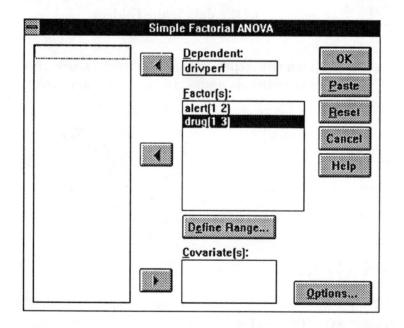

Figure 4.

The completed Simple Factorial ANOVA dialog box

8.2.3 Output listing for a two-way ANOVA

8.2.3.1 The two-way ANOVA summary table

The ANOVA table (see Output Listing 1) tabulates the F ratios and their associated significance levels for the main effects and the two-way interaction. Note the **Signif of F** (ie p-value, or tail probability) value for each F ratio. There are significant main effects for both the *alert* and *drug* factors: the former is significant beyond the 0.01 level; the latter beyond the 0.05 level, but not beyond the 0.01 level. In addition to main effects of both treatment factors, there is a significant interaction. The p-value is given as *0.000*, which means that it is less than *0.0005*. Clearly, the *drug* factor has different effects upon fresh and tired subjects; but to ascertain the nature of these effects, we shall need to explore further the pattern of the treatment means.

Output Listing 1. The two-way ANOVA summary table

```
* * *   A N A L Y S I S   O F   V A R I A N C E   * * *

        DRIVPERF Driving Performance
   by   ALERT    Alertness
        DRUG     Drug Treatment

        UNIQUE sums of squares
        All effects entered simultaneously
```

Source of Variation	Sum of Squares	DF	Mean Square	F	Sig of F
Main Effects	391.667	3	130.556	5.640	.002
ALERT	201.667	1	201.667	8.712	.005
DRUG	190.000	2	95.000	4.104	.022
2-Way Interactions	763.333	2	381.667	16.488	.000
ALERT DRUG	763.333	2	381.667	16.488	.000
Explained	1155.000	5	231.000	9.979	.000
Residual	1250.000	54	23.148		
Total	2405.000	59	40.763		

```
60 cases were processed.
0 cases (.0 pct) were missing.
```

8.2.3.2 Obtaining cell means and standard deviations

To interpret the ANOVA summary table, it is necessary to obtain the mean performance levels under each of the six treatment combinations. These are easily found by running the **Means** procedure.

Choose
Statistics
    Compare Means
        Means

to open the **Means** dialog box (see Figure 14, Chapter 4). In the box on the left are the variables *alert*, *drug* and *drivperf*. Highlight *drivperf* and click on > to transfer it to the **Dependent List** box. Highlight *alert* and click on > to transfer it to the **Independent List** box.

Notice that the box above the **Independent List** box contains the caption **Layer 1 of 1**. So far, SPSS knows only of one layer of classification, created by classifying the dependent variable *drivperf* by the coding variable *alert*. Click the **Next** subdialog button and enter the next layer according to the grouping variable *drug*. The central caption will now read **Layer 2 of 2**, indicating that SPSS now knows of the two layers of classification. Click on **OK** to run the **Means** procedure, the output for which is shown in Output Listing 2.

Output Listing 2. The means and standard deviations for each cell and for levels of Alert

```
         - - Description of Subpopulations - -

Summaries of      DRIVPERF   Driving Performance
By levels of      ALERT      Alertness
                  DRUG       Drug Treatment


Variable          Value  Label              Mean      Std Dev   Cases

For Entire Population                       16.5000   6.3846    60

ALERT               1    Fresh              18.3333   6.3481    30
   DRUG             1    Placebo            21.0000   4.2947    10
   DRUG             2    Drug A             12.0000   4.4222    10
   DRUG             3    Drug B             22.0000   4.9441    10

ALERT               2    Tired              14.6667   5.9731    30
   DRUG             1    Placebo            10.0000   5.6569    10
   DRUG             2    Drug A             18.0000   4.6428    10
   DRUG             3    Drug B             16.0000   4.7842    10

   Total Cases = 60
```

Unfortunately Output Listing 2 does not show the means for the levels of *drug* (ie for *Placebo*, *Drug A*, *Drug B*). To get those means, it is necessary to reset the dialog box and re-run it with *drivperf* as before in the **Dependent List** box but with just *drug* in the **Independent List** box.

8.2.3.3 Exploring the interaction by graphing the cell means

The two-way table of means and standard deviations certainly explains any significant main effects in the ANOVA summary table. The pattern of the cell means, however, will emerge much more clearly from a graphical representation. Select

Graphs
    Line

which will bring the **Line Charts** dialog box into view (Figure 5).

Highlight the **Multiple** box and click on **Define** to open the **Define Multiple Line: Summaries for Groups of Cases** dialog box (the completed version is shown in Figure 6).

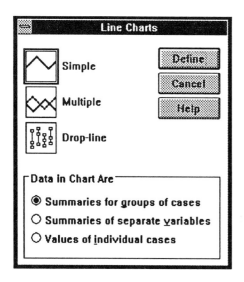

Figure 5.

The Line Charts selection box

Within the **Lines Represent** box (Figure 6), mark the **Other Summary Function** radio button. By default, this choice selects the mean of whatever variable is entered into the **Variable** box (other functions, such as the median, can be selected by clicking on the **Change Summary** button.) When the dialog box is first opened, the variable names are listed alphabetically in the panel on the left. Since we want to plot the cell means on the dependent variable, highlight *drivperf* and click on > to make it the argument of the function **MEAN[ ]** in the **Variable** box, the entry in which will then be **MEAN[drivperf]**. Since we want to profile the fresh and tired subjects over the three levels of the *drug* factor, we transfer the variable *drug* into the **Category Axis** box and the variable *alert* into the **Define Lines by** box. Click on **OK** to obtain the graph in Figure 7.

Figure 6. The Define Multiple Line: Summaries for Groups of Cases dialog box

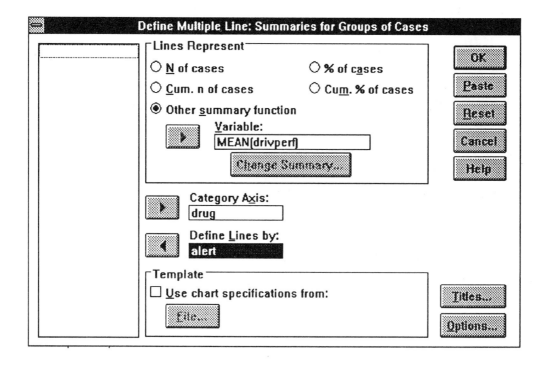

Figure 7. The graph showing the profile of fresh and tired subjects over the levels of drug treatment

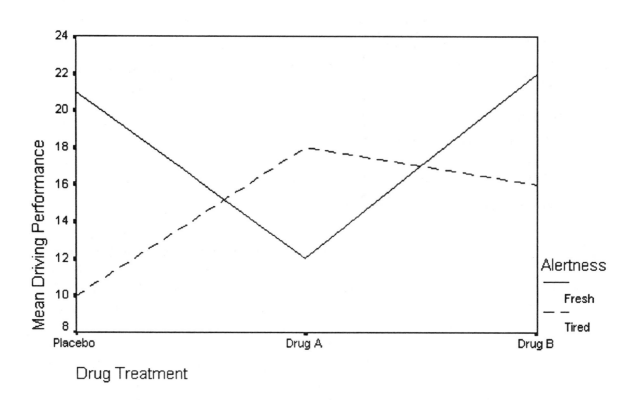

Since the profiles of the fresh and tired subjects are obviously far from being parallel, there is clear evidence of an interaction between the two factors, which arises from the different effects of the drug on fresh and tired subjects.

8.2.3.4 Unplanned multiple pairwise comparisons with Tukey's HSD test

Following a significant main effect or interaction, the user will often want to make comparisons among either (in the former case) the marginal means or (in the latter) the cell means.

In the present case, the ANOVA showed a significant main effect of the *drug* factor, and the user would naturally wish to know which of the pairwise differences among the three treatment means are significant. Here the trick is to pretend that the experiment had only one treatment factor *drug*, and run a one-way ANOVA with the **Tukey HSD** test. Simply choose the one-way ANOVA procedure and specify the *Drug* factor as the independent variable, ignoring the *Alertness* factor.

Should an interaction prove significant (as in the present example), it will often be illuminating to make comparisons among the *cell means* rather than the marginal means. The **Tukey HSD** test can be used for inter-cell comparisons; but this time we must pretend the data are from a one-factor experiment with as many levels in its single factor as there are cell means in the original two-way table of results. To achieve this, we must construct a new coding variable *cellcode*, containing a code number for each of the combinations *(1,1)*, *(1,2)*, *(2,1)*, *(2,2)*, *(3,1)*, *(3,2)* that coded the treatment combinations *(placebo, fresh)*, *(placebo, tired)*, *(drugA, fresh)*, *(drugA, tired)* and so on.

The first step is to define the variable *cellcode*, which has the value *1* if *drug = 1* and *alert = 1*. Proceed as follows:

(1)   Click on **Transform** and **Compute** to obtain the **Compute Variable** window (Chapter 4, Figure 23). In the **Target Variable** box, type the name of the new variable *cellcode*.

(2)   Click on **If** to bring the **Compute Variable: If Cases** dialog box. Click the radio button labelled **Include if case satisfies condition**. Enter the statement *drug = 1 & alert = 1* into the box.

(3)   Click on **Continue** to return to the **Compute Variable** window. In the box labelled **Numeric Expression**, type *1*. Press **OK** to run the procedure, which will result in the creation, in the **Data Editor**, of a new variable *cellcode* which will have entries of *1* in all rows where *drug = 1* and *alert = 1* and the system-missing symbol (.) elsewhere. You can check that this has been done by inspecting the **Data Editor** grid.

Repeat steps 1, 2 and 3, substituting the statement *drug = 1 & alert = 2* and typing *2* for the value of *cellcode*. Continue repeating these three steps until the assignment rules for the six values of *cellcode* have been completed.

Now simply run the **one-way ANOVA** procedure, with *drivperf* as the dependent variable and *cellcode* as the independent variable, opting for the **Tukey HSD** test.

8.3 EXPERIMENTS WITH THREE OR MORE TREATMENT FACTORS

SPSS can readily be used to analyse data from more complex factorial experiments, with three or more treatment factors. We should warn the reader, however, that experiments with more than three factors should be avoided, because interpretation of complex interactions involving four or more factors is often extremely difficult.

The ANOVA of data from an experiment with three or more factors, however, is simple on SPSS: it is only necessary to remember that a code variable is needed for each factor.

8.4 A NONPARAMETRIC ALTERNATIVE TO THE TWO-WAY ANOVA

As with the one-factor ANOVA, the use of the factorial ANOVA presupposes that the assumptions of a statistical model hold for the data: for example, homogeneity of cell variance is assumed, and normality of distribution. If there is marked violation of these assumptions, it may be better to use a nonparametric analysis. Meddis (1984) describes the procedure. Unfortunately, it is not available on SPSS.

8.5 SUMMARY

1)   This chapter has considered the analysis of variance of data from a two-factor factorial experiment, with no repeated measures. The use of the technique assumes normality of distribution and homogeneity of cell variance.

2)   The **two-way ANOVA** tests for the presence of a **main effect** of each factor considered separately and for an **interaction** between the factors. A factor is said to have a **main effect** if performance is not the same at all levels. Two factors are said to **interact** if the effect of either is heterogeneous across the levels of the other factor.

3)   For a two-way **ANOVA**, choose
        Statistics
           ANOVA models
              Simple Factorial

4)   Graphs of means can be drawn by choosing
        Graphs
           Line
              Multiple

CHAPTER 9

EXPERIMENTS WITH REPEATED MEASURES ON ALL FACTORS

9.1 INTRODUCTION

An experiment is said to have **repeated measures** on a treatment factor if each subject's performance is measured at every level of the factor. When a factor has repeated measures, its conditions can be said to vary **within subjects**, as opposed to **between subjects**. In Chapter 7, a one-factor experiment was described, in which the recall of a text by three groups of subjects was compared, each group being tested at a different level of the treatment factor (Mnemonic Training History). That experiment was said to have **no repeated measures** on its single treatment factor. It could also be described as a one-factor, **between subjects experiment**. In other circumstances, however, it would be better to have just one sample of subjects, and to test each subject under all the conditions making up the treatment factor. In that case, the experiment could be described as a **one-factor experiment with repeated measures**, or as a one-factor **within subjects experiment**.

As an example, suppose that in a study of performance, the independent variable is task complexity, with three levels: simple, medium and high. The experimental design can be represented in Table 1.

Table 1. A one-factor experiment with repeated measures

COMPLEXITY

simple	medium	complex

same group of subjects

The same design, however, can be represented somewhat differently, as in Table 2.

Table 2. Another representation of the design shown in Table 1

COMPLEXITY

	simple	medium	complex
Subject 1	—	—	—
Subject 2	—	—	—
....	......	......	......
....	......	......	......
Subject 30	—	—	—

In each row, the dashes represent the scores that one particular subject achieves under the three conditions. It can be seen from Table 2 that, although there is just one treatment factor (complexity), the design could be thought of as having two factors:

(1)   The **treatment factor** (with 3 levels).

(2)   **Subjects**, with 30 levels (if there are 30 subjects in the experiment).

Moreover, the two factors, treatment and subjects, **cross**: each level of either factor is to be found in combination with every level of the other. The one-factor repeated measures design, in fact, resembles a two-factor experiment (Chapter 8) with just one observation in each cell. For this reason, the one-factor repeated measures experiment is sometimes termed a **subjects by treatments** experiment.

In this chapter, we shall consider only the analysis of experiments that have repeated measures on **all** their treatment factors. In principle, of course, as with between subjects experiments, there can be any number of treatment factors.

9.2 ADVANTAGES AND DISADVANTAGES OF REPEATED MEASURES EXPERIMENTS

A potential problem with between subjects experiments (Chapters 7 & 8) is that if there are large individual differences in performance, searching for a meaningful pattern in the data is like trying to listen to a radio programme against a background of interference. For example, in the mnemonics methods experiment described in Chapter 7, some of the scores obtained by subjects in the control condition may well be higher than those of subjects who were trained to use a mnemonic. This is because there are some people who, when asked to read through a long list, can, **without any training at all**, reproduce most of the items accurately; whereas others, even after training, would recall very few items. Individual differences, therefore, can introduce considerable **noise** into the data from between subjects experiments.

Essentially, the within subjects experiment uses each subject as their own control; and the crossed nature of the design makes it possible to separate the variance that has resulted from the manipulation of the treatment factor from that arising from individual differences.

Another drawback with the between subjects experiment is that it is wasteful of subjects: if the experimental procedure is a short one, a subject may spend more time travelling to and from the place of testing than actually performing the experiment. The great appeal of the within subjects experiment is that much more extensive use can be made of the subject who has taken the trouble to attend.

In summary, therefore, the within subjects experiment has two advantages over the between subjects experiment:

(1)   It cuts down data noise.

(2)   It is a more efficient use of time and resources.

Nevertheless, the within subjects experiment also has disadvantages, which in some circumstances can outweigh considerations of convenience and maximising of the signal-to-noise ratio. In designing an experiment, it is essential to try to ensure that the independent variable does not co-vary with an unwanted, or **extraneous** variable, so that the effects of the two are entangled, or **confounded**.

Suppose the mnemonics experiment had been of repeated measures design, and that each subject had first performed under the control condition, then under *Mnemonic A* and finally under *Mnemonic B*. Perhaps the improvement under mnemonic A was simply a **practice effect**: the more lists one learns, the better one becomes at learning lists. A practice effect is one kind of **carry-over effect**. Carry-over effects do not always have a positive effect upon performance: recall of the items in a list is vulnerable to interference from items in previous lists. Carry-over effects may depend upon the sequence of conditions: for example, while performance under mnemonic A may be unaffected by previous performance under the control condition, the converse may not true: it may be difficult for subjects who have been trained in the use of a mnemonic to cease to use it on demand. This is an example of an **order effect**. Carry-over and order effects can act as extraneous, confounding variables, making it impossible to interpret the results of a within subjects experiment.

One approach to the problem of carry-over effects and order effects is the procedure known as **counterbalancing**, whereby the order of presentation of the conditions making up a repeated measures factor is varied from subject to subject, in the hope that carry-over and order effects will balance out across conditions. Counterbalancing is not always sensible, however, as in the mnemonics experiment, where (as we have seen) it would make little sense to have the control condition coming last. These matters must be carefully considered before deciding to perform an experiment with repeated measures on its treatment factors.

An additional problem with repeated measures is that if there is **heterogeneity of covariance** (see next section), there is a heightened risk of statistical error.

9.3 REPEATED MEASURES ANOVA WITH SPSS

To perform a univariate repeated measures ANOVA on SPSS, the user must turn to the **repeated measures** option within the **ANOVA Models** which, paradoxically, is based on its multivariate MANOVA program. This program interprets the data obtained at the various levels of a factor with repeated measures as **dependent** variables. Provided these are all linked with the name of the within subjects factor concerned, MANOVA will include a univariate repeated measures ANOVA in its output. Unfortunately, however, the output contains other items, many of which will be unfamiliar to one unaccustomed to working with computing packages. In the space available to us here, we can only offer the briefest outline of the rationale of MANOVA. We strongly recommend readers who wish to deepen their understanding of the topic to study the readable text by Tabachnick & Fidell (1989).

Basically, MANOVA finds a linear function of the dependent variables such that it maximises differences among the treatment groups. It then performs something similar to an ANOVA on a derived data set comprising subjects' scores on the new variable. Instead of performing an F test, however, a multivariate statistic is used such as **Wilks' Lambda, Hotelling's trace criterion**, or **Pillai's criterion**.

Provided the correct command is given, however, the MANOVA output will also include the usual **univariate ANOVA summary table** appropriate for a within subjects experiment. It is important to be aware that the model underlying the use of the repeated measures univariate ANOVA specifies certain additional requirements, over and above those required for between subjects experiments. The most important of these is that the correlations among the scores at the various levels of the within subjects factor are homogeneous. This is known as the assumption of **homogeneity of covariance**. Should that assumption be violated, the true Type I error rate may be greatly inflated. (A Type I error is the probability of rejecting H_0 when it is true.)

The MANOVA program tests for heterogeneity of covariance with the **Mauchly sphericity test**. Should the data fail the sphericity test, the ANOVA F test must be modified to make it more conservative. The **Greenhouse-Geisser** test reduces the degrees of freedom of the numerator and denominator of the F test by multiplying the original values by a factor **e**, the value of which is given in the SPSS output under **Greenhouse-Geisser epsilon**. (The value of F remains the same as before: only the degrees of freedom are reduced.) For a helpful discussion, see Howell (1992: Chapter 14).

9.4 A ONE-FACTOR REPEATED MEASURES ANOVA

9.4.1 Some experimental results

In an exercise in experimental aesthetics, each subject was asked to produce three pictures using just one of three different materials for any one picture: *crayons*, *paints* or *felt-tip* pens. The dependent variable was the *rating* a picture received from a panel of judges. The independent variable was the type of implement used to produce the picture. Since the subjects would certainly vary in artistic ability, it was decided to ask each to produce three pictures, one with each type of implement. In an attempt to neutralise order effects, the order of implements is counterbalanced across subjects. This is a one-factor experiment with repeated measures. Alternatively, it could be described as a **one-factor within subjects** or **subjects by treatments** experiment. Suppose the results are as in Table 3.

Table 3. Results of a one-factor repeated measures experiment

	IMPLEMENT		
	Crayon	Paint	Felt-tip
S1	10	12	14
S2	18	10	16
S3	20	15	16
S4	12	10	12
S5	19	20	21
S6	25	22	20
S7	18	16	17
S8	22	18	18
S9	17	14	12
S10	23	20	18

9.4.2 Preparing the SPSS data set

No coding (grouping) variables are necessary since the three samples of scores are already separate. Using the technique described in Section 3.5, define the variables *crayon*, *paint*, and *felttip*, and enter the data of Table 3 into the three columns.

Save the data to a file with a pathname such as **a:implem.sav**, by choosing
File
    Save as.

9.4.3 Procedure for the repeated measures ANOVA

Select the **Repeated Measures** item from the **ANOVA Models** menu (Figure 1) by choosing
Statistics
    ANOVA Models
        Repeated Measures
to open the **Repeated Measures Define Factor(s)** dialog box (Figure 2).

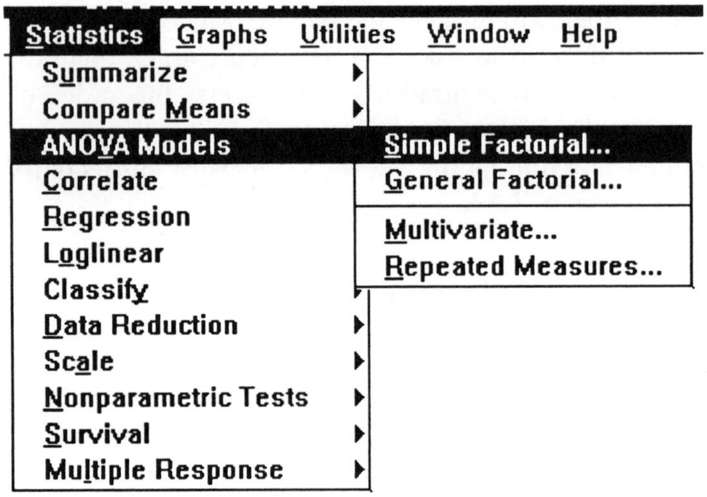

Figure 1.
The ANOVA Models
menu

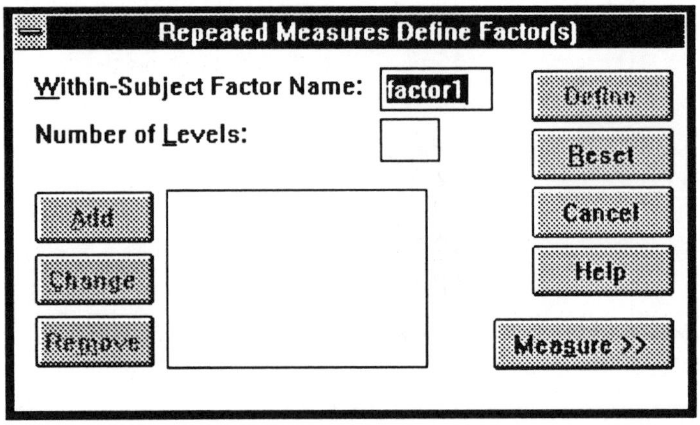

Figure 2.
The Repeated
Measures Define
Factor(s) dialog box

In the **Within-Subject Factor Name** box, delete *factor1* and type a generic name (such as *implem*), bearing in mind that the new name must not be that of any of the variables in the data set; moreover, it must not exceed 8 characters in length. In the **Number of Levels** box, type the number of conditions (*3*) making up the *implem* factor. Click on **Add** to paste the factor name and number of levels into the lowest box (Figure 3).

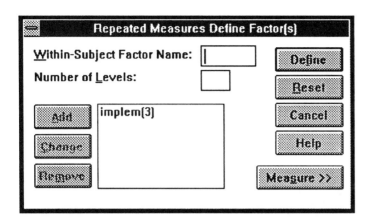

**Figure 3.
The completed
Repeated Measures
Define Factor(s) dialog
box**

Click on **Define** to open the **Repeated Measures ANOVA** dialog box (Figure 4). Click-and-drag the arrowhead cursor down all three variables and click on > to transfer them into the box labelled **Within-Subjects Variables [implem]**. The question marks will be replaced by the variable names as shown in Figure 5.

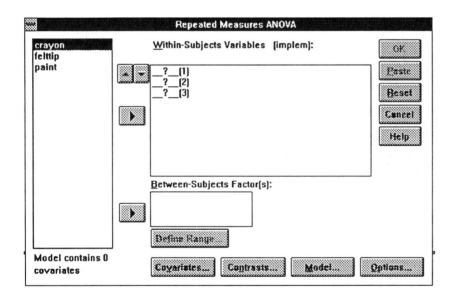

**Figure 4.
The
Repeated
Measures
ANOVA
dialog box**

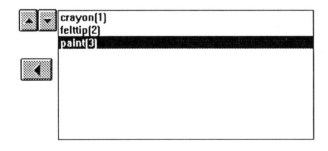

**Figure 5.
The completed Within-
Subjects Variables box**

Finally the multivariate listing can be suppressed (thus leaving just the univariate listing) by clicking on **Model** to open the **Repeated Measures ANOVA: Model** dialog box (not

127

reproduced). In the bottom left-hand corner is a box labelled **Within-Subjects Tests** containing three check boxes (Figure 6). Click on the check box beside **Multivariate tests to** remove the X.

```
┌Within-Subjects Tests──────────┐
│ ☐ Multivariate tests          │
│                               │
│ ☒ Averaged F                  │
│                               │
│ ☐ Epsilon corrected averaged F│
│                               │
└───────────────────────────────┘
```

**Figure 6
The Within-Subjects Tests
check boxes**

Click on **Continue** and then on **OK** to run the analysis.

9.4.4 Output listing for a one-factor repeated measures ANOVA

The first part of the listing (not reproduced here) is subtitled **Tests of Between-Subjects Effects** and can be ignored since this example has no between-subjects variable.

The next section (Output Listing 1) uses the **Mauchly Sphericity Test** to evaluate the homogeneity of covariance assumption, which is important for the univariate approach. If the test is not significant (ie **Significance**, the p-value, has a value greater than 0.05), then the p-value given in the ANOVA summary table, which appears under the title **Averaged Tests of Significance**, can be accepted; otherwise, one can make a more conservative test, such as the Greenhouse-Geisser by returning to the **Within-Subjects Tests** check boxes (Figure 6), clicking on the **Epsilon corrected averaged F** check box and then re-executing the analysis. In the present case, the Mauchly test gives a p-value of 0.684, so the usual ANOVA F test can be used. In the situation where there is no evidence of heterogeneity of covariance, the univariate ANOVA F test is more **powerful** than MANOVA: H_0, if false, is more likely to be rejected.

Output Listing 1. The Mauchly sphericity test and epsilon

```
* * * A n a l y s i s   o f   V a r i a n c e  -- design  1 * * *

Tests involving 'IMPLEM' Within-Subject Effect.


Mauchly sphericity test, W =        .90942
Chi-square approx. =                .75963 with 2 D. F.
Significance =                      .684

Greenhouse-Geisser Epsilon =        .91694
Huynh-Feldt Epsilon =              1.00000
Lower-bound Epsilon =               .50000

AVERAGED Tests of Significance that follow are equivalent to
univariate or split-plot or mixed-model approach to repeated measures.
Epsilons may be used to adjust d.f. for the AVERAGED results.
```

In Output Listing 2 is shown the ANOVA summary table. Note the **Signif of F** value for the *implem* within-subject factor is 0.021 (ie the obtained value of F is significant beyond the 5 per cent level, but not beyond the 0.01 level). Thus the type of implement used does affect the ratings that a painting receives.

Output Listing 2. The ANOVA summary table

```
***A n a l y s i s   o f   V a r i a n c e -- design  1 ***

Tests involving 'IMPLEM' Within-Subject Effect.

AVERAGED Tests of Significance for MEAS.1 using UNIQUE sums of squares
Source of Variation         SS      DF      MS       F  Sig of F

WITHIN+RESIDUAL            72.73    18     4.04
IMPLEM                     39.27     2    19.63     4.86      .021
```

9.4.5 Unplanned pairwise multiple comparisons

Unfortunately, SPSS does not offer pairwise multiple comparisons tests for repeated measures ANOVA. From the output statistics, however, it is a simple matter to arrange the means in order of magnitude, calculate the pairwise differences among them and obtain a **Tukey critical difference (CD)** from the formula

$$CD = q_{critical} \sqrt{(MS_{error}/n)}$$

where q is the value from the table of critical values for the **Studentized Range Statistic** (available in Howell, 1992), MS_{error} is the ANOVA error mean square (called WITHIN CELLS in the output listing) and n is the number of subjects in the experiment.

To obtain $q_{critical}$, enter the table with *number of steps* = the number of levels in the treatment factor, and *error df* = the degrees of freedom for the ANOVA error mean square.

9.5 NONPARAMETRIC TESTS FOR A ONE-FACTOR REPEATED MEASURES EXPERIMENT

As with the one-factor completely randomised experiment, there are available nonparametric methods for the analysis of ordinal and nominal data.

9.5.1 The Friedman test

Suppose that six people rank five objects (O1 to O5) in order of pleasingness. Their decisions might appear as in Table 4.

Table 4. The ranking, by six people, of five aesthetic objects in order of pleasingness

	O1	O2	O3	O4	O5
Person 1	2	1	5	4	3
Person 2	1	2	5	4	3
Person 3	1	3	4	2	5
Person 4	2	1	3	5	4
Person 5	2	1	5	4	3
Person 6	1	2	5	3	4

If we assume that the highest rank is given to the most pleasing object, it would appear, from inspection of Table 4, that Object 3 (O3) seems to be more pleasing to most of the raters than is Object 1. Since, however, each of the entries in Table 4 is not an independent measurement but a rank, the one-factor repeated measures ANOVA cannot be used here.

The Friedman test is suitable for ordinal data of the type shown in Table 4. Enter the data in the usual way into the **Data Editor** grid.

Choose
Statistics
    Nonparametric Tests
        K Related Samples

to obtain the **Tests for Several Related Samples** dialog box (not shown).

On the left, will appear a list of the variables in the **Data Editor** grid. This list should include the items *O1*, *O2*, ..., *O5*, which will contain the numbers shown in Table 4. Simply transfer these names to the **Test Variables** box in the usual way. Make sure the **Friedman** check box has been marked and click on **OK** to run the Friedman test.

9.5.2 Cochran's Q test

Suppose that each of six children is asked to imagine they were in five different situations and had to choose between course of action *A* (coded *0*) and *B* (coded *1*). The results might appear as in Table 5.

Table 5. Courses of action chosen by six children in five scenarios

	Scen1	Scen2	Scen3	Scen4	Scen5
Child 1	0	0	1	1	1
Child 2	0	1	0	1	1
Child 3	1	1	1	1	1
Child 4	0	0	0	1	0
Child 5	0	0	0	0	0
Child 6	0	0	0	1	1

From inspection of Table 5, it would seem that *Course of Action B* is chosen more often in some scenarios than in others. A suitable confirmatory test is **Cochran's Q** test, which was designed for use with related samples of dichotomous nominal data.

The **Cochran Q** test is run by bringing the **Test for Several Related Samples** dialog box to the screen (see previous section). Click off the **Friedman** check box and click on the **Cochran** check box.

9.6 THE TWO-FACTOR WITHIN SUBJECTS ANOVA

9.6.1 Results of a two-factor within subjects experiment

An experiment is designed to investigate the detection of patterns on a screen. The patterns vary in shape and in solidity. The dependent variable (DV) is the number of errors made in responding to the pattern, and the two independent variables are *shape* (*circle*, *square*, or *triangle*) and *solidity* (*outline* or *solid*). The experimenter suspects that a shape's solidity affects whether it is perceived more readily than another shape. The same sample of subjects is used for all the possible treatment combinations, that is, there are repeated measures on both factors in the experiment. As with the one-factor repeated measures experiment, the univariate ANOVA is performed by using SPSS's **Repeated Measures** option within the **ANOVA Models** menu based on its MANOVA program. In this case, although each treatment combination will be treated as a separate dependent variable, the listing will contain a univariate ANOVA summary table with F tests of main effects and the interaction.

The results are shown in Table 6.

Table 6. Results of a two-factor within subjects experiment

| SHAPE:- | Circle | | Square | | Triangle | |
SOLIDITY:-	Solid	Outline	Solid	Outline	Solid	Outline
S1	4	2	2	8	7	5
S2	3	6	2	6	8	9
S3	2	10	2	5	5	3
S4	1	8	5	5	2	9
S5	4	6	4	5	5	10
S6	3	6	4	6	9	12
S7	7	12	2	6	4	8
S8	6	10	9	5	0	10
S9	4	5	7	6	8	12
S10	2	12	12	8	10	12

Extra care is needed when analysing data from experiments with two or more within subjects factors. It is essential to ensure that SPSS understands which data were obtained under which combination of factors. In the present example, there are six data for each subject, each datum being a score achieved under a different combination of the two factors. We can label the data variables as *circsol, circlin, squarsol, squarlin, triansol* and *trianlin,* representing all possible combinations of the shape and solidity factors. Should there be many treatment combinations in the experiment, however, it would be very tedious to name the variables individually. In such cases, it is much more convenient to use the default variable names provided by the computer (ie *var00001, var00002, var00003* etc), but a careful note must be kept about which combinations of levels of the within subjects factors are represented by which of these default variable names. This information has repercussions for the naming of the within-subjects factors within the **Repeated-Measures Define Variable(s)** dialog box, as will be explained later.

In the present example, remembering that the program initially treats each combination of levels of within subjects factors as a separate dependent variable, it can be seen that the sequence of names *circsol, circlin, squarsol, squarlin, triansol* and *trianlin,* represents successive columns of data in Table 6.

9.6.2 Preparing the data set

The data file (part of which is shown in Figure 7) is prepared as before, except that there are now six columns rather than three. Care must be taken with the ordering of the columns - see the previous section.

Figure 7. Part of the SPSS data file for the two-factor within subjects ANOVA

	circsol	circlin	squarsol	squarlin	triansol	trianlin
1	4	2	2	8	7	5
2	3	6	2	6	8	9
3	2	10	2	5	5	3
4	1	8	5	5	2	9

9.6.3 Performing the analysis

The analysis is executed by choosing

Statistics
> **ANOVA Models**
>> **Repeated Measures**

and then completing the various dialog boxes as in the previous example (except that there is an extra repeated-measures factor to be defined). The completed **Repeated Measures Define Factor(s)** dialog box, with two generic names *shape* and *solidity* (together with their respective numbers of levels) is shown in Figure 8. After the **Define** button has been clicked on, the **Repeated Measures ANOVA** dialog box appears (see Figure 9). On the left, the six variables are listed in alphabetical order. On the right, in the box labelled **Within-Subjects Variables [shape,solidity]**, appears a list of the various combinations of the code numbers representing the levels of each of the two treatment factors. It will be noticed that, as one reads down the list, the first number in each pair changes more slowly than the second.

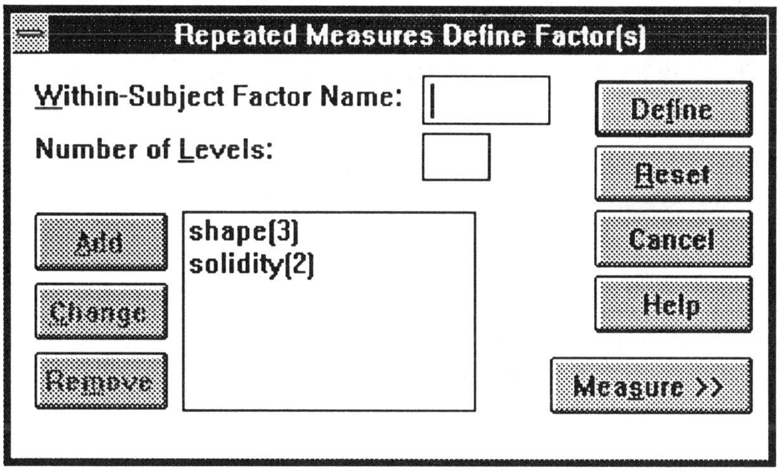

Figure 8. The completed Repeated Measures Define Factor(s) dialog box

Figure 9. The upper part of the Repeated Measures ANOVA dialog box

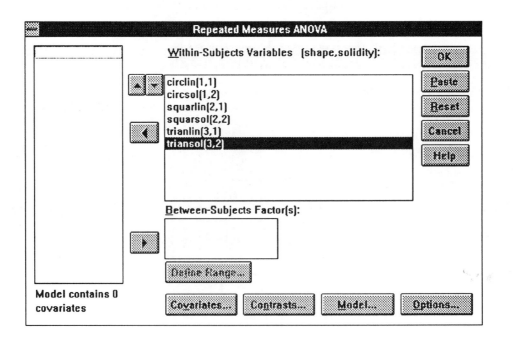

When there is more than one within subjects factor, it is not advisable to transfer the variable names in a block from the left-hand box to the **Within-Subjects Variables** box by a click-and-drag operation, as was done in the case of one within subjects factor. Care must be taken to ensure that the correct variable name is transferred to the correct slot; it is recommended that the variables are transferred one at a time, by noting the numbers in the square brackets and referring to the names of the defined within subjects factors within the square brackets at the head of the box. Remember that the order of variables listed in the left-hand box is alphabetic, rather than the order of successive columns within the **Data Editor** window.

The completed **Repeated Measures ANOVA** dialog box is shown in Figure 10.

Figure 10. The completed Repeated Measures ANOVA dialog box for two within subjects factors [shape and solidity]

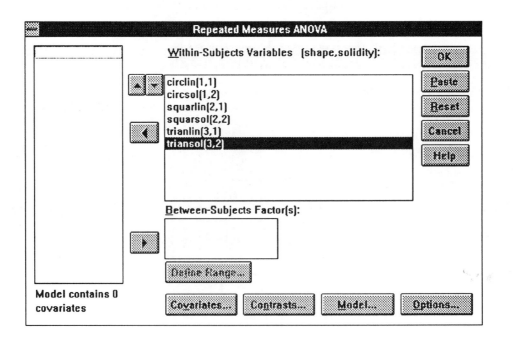

9.6.4 Output listing for a two-factor within subjects ANOVA

The section subtitled **Tests of Between-Subjects Effects** (not reproduced here) can be ignored: here we are interested only in within subjects effects.

9.6.4.1 Tests for main effects

Output Listing 3 contains the **Mauchly sphericity test**, which is used to check the homogeneity of covariance assumption for the SHAPE within subject effect. In this case it is not significant, because the p-value (0.197) is greater than 0.05. Accordingly, the **Averaged Tests of Significance** (the univariate ANOVA) for SHAPE can be accepted.

Output Listing 3. Some statistics of the SHAPE factor

```
* * * A n a l y s i s   o f   V a r i a n c e -- design  1 * * *
Tests involving 'SHAPE' Within-Subject Effect.


Mauchly sphericity test, W =        .66634
Chi-square approx. =                3.24763 with 2 D. F.
Significance =                      .197

Greenhouse-Geisser Epsilon =        .74982
Huynh-Feldt Epsilon =               .86638
Lower-bound Epsilon =               .50000

AVERAGED Tests of Significance that follow multivariate tests are equivalent
univariate or split-plot or mixed-model approach to repeated measures.
Epsilons may be used to adjust d.f. for the AVERAGED results.
```

Output Listing 4 shows that with a **Significance of F** = 0.076, the differences attributable to the factor SHAPE are not significant.

Output Listing 4. The ANOVA summary table for SHAPE

```
* * * A n a l y s i s   o f   V a r i a n c e -- design  1 * * *
Tests involving 'SHAPE' Within-Subject Effect.

AVERAGED Tests of Significance for SCORE using UNIQUE sums of squares
Source of Variation       SS        DF        MS        F  Sig of F

WITHIN CELLS           138.97       18       7.72
SHAPE                   46.03        2      23.02      2.98     .076
```

Output Listing 5 examines the within subject factor SOLIDITY. With only two levels in this factor, the multivariate and univariate approaches are identical, and no sphericity test is necessary. This factor is significant beyond the 1 per cent level, since the **Significance of F** is listed as 0.000 (meaning that the p-value is less than .0005).

Output Listing 5. The ANOVA summary table for SOLIDITY

```
***Analysis   of   Variance -- design   1***

Tests involving 'SOLIDITY' Within-Subject Effect.

AVERAGED Tests of Significance for SCORE using UNIQUE sums of squares
Source of Variation          SS        DF        MS         F   Sig of F

WITHIN CELLS               19.40        9       2.16
SOLIDITY                  117.60        1     117.60      54.56      .000
```

9.6.4.2 Test for an interaction

The next sections of the listing examine the interaction of the two within subject factors (SHAPE BY SOLIDITY). Since the **Mauchly sphericity test** is not significant (Significance = 0.663), the univariate test can be used (Output Listing 6). The ANOVA summary table, however, shows that this interaction is not significant (**Significance of F** = 0.270).

Output Listing 6. Some statistics and the ANOVA summary table for the interaction

```
***Analysis   of   Variance -- design   1***

Tests involving 'SHAPE BY SOLIDITY' Within-Subject Effect.

Mauchly sphericity test, W =        .90250
Chi-square approx. =                .82067 with 2 D. F.
Significance =                      .663

Greenhouse-Geisser Epsilon =        .91116
Huynh-Feldt Epsilon =              1.00000
Lower-bound Epsilon =               .50000

AVERAGED Tests of Significance that follow are equivalent to
univariate or split-plot or mixed-model approach to repeated measures.
Epsilons may be used to adjust d.f. for the AVERAGED results.

- - - - - - - - - - - - - - - - - - - - - - - - - - - - - - - - -

***Analysis   of   Variance -- design   1***

Tests involving 'SHAPE BY SOLIDITY' Within-Subject Effect.

AVERAGED Tests of Significance for SCORE using UNIQUE sums of squares
Source of Variation          SS        DF        MS         F   Sig of F

WITHIN CELLS              151.30       18       8.41
SHAPE BY SOLIDITY          23.70        2      11.85       1.41      .270
```

In conclusion, the listing shows that only *solidity* is significant: the other systematic sources, namely, *shape* and its interaction with *solidity*, are not significant.

9.6.4.3 Unplanned multiple pairwise comparisons following a factorial within subjects experiment

The researcher will often want to follow up the ANOVA of a set of data from a factorial within subjects experiment with pairwise comparisons among either the marginal or the cell means, in order to elucidate a significant main effect or interaction, respectively. Unfortunately, tests such as the **Tukey HSD** are not available on SPSS with repeated measures ANOVA. The user must arrange the relevant means from left to right in order of magnitude and calculate the appropriate **critical difference (CD)** from the formula:

$$CD = q_{critical} \sqrt{(MS_{error} / n^*)}$$

where n^* is the number of scores from which the treatment means to be compared have been calculated. The term MS_{error} is the denominator of the F ratio for the test of the treatment effect concerned, and $q_{critical}$ is the value obtained from the table of critical values of the **Studentized Range Statistic** (available in Howell, 1992).

In the present example, for instance, had the *shape* factor proved significant, one would have wished to make pairwise comparisons among the mean scores for the three different shapes. In that case, $n^* = 20$, i.e. the number of subjects times the number of levels in the *solidity* factor. If, on the other hand, following a significant interaction, you wanted to make comparisons among the individual cell means, $n^* = 10$, because only ten scores contributed to the mean performance under each combination of the factors of *shape* and *solidity*.

To obtain the correct value of q, enter the table with two parameters:

(1) The number of means in the whole comparison set (the number of cell or marginal means).

(2) The degrees of freedom of the error term.

9.7 SUMMARY

1) When an experiment has **repeated measures on all factors**, the analysis can be obtained from the **repeated measures** option within the **ANOVA Models** menu. **Univariate** analyses are preferred to **multivariate** analyses when the sphericity assumption (ie the homogeneity of covariance) holds. If the **Mauchly sphericity test** is significant, however, a **conservative F test** can be used to make a more conservative test.

2) The procedure for repeated-measures ANOVA is
Statistics
   ANOVA Models
     Repeated Measures
Repeated measures factors are defined in the **Repeated Measures Define Factor(s)** dialog box. After clicking on **Define**, the **Repeated Measures ANOVA** dialog box is opened. Here the variable names are arranged in alphabetical order within the left-hand box. The names of the within subjects levels (or the combinations of within subjects levels when there is more than one factor) are transferred to the **Within-Subjects Variables** box, taking particular care when there is more than one within subjects factor, to enter the correct name in the appropriate slot.

3) Multivariate output can be suppressed by clicking on **Model** and switching off the check box for **Multivariate tests.**

4) Nonparametric tests for a one-factor repeated measures experiment include the **Friedman test** for ordinal data and **Cochran's Q test** for dichotomous nominal data.
Choose
Statistics
   Nonparametric Tests
     K Related Samples
to open the **Tests for Several Related Samples** dialog box. Click on the **Friedman** or **Cochran** check box as required.

CHAPTER 10

EXPERIMENTS OF MIXED DESIGN

10.1 INTRODUCTION

10.1.1 Mixed (or split-plot) factorial experiments

It is very common for factorial designs to have repeated measures on **some** (but not all) of their treatment factors. Since such experiments have a mixture of between subjects and within subjects factors, they are often said to be of **mixed** design. The term **split-plot** is also used, reflecting the agronomic context in which this type of experiment was first employed.

In psychological and educational research, the researcher often selects two samples of subjects (eg male and female groups) and performs the same repeated measures experiment upon each group. Suppose, for example, that samples of male and female subjects are tested for recall of a written passage with three different line spacings, the order of presentation of the three levels of the spacing factor being counterbalanced across subjects to neutralise order effects. In this experiment, there are two factors:

(1) Gender (male, female).
(2) Spacing (narrow, medium, wide).

The levels of gender vary **between** subjects, whereas those of spacing vary **within** subjects. The experiment has thus one between subjects and one within subjects factor.

10.1.2 A notational scheme for mixed factorial experiments

In the foregoing experiment on the effects of *gender* and *spacing* upon *recall* of written passages, the *gender* factor was between subjects and the spacing factor was within subjects. We shall adopt the convention whereby within subjects factors are bracketed, so that if A is *gender* and B is *spacing*, the new reading experiment is of type Ax(B), signifying a mixed design with repeated measures on factor B.

With three treatment factors, two mixed designs are possible: there may be one or two repeated measures factors, the former being denoted by AxBx(C), the latter by Ax(BxC).

10.2 THE TWO-FACTOR MIXED FACTORIAL ANOVA

10.2.1 Mixed factorial ANOVA with SPSS

The SPSS **Repeated Measures** program from the **ANOVA Models** menu is used for the analysis of data from experiments with repeated measures on their treatment factors. The procedure for defining the repeated measures factors was explained in Chapter 9. In experiments with mixed designs, however, there are also between subjects factors. As in between subjects experiments, their levels are identified by means of a numerical code in the data file.

10.2.2 Results of a mixed Ax(B) experiment

A psychologist designs an experiment to explore the hypothesis that engineering students, because of their training in two-dimensional representation of three-dimensional structures, have a more strongly developed sense of shape and symmetry than do psychology students. Three types of shapes are presented to samples of psychology and engineering students under sub-optimal conditions on a monitor screen. All three types of shape are presented to each subject: hence shape is a within subjects factor. The category of student (psychology or engineering) on the other hand, is a between subjects factor. The dependent variable is the number of shapes correctly identified.

The results of the experiment are shown in Table 1.

Table 1. Results of a two-factor mixed factorial experiment of type A×(B)

TYPE OF STUDENT		Triangle	SHAPE Square	Rectangle
Psychology	S1	2	12	7
	S2	8	10	9
	S3	4	15	3
	S4	6	9	7
	S5	9	13	8
	S6	7	14	8
Engineering	S7	13	3	35
	S8	21	4	30
	S9	26	10	35
	S10	22	8	30
	S11	20	9	28
	S12	19	8	27

10.2.3 Preparing the SPSS data set

In Table 1, we chose to represent the experimental design with the levels of the within subjects factor arrayed horizontally and those of the between subjects factor stacked vertically, with the level *engineering* under *psychology*. We did so because this arrangement corresponds to the arrangement of the results in the SPSS data set.

The first column of the **Data Editor** grid will contain a single grouping variable representing the psychologists (*1*) and the engineers (*2*). The second, third and fourth columns will contain the results at the three levels of the shape factor (ie *triangle*, *square*, and *rectangle*).

Using the techniques described in Section 3.5, define four variables: *category* (the grouping variable), *triangle*, *square*, and *rectangl* (remember the variable names must not exceed 8 characters in length). Using the **Define Labels** procedure (Section 3.5.3.4), assign to the values of the *category* variable the value labels *Psychology Student* and *Engineering Student*. When the data of Table 1 have been entered into the **Data Editor** grid, they should appear as shown in Figure 1. Save the SPSS data set to a file with a name such as **a:shapes.sav.**

	category	triangle	square	rectangl
1	1	2	12	7
2	1	8	10	9
3	1	4	15	3
4	1	6	9	7
5	1	9	13	8

Figure 1.

The upper part of the SPSS data set from the results in Table 1

10.2.4 Exploring the results: obtaining a table of means and standard deviations

As always, the first step is to explore the data set. What we shall want immediately is a table of cell means and standard deviations, together with the marginal means for the three different shapes. Inspection of this table will indicate whether there has been a main effect of the within subjects factor *shape* or a *shape by category* interaction. The table can be obtained directly, by using the **Means** procedure.

We shall want the marginal means for the between subjects factor to ascertain whether it had a main effect, too. These also can be obtained by running **Means**; but first it is necessary to use **Compute** to calculate the mean score over the three different shapes that each subject achieved.

10.2.4.1 Obtaining the cell means and the marginal means for the within subjects factor

Choose
Statistics
    Compare Means
        Means

to open the **Means** dialog box. Detailed instructions are given in Section 4.3.3.3. Transfer the names of the three *shape* variables into the **Dependent List** box. Transfer *category* into the **Independent List** box. Click on **OK** to obtain a table showing the cell means and the marginal means for the *shape* factor. This table, however, does not include the marginal means for the between subjects factor, *category*.

10.2.4.2 Obtaining the marginal means for the between subjects factor

In order to use **Means** to calculate the marginal means for *category*, one must first define a new variable (eg *meancat*) which is the mean score that a subject achieves over the three different shapes.

Choose
Transform
    Compute

to open the **Compute Variable** dialog box. Detailed instructions are given in Section 4.4.2. Type *meancat* into the **Target Variable** box. In the **Functions** box, scroll down to, and highlight, the function **MEAN[numexpr, numexpr ....]** and click on ^ to transfer the function to the **Numeric Expression** box, where question marks will replace **numexpr**, inviting specific variable names. Delete the question marks and then successively highlight and transfer the variable names *triangle, square,* and *rectangl,* taking care to ensure that there is a comma between each name. The final entry is now **MEAN[triangle, square, rectangl].** Click on **OK** to run the procedure.

Note that in order to display the values of the *meancat* variable in the **Data Editor** window to, say, two places of decimals, it may be necessary to override the general format instruction specified in **Preferences**, which may have specified that all variables will be displayed as integers. Within the **Define Variable** dialog box (brought by double-clicking on the heading *meancat* column), click on **Type** and make the necessary adjustment to the value in the **Decimal Places** box. Now it is possible to compute the marginal means and standard deviations for *category* by returning to **Means** and transferring *meancat* to the **Dependent List** box, and *category* to the **Independent List** box. Click on **OK**.

10.2.4.3 The complete table of marginal and cell means and standard deviations

Table 2 combines the information from the computations described in the previous subsections.

Table 2. Mean levels of performance by two groups of students with three different shapes (standard deviations are given in brackets)

		SHAPE		
	Triangle	Square	Rectangl	
Psychology	6.00 (2.61)	12.17 (2.32)	7.00 (2.10)	8.39
CATEGORY				
Engineering	20.20 (4.26)	7.00 (2.83)	30.83 (3.83)	19.33
	13.08	9.58	18.92	

The values of the marginal means in Table 2 strongly suggest main effects of both the *shape* and *category* factors. Moreover, the markedly superior performance of the engineers on triangles and rectangles is reversed with squares, suggesting the presence of an interaction.

10.2.5 Procedure for a mixed A×(B) ANOVA

Choose
Statistics
    ANOVA Models
        Repeated Measures

to open the **Repeated Measures Define Factor(s)** dialog box (Chapter 9, Figure 2).

In the **Within-Subject Factor Name** box, delete *factor1* and type a generic name (such as *shape*) for the repeated factor. This name must not be that of any of the three levels making up the factor and must also conform to the rules governing the assignment of variable names. In the **Number of Levels** box, type the number of levels (*3*) making up the repeated measures factor. Clicking on **Add** will result in the appearance of the entry *shape(3)* in the lowest box (Figure 2).

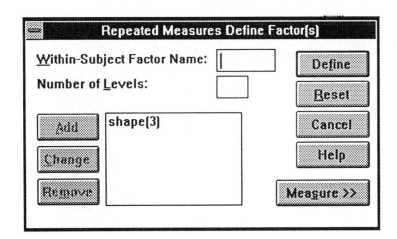

Figure 2.

The completed Repeated Measures Define Factor(s)

Click on **Define** to open the **Repeated Measures ANOVA** dialog box (part of which is shown in Figure 3). Click-and-drag the arrowhead down the variable names to highlight them, and click on > to transfer them into the **Within-Subjects Variable(s) [shape]** box (Figure 4). So far, the procedure has been as described in Chapter 9.

Figure 3. Part of the Repeated Measures ANOVA dialog box before entering the names of the levels

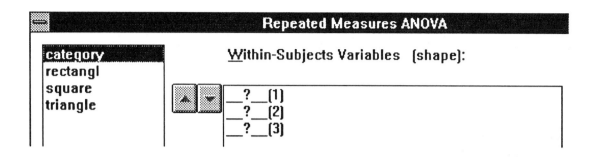

The new element is the presence of the between subjects factor *category*. Click on that variable name and transfer it to the **Between-Subjects Factor(s)** box by clicking on > to the left of that box. On transferral, click on **Define Range** and type the value *1* into the **Minimum** box and *2* into the **Maximum** box. Click on **Continue** to return to the **Repeated Measures ANOVA** dialog box which now appears as shown in Figure 4.

Figure 4. The completed Repeated Measures ANOVA dialog box with one Within Subjects variable (shape) and one Between Subjects variable category

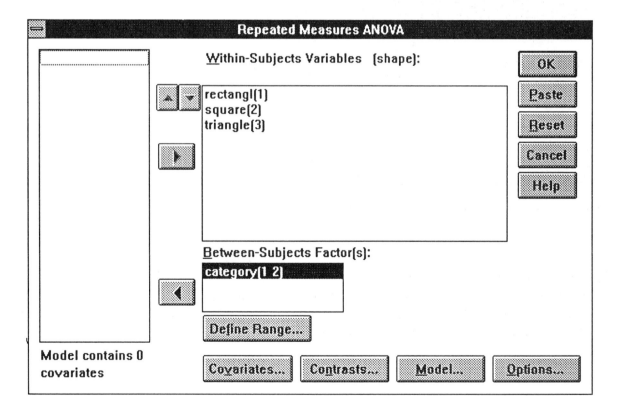

Finally, before running the ANOVA, we suggest that **Multivariate tests** should be turned off. Click on **Model** to open the **Within-Subjects Tests** dialog box, within which are the check boxes of the **Within-Subjects Tests** menu. Cancel the X beside **Multivariate tests** to disable that function (Figure 5).

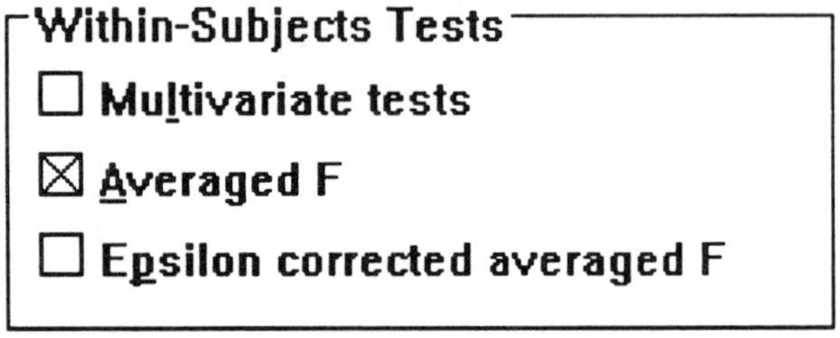

```
┌Within-Subjects Tests──────────────┐
│  □ Multivariate tests              │
│                                    │
│  ⊠ Averaged F                      │
│                                    │
│  □ Epsilon corrected averaged F    │
│                                    │
└────────────────────────────────────┘
```

Figure 5.

The Within-Subjects Tests check boxes within the Repeated Measures ANOVA: Model dialog box

Click on **Continue** to return to the **Repeated Measures ANOVA** dialog box, and then on **OK** to run the ANOVA.

10.2.6 Output listing for the two-factor mixed ANOVA

10.2.6.1 Between subjects effects

The tests for between subjects effects are shown in Output Listing 1.

Output Listing 1. Tests for Between Subjects Effects

```
***Analysis   of   Variance -- design   1***

Tests of Between-Subjects Effects.

Tests of Significance for T1 using UNIQUE sums of squares
Source of Variation        SS       DF       MS          F   Sig of F

WITHIN+RESIDUAL          108.94     10     10.89
CATEGORY                1078.03      1   1078.03      98.95      .000
```

Note that the factor *category* is significant beyond the 1 per cent level: the **Sig of F** (0.000) is less than 0.0005. There is thus a difference in performance between the two groups of students.

10.2.6.2 Tests for within subjects and interaction effects

Output Listing 2 shows the Mauchly test for homogeneity of covariance in the within subjects *shape* factor.

Output Listing 2. Statistics of the Within Subjects shape factor

```
* * * A n a l y s i s   o f   V a r i a n c e -- design   1 * * *
Tests involving 'SHAPE' Within-Subject Effect.


Mauchly sphericity test, W =        .90277
Chi-square approx. =                .92059 with 2 D. F.
Significance =                      .631

Greenhouse-Geisser Epsilon =        .91139
Huynh-Feldt Epsilon =              1.00000
Lower-bound Epsilon =               .50000

AVERAGED Tests of Significance that follow multivariate tests are equivalent
univariate or split-plot or mixed-model approach to repeated measures.
Epsilons may be used to adjust d.f. for the AVERAGED results.
```

The **Mauchly sphericity test** is not significant (**Significance** is greater than 0.05). Had it been significant, it would have been necessary to make a conservative Greenhouse-Geisser test with fewer degrees of freedom (obtained by multiplying the original numerator and denominator degrees of freedom by the value of **epsilon**, which is given in the output). This could also be done by clicking on the **Epsilon corrected averaged F** test in the **Within-Subjects Tests** box (Figure 5).

Output Listing 3 shows the ANOVA summary table for the within subjects factor *shape* and the *category by shape* interaction.

Output Listing 3. ANOVA summary table for shape main effect and for category by shape interaction

```
* * * A n a l y s i s   o f   V a r i a n c e -- design   1 * * *
Tests involving 'SHAPE' Within-Subject Effect.

AVERAGED Tests of Significance for MEAS.1 using UNIQUE sums of squares
Source of Variation          SS        DF        MS         F   Sig of F

WITHIN+RESIDUAL            163.56       20       8.18
SHAPE                     533.56        2     266.78     32.62      .000
CATEGORY BY SHAPE        1308.22        2     654.11     79.99      .000
```

The ANOVA strongly confirms the patterns that were discernible in Table 2: the *shape* and *category* factors both have significant main effects and the interaction between the factors is also significant.

10.3 THE THREE-FACTOR MIXED ANOVA

The procedures described in Section 10.2 can readily be extended to the analysis of data from mixed factorial experiments with three treatment factors. In Section 10.1.2, we introduced a notation for specifying a particular mixed design, whereby a within subjects factor is written in brackets, so that the designation A×(B) denotes a mixed, two-factor factorial experiment, where factor A is between subjects and factor B is within subjects. Here we consider the two possible mixed three-factor factorial designs:

    (1)   The A×(B×C) experiment, with two within subjects factors.
    (2)   The A×B×(C) experiment, with one within subjects factor.

10.3.1 The mixed A×(B×C) experiment

Suppose the A×(B) experiment described in Section 10.2.2 has an additional within subjects factor C added, such as the solidity of the shape (*solidity*) with two levels, either *solid* or *outline*. Thus the subjects (either Psychology or Engineering students) have to try to recognise either solid or outline triangles, squares, or rectangles. This now becomes an A×(B×C) experiment.

There will now be 3×2 = 6 within subjects variables in the **Data Editor** window, each variable containing the data for a combination of *shape* and *solidity*. It is convenient (though not essential) to prepare these columns in the **Data Editor** window systematically by taking the first level of one variable and combining it in turn with each of the levels of the second variable, followed by the second level of the first variable combined with each level of the second variable, and so on. Thus for this experiment the **Data Editor** window might appear as in Figure 6.

Figure 6. The variable names for an A×(B×C) experiment

category	trisolid	trioutln	squsolid	squoutln	recsolid	recoutln

Care must be taken in transferring variable names within the **Repeated Measures ANOVA** dialog box. The names are listed alphabetically within the left-hand box and may not necessarily be in the right order for a block transfer (using the click-and-drag technique) to the **Within-Subjects Variables** box. It may be necessary to transfer the variable names one at a time to ensure that the correct name is fitted into the various slots, bearing in mind that the order of the defined factors is shown in square brackets above the box. The completed dialog box is shown in Figure 7.

Figure 7. The completed Repeated Measures ANOVA dialog box for an A×(B×C) experiment with category as A, shape as B, and solidity as C

Figure 7. **The completed Repeated Measures ANOVA dialog box for an A×(B×C) experiment with category as A, shape as B, and solidity as C**

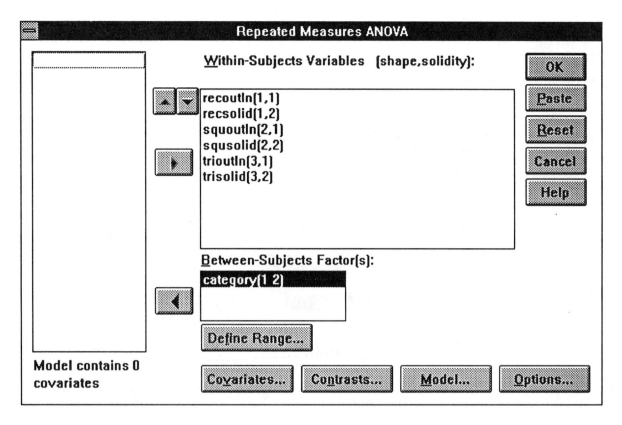

10.3.2 The mixed A×B×(C) experiment

This experiment has two between subjects factors (A and B) and one within subjects factor (C). Suppose the A×(B) experiment described in Section 10.2.2 has an additional between subjects factor added, such as the sex of the subjects (*sex*). This variable has two levels *male* and *female*. Thus the subjects (either Psychology or Engineering students, and either male or female) have to try to recognise shapes (either triangles, squares, or rectangles). This now becomes an A×B×(C) experiment.

There will now be two coding variables *category* and *sex*, and the three levels of the within subjects variable *rectangl*, *square*, and *triangle*. Thus for this experiment the **Data Editor** window might appear as in Figure 8.

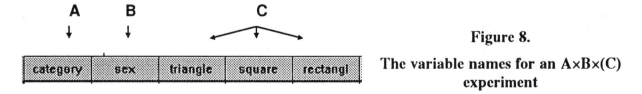

Figure 8.

The variable names for an A×B×(C) experiment

The completed **Repeated Measures ANOVA** dialog box would then be as shown in Figure 9.

Figure 9. The completed Repeated Measures ANOVA dialog box for an A×B×(C) experiment with category as A, sex as B, and shape as C

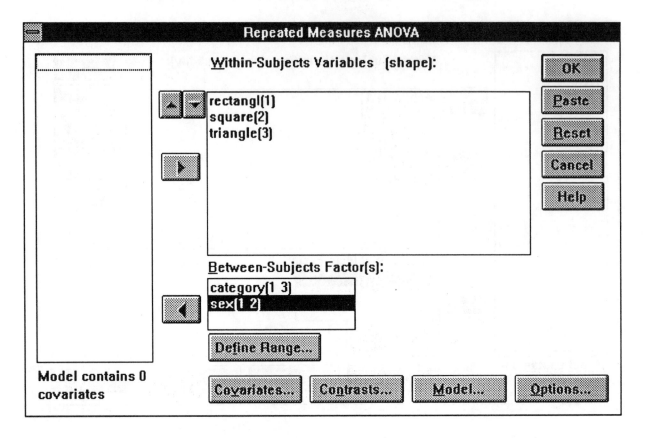

10.4 FURTHER ANALYSIS: SIMPLE EFFECTS AND MULTIPLE COMPARISONS

The analysis of variance is a large topic in statistics, and there are available many more techniques than we can mention in this book, which is primarily concerned with computing, rather than statistics as such. For example, following the confirmation that an interaction is significant, it is often useful to follow up the initial ANOVA with additional tests of the effects of one factor at specific levels of another. Such analyses of **simple effects** can be combined with both planned and unplanned multiple comparisons. We urge the reader who is unfamiliar with such methods to read the relevant chapters in a lucid textbook such as Howell (1992).

10.5 SUMMARY

1) An ANOVA design that includes both between subjects and within subjects factors is called a **mixed,** or **split-plot**, design. In SPSS, the results of such an experiment are analysed with the **Repeated Measures** item from the **ANOVA Models** menu.

2) The procedure for mixed designs is
Statistics
    ANOVA Models
        Repeated Measures

Generic names for repeated measures are defined in the **Repeated Measures Define Factor(s)** dialog box. After each within subjects factor name has been entered, the number of levels it contains is typed into the **Number of Levels** box. Click on **Add** to transfer the factor name and its levels into the **Factor Name** box.

The variable names are then entered in the **Repeated Measures ANOVA** dialog box, taking care if there is more than one within subjects factor to ensure that the correct name is transferred to the appropriate slot in the **Within-Subjects Variables [factor1 , factor2]** box. Between subjects factor names, along with their ranges of levels, are entered in the **Between-Subjects Factor(s)** box.

Multivariate output can be suppressed by clicking on the **Model** box and clicking off the **Multivariate tests** check box.

3) Tables of means and standard deviations can be obtained by using the **Means** procedure. The mean scores at different levels of between subjects factors are obtained by computing a new variable of means across all levels of the within subjects factors using the **Compute** procedure, and then applying the **Means** procedure to this new variable.

CHAPTER 11

MEASURING STATISTICAL ASSOCIATION

11.1 INTRODUCTION

11.1.1 Statistical association in interval data

So far, this book has been concerned with statistical methods devised for the purpose of comparing averages between or among samples of data that might be expected to differ in general level: for example, right-handed people might be compared with left-handed people; the trained might be compared with the untrained; males might be compared with females.

Consider, however, a set of paired data of the sort that might be produced if one were to weigh each of a sample of one hundred men before and after they had taken a fitness course. Previously, our concern would have been with the **comparison** of the men's average weight before the course with their average weight afterwards. One would expect these data to show another feature, however: the person who was heaviest before the course is likely to be among the heaviest in the group afterwards; the lightest person before the course should be among the lightest afterwards; and one with an intermediate score before the course is likely to be in the middle of the group afterwards. In other words, there should be a statistical **association** or **correlation** between people's weights before and after the course.

11.1.2 Depicting an association: the scatterplot

The existence of a statistical association between two variables is most apparent in the appearance of a diagram called a **scatterplot** which, in the foregoing example, would be constructed by representing each person as a point in space, using as coordinates that person's weights before and after taking the course. The cloud of points would take the shape of an ellipse, whose longer axis slopes upwards from left to right across the page. An elliptical scatterplot indicates the existence of a **linear relationship** between two variables. If the slope of the major axis is positive, the variables are said to be **positively correlated**; if it is negative, they are **negatively correlated**. The thinner the ellipse, the stronger the degree of linear relationship; the fatter the ellipse, the weaker the relationship. A circular scatterplot indicates the absence of any relationship between the two variables.

11.1.3 Linear association

The term **linear** means 'of the nature of a straight line'. In our current example, a straight line (known as a **regression line**) can be drawn through the points in the elliptical scatterplot so that it is rather close to most of the points (though there may be one or two atypical scores, or **outliers** as they are termed). We can use the regression line to make quite a good **estimate** of a particular man's weight after the course from a knowledge of his weight before the course: if we have *weight before* on the horizontal axis and *weight after* on the vertical axis, we need only move up to the point on the regression line vertically above his first weight, and then move across to the vertical scale to estimate his second weight. If we do that, we shall probably be in error, the difference between his true weight after the course and his estimated weight from the regression line being known as a **residual**. The value of the residual, however, is likely to be small in comparison with the man's true weight after the course.

11.1.4 Measuring the strength of a linear association: the Pearson correlation

A **correlation coefficient** is a statistic devised for the purpose of measuring the strength, or degree, of a supposed linear association between two variables, each of which has been measured on a scale with units. The most familiar correlation coefficient is the **Pearson correlation (r)**. The Pearson correlation is so defined that it can take values only within the range from -1 to +1, inclusive. The larger the absolute value (ie ignoring the sign), the narrower the ellipse, and the closer to the regression line the points in the scatterplot will fall. A perfect correlation arises when the values of one variable are exactly predictable from those of the other and the Pearson correlation takes a value of ± 1, in which case all the points in the scatterplot lie on the regression line. In other cases, the narrower the elliptical cloud of points, the stronger the association, and the greater the absolute value of the Pearson correlation. When there is no association whatever between two variables, their scatterplot should be a roughly circular cloud, in which case the Pearson correlation will be about zero and the regression line will be horizontal, ie have a slope of zero (see Figure 1).

Figure 1. The scatterplots of sets of data showing varying degrees of linear association: top left r = +1.0; bottom left r = -1.0; top right r = 0; bottom right r = +0.6

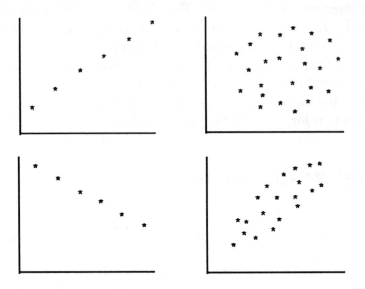

11.1.5 A word of warning

It is quite possible, from inspection of a scatterplot, to do two things:

(1)   See whether there is indeed a linear relationship between the variables, in which case the Pearson correlation would be a meaningful statistic to use.

(2)   Guess fairly accurately what the value of the Pearson correlation would be if calculated.

In other words, from inspection of their scatterplot alone, one can discern all the essential features of the true relationship (if any) between two variables. So if we reason from the scatterplot to the statistics, we shall not go seriously wrong.

The converse, however, is not true: **given only the value of a Pearson correlation, one can say nothing whatsoever about the relationship between two variables.** In a famous paper, the statistician Anscombe (1973) presents data which illustrate how misleading the value of the Pearson correlation can be. Basically, he shows that, wherever the scatterplot is neither elliptical nor circular (ie the variables are neither in a linear relationship nor independent), the value of the Pearson correlation is misleading. (Exercise 13 uses Anscombe's data to show this.) For example, data giving a zero Pearson correlation may show a very strong **nonlinear** association in their scatterplot. Two variables may be unrelated (and most of the data may show a circular scatterplot), but the presence of one or two outliers can exert considerable **leverage** and yield a high Pearson correlation, suggesting a strong linear relationship.

The moral of this cautionary tale is clear: when studying the association between two variables, always construct a scatterplot, and interpret (or disregard) the Pearson correlation accordingly. In the same paper, Anscombe gives a useful rule for deciding whether there really is a robust linear relationship between two variables: should the shape of the scatterplot be unaltered by the removal of a few observations at random, there is probably a real relationship between the two variables.

To sum up, the **Pearson correlation** is a measure of a **supposed** linear relationship between two variables; and the supposition of linearity must be confirmed by inspection of the scatterplot.

11.2 CORRELATIONAL ANALYSIS WITH SPSS

The principal of a tennis coaching school thinks that tennis proficiency depends upon the possession of a degree of general hand-eye coordination. To confirm this hunch, she measures the hand-eye coordination of some pupils who are beginning the course and their proficiency in tennis at the end of the course.

The data are shown in Table 1.

Table 1. A set of paired data

Pupil	Initial Co-ordination	Final Tennis Proficiency
1	4	4
2	4	5
3	5	6
4	2	2
5	10	6
6	4	2
7	7	5
8	8	6
9	9	9
10	5	3

11.2.1 Preparing the SPSS data set

Using the techniques described in Section 3.5, define the variables *coordin* and *proficy* (fuller names, such as *Initial Co-ordination* and *Final Tennis Proficiency*, can be assigned by using the **Define Labels** procedure). Type in the data and save to a file such as **a:corr.sav**.

11.2.2 Obtaining a scatterplot

Choose
Graphs
    Scatter

When the **Scatterplot** selection box (Figure 2) appears, click on **Define** (with a **Simple** scatterplot selected by default).

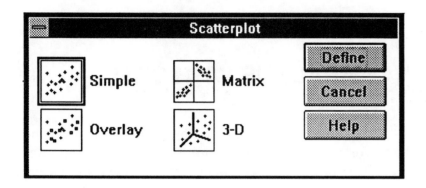

The scatterplot selection box

Enter the variable names proficy and coordin into the **y-axis** and the **x-axis** box, respectively. Click on **OK**.

The scatterplot is shown in Figure 3. The plot shows a consistent trend, with no outliers.

Figure 3. Scatterplot of Final Tennis Proficiency against Initial Co-ordination

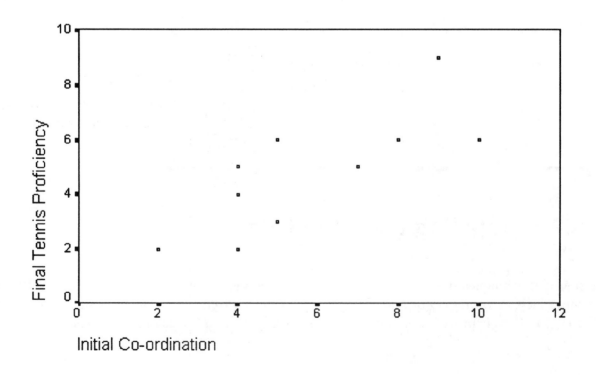

11.2.3 Procedure for the Pearson correlation

Choose (Figure 4)
Statistics
    Correlate
        Bivariate

to open the **Bivariate Correlations** dialog box (the completed version is shown in Figure 5).

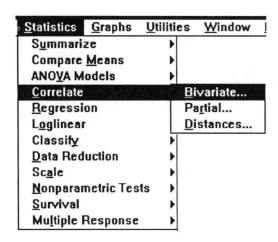

Figure 4.

The Correlate menu

Highlight both variables and click on > to transfer the names to the **Variables** box. Click on **Options** and then click on the **Means and Standard Deviations** check box. Click on **Continue** and then on **OK** to run the correlation coefficient and the optional additional statistics.

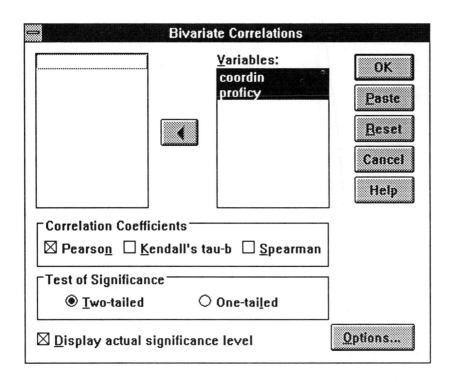

Figure 5.

The completed Bivariate Correlations dialog box

11.2.4 Output listing for the Pearson correlation

The output listing (Output Listing 1) begins with a tabulation of the means and standard deviations of the two variables, as requested with **Options**. Then the correlation coefficient, together with its exact p-value, is listed. With a value for r of 0.7752 and a two-tailed p-value of 0.008, it can be concluded that the correlation coefficient is significant beyond the 1 per cent level.

```
Variable      Cases           Mean          Std Dev
COORDIN        10            5.8000          2.5734
PROFICY        10            4.8000          2.1499
     - -  Correlation Coefficients  - -

               COORDIN        PROFICY

COORDIN        1.0000          .7752
               <   10>        <   10>
               P= .           P= .008

PROFICY         .7752         1.0000
               <   10>        <   10>
               P= .008        P= .

(Coefficient / (Cases) / 2-tailed Significance)

" . " is printed if a coefficient cannot be computed
```

Output Listing 1.

Pearson correlation and statistics of the two variables

If the **Display actual significance level** check box at the bottom left of the **Bivariate Correlations** dialog box is turned off (see Figure 5), the correlation is displayed as in Output Listing 2.

```
     - -  Correlation Coefficients  - -

               COORDIN        PROFICY

COORDIN        1.0000          .7752**
PROFICY         .7752**       1.0000

* - Signif. LE .05     ** - Signif. LE .01     (2-tailed)

" . " is printed if a coefficient cannot be computed
```

Output Listing 2.

Brief display of the significance of r

11.2.5 Obtaining a correlation matrix

When there are more than two variables, SPSS can be commanded to construct a **correlation matrix,** a rectangular array whose entries are the correlations between each variable and every other variable.   This is done by entering as many variable names as required into the **Variables** box within the **Bivariate Correlations** dialog box (Figure 5).

11.3 OTHER MEASURES OF ASSOCIATION

The Pearson correlation is suitable only for interval data. With nominal or ordinal data, other measures must be used. (**Ordinal** data are either ranks or records of **ordered** category membership; **nominal** data are records of **qualitative** category membership.)

11.3.1 Measures of association strength for ordinal data

The term ordinal data embraces all data relating to quantitative variables that are not measures on an independent scale with units. For example, if we rank a group of 10 people with respect to height, giving 10 to the tallest and 1 to the shortest, the resulting set of ranks is an ordinal data set, because an individual rank does not signify so many inches, centimetres (or some other unit of height): a rank merely expresses an individual's height in relation to the heights of the other people in that particular group.

If two judges are asked to rank, say, ten paintings in order of preference, they may well disagree in their orderings, especially if each judge is required to assign a different rank to each object and avoid 'ties'. (This stricture, however, is not always enforced and one or two ties may be tolerated.) The result of such an exercise would be a set of paired ordinal data.

In a rather different procedural paradigm, however, ties, rather than being, at best, tolerable may actually be built into the judgmental process. Judges may be asked to assign objects to a pre-specified set of ordered categories. If, as is usual, there are more objects than categories, tied observations are inevitable. Rating scales yield data in the form of assignments to ordered categories.

The term **ordinal data** includes both ranks and assignments to ordered categories. When, as in the case of the two judges, ordinal data are paired, the question arises as to the extent to which the two sets of ranks of category assignments agree. This is a question about the strength of association between two variables which, although quantitative, are measured at the ordinal, rather than the interval level.

11.3.1.1 The Spearman rank correlation

Suppose that the ranks assigned to the ten paintings by the two judges are as in Table 2.

It is obvious from Table 2 that the judges generally agree closely in their rankings: at most, the ranks they assign to a painting differ by a single rank. One way of measuring the level of agreement between the two judges is by calculating the Pearson correlation between the two sets of ranks. This correlation is known as the **Spearman rank correlation** (or as **Spearman's rho**). The Spearman rank correlation is usually presented in terms of a formula which, although it looks very different from that of the Pearson correlation, is actually equivalent, provided that no ties are allowed.

Table 2. Ranks assigned by two judges to each of ten paintings

Painting	A	B	C	D	E	F	G	H	I	J
First Judge	1	2	3	4	5	6	7	8	9	10
Second Judge	1	3	2	4	6	5	8	7	10	9

The use of the Spearman rank correlation is not confined to ordinal data. Should a scatterplot show that the Pearson correlation is unsuitable as a measure of the strength of association between two quantitative variables which have been measured at the interval level, the scores on both variables can be converted to ranks and the Spearman rank correlation calculated instead.

With small samples, it is difficult to obtain an accurate p-value for a Spearman correlation, especially when there are tied ranks. When there are no tied ranks, one can obtain critical values for the Spearman rank correlation from tables in textbooks such as Neave & Worthington (1988). When ties are present, they must reduce one's confidence in the critical values given in the tables. The user can but hope that when there is only a tie or two here and there, the tables will still give serviceable p-values.

11.3.1.2   Kendall's tau statistics

Kendall's tau statistics provide an alternative to the Spearman rank correlation as measures of agreement between rankings, or assignments to ordered categories. The basic idea is that one set of ranks can be converted into another by a succession of reversals of pairs of ranks in one set: the fewer the reversals needed (in relation to the total number of possible reversals), the larger the value of tau. The numerator of Kendall's tau is the difference between the number of pairs of objects whose ranks are concordant (i.e. they go in the same direction) and the number of discordant pairs. If the former predominate, the sign of tau is positive; if the latter predominate, tau is negative.

There are three different versions of Kendall's tau: **tau-a**, **tau-b** and **tau-c**. All three measures have the same numerator, the difference between the numbers of concordant and discordant pairs. It is in their denominators that they differ, the difference lying in the way they handle tied observations. The denominator of tau-a is simply the total number of pairs. The problem with tau-a is that when there are ties, its range quickly becomes restricted, to the point where it becomes difficult to interpret. The correlation tau-b has terms in the denominator that consider, in either variable, pairs that are tied on one variable but not on the other. (When there are no ties, the values of tau-a and tau-b are identical.) The correlation tau-c was designed for situations where one wishes to measure agreement between assignments to unequal-sized sets of ordered categories. Provided the data meet certain requirements, the appropriate tau correlation can vary throughout the complete range from -1 to +1.

Kendall's tau correlations have advantages over the Spearman correlation, especially with small data sets, in which there are tied assignments, where serviceable p-values can still be obtained.

11.3.1.3   Obtaining the Spearman and Kendall rank correlations

In the **Data Editor** grid, define two variables, *judge1* and *judge2*. From Table 2, enter the ranks assigned by the first judge into the *judge1* column and those assigned by the second judge into the *judge2* column.

Choose
Statistics
 Correlate
  Bivariate

to obtain the **Bivariate Correlations** dialog box (Figure 5).

By default, the **Pearson** check box will be marked. Mark also the **Kendall's tau-b** and the **Spearman** check boxes and click on **OK** to obtain all three statistics (Output Listing 3). Note that the calculation of Kendall's statistics with **categorial** data, in the form of assignments of target objects to ordered categories, is best handled by the **Crosstabs** procedure (see next section); indeed, tau-c can only be obtained in **Crosstabs**.

Output Listing 3   The Pearson correlation between two sets of ranks

```
                        - -  Correlation Coefficients  - -

                   JUDGE1        JUDGE2

       JUDGE1      1.0000         .9515
                 (   10)       (   10)
                 P= .          P= .000

       JUDGE2       .9515        1.0000
                 (   10)       (   10)
                 P= .000        P= .


K E N D A L L    C O R R E L A T I O N    C O E F F I C I E N T S  ·


       JUDGE2          .8222
                  N(   10)
                  Sig .001

                   JUDGE1


S P E A R M A N    C O R R E L A T I O N    C O E F F I C I E N T S


       JUDGE2          .9515
                  N(   10)
                  Sig .000

                   JUDGE1
```

Output Listing 3 shows the Pearson correlation between the two sets of ranks as *0.9515*, and the Kendall correlation as *0.8222*. This value is different from that of the Pearson correlation, but there is nothing untoward in this: the two statistics are based on quite different theoretical foundations and often take noticeably different values. Finally the Spearman rank correlation is *0.9515*, which is exactly the value given for the Pearson correlation.

11.3.2 Measures of association strength for categorial data

When people's membership of two sets of mutually exclusive and exhaustive categories (such as sex or blood group) is recorded, it is possible to construct a **crosstabulation**, or **contingency table** (see Section 3.9.2). In the analysis of categorial data, the crosstabulation is the analogue of the scatterplot. Note that the categories of each variable must be mutually exclusive, that is no individual or case can fall into more than one combination of categories.

In SPSS, crosstabulations are handled by **Crosstabs**, which is found in the **Summarize** menu. Within the **Crosstabs** dialog box, there is a **Statistics** subdialog box (this chapter, Figure 11) containing check boxes for several measures of association. Many of these are based on the familiar **chi-square** statistic, which is used for determining the presence of an association between two qualitative variables. The rejection of H_0 by means of chi-square, however, only establishes the **existence** of a statistical association: it does not measure its **strength**. In fact, the chi-square statistic is unsuitable as a **measure** of association, because it is affected by the total frequency.

{A word of warning about the misuse of chi-square should be given here. It is important to realise that the calculated statistic is only **approximately** distributed as the theoretical chi-square distribution: the greater the expected frequencies, the better the approximation, hence the rule about minimum expected frequencies, which is stated in Section 11.3.2.2. It is also important to note that the use of the chi-square statistic requires that **each individual studied contributes to the count in only one cell in the crosstabulation**. There are several other potential problems the user should be aware of. A lucid account of the rationale and assumptions of the chi-square test is given by Howell (1992), and a survey of the errors and misconceptions about chi-square that abound in the research literature is given by Delucchi (1983).}

Several measures of strength of association for nominal data have been proposed (see Reynolds, 1984). An ideal measure should mimic the correlation coefficient by having a maximum absolute value of 1 for perfect association, and a value of 0 for no association. The choice of the appropriate statistic depends on whether the variables are ordinal or nominal, and whether the contingency (crosstabulation) table is 2×2 (each variable has two categories) or larger. Guidance can be found by clicking on the **Help** box and choosing the various statistics in turn to find the most appropriate one. One such statistic, for example, is the **phi coefficient**, obtained by dividing the value of chi-square by the total frequency and taking the square root. For two-way contingency tables involving variables with more than two categories, however, another statistic, known as **Cramer's V**, is preferred because with more complex tables, Cramer's measure can still, as in the 2×2 case, achieve its maximum value of unity. Other measures of association, such as **Goodman & Kruskal's lambda**, measure the proportional reduction in error achieved when membership of a category on one attribute is used to predict category membership on the other. If the categories in the cross-tabulation are

ordered, we have ordinal, not nominal, data and Kendall's statistics **tau-b** and **tau-c** are appropriate.

11.3.2.1 A 2×2 contingency table

Suppose that 50 boys and 50 girls are individually asked to select toys from a cupboard. The available toys have previously been categorised as mechanical or non-mechanical. The hypothesis is that the boys should prefer mechanical toys, and the girls non-mechanical toys. There are two nominal variables here: *group* (boys or girls); and *children's choice* (mechanical or non-mechanical). The null hypothesis (H_0) is that there is no association between the variables. Table 3 shows the children's choices.

Table 3. A contingency table

		CHILDREN'S CHOICE		
		Mechan-ical	Non-mechanical	Total
GROUP	Boys	30	20	50
	Girls	15	35	50
	Total	45	55	100

From inspection of this 2×2 contingency table, it would appear that there is an association between the group and choice variables: the majority of the boys did, in fact, choose mechanical toys; whereas the majority of the girls chose non-mechanical toys.

11.3.2.2 Procedure for crosstabulation and associated statistics (chi-square, phi and Cramer's V)

The SPSS data set for a contingency table must include two coding variables to identify the various cell counts, one representing the rows (*group*), the other the columns (*choice*). Using the techniques described in Section 3.5, define the variables *group*, *choice*, and *count*. In the *group* variable, the code numbers *1* and *2* can represent *boys* and *girls*, respectively; in the *choice* variable, the values *1* and *2* can represent *mechanical* and *non-mechanical*, respectively.

Type the data into the three columns, as shown in Figure 6.

	group	choice	count
1	1	1	30
2	1	2	20
3	2	1	15
4	2	2	35

Figure 6.

Part of the Data Editor window showing the coding of the children's choices

The next step is essential. Since the data in the *count* column represent cell frequencies of a variable (not values), SPSS must be apprised of this by means of the **Weight Cases** item within the **Data** menu (Figure 7).

Choose
Data
    Weight Cases

to open the **Weight Cases** dialog box (Figure 8).

Figure 7. The Data menu

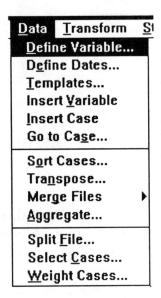

Figure 8. The Weight Cases dialog box

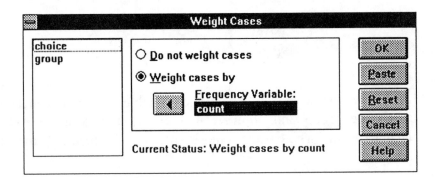

Click on the name of the variable that is to be weighted (*count*), then on the item **Weight cases by** (which cancels the default item **Do not weight cases**), and finally on > to enter *count* into the **Frequency Variable** box. Click on **OK**. The completed dialog box is shown in Figure 8.

To analyse the contingency table data, choose
Statistics
    Summarize

and then click on **Crosstabs** (Figure 9). This will open the **Crosstabs** dialog box (Figure 10).

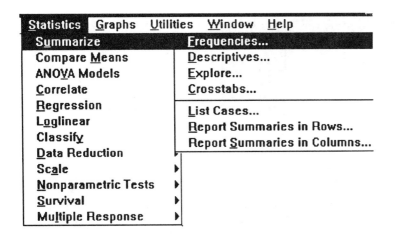

Figure 9.

Finding Crosstabs in the Statistics menu

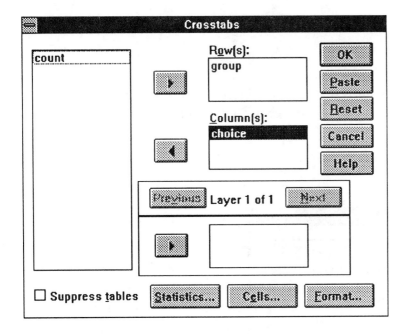

Figure 10.

The completed Crosstabs dialog box

Within the **Crosstabs** dialog box, click on *group* and then on > to transfer the name into the **Row(s)** box. Click on *choice* and then on > to transfer the name into the **Column(s)** box (Figure 10).

Click on **Statistics** to open the **Crosstabs: Statistics** dialog box (Figure 11). Within the **Nominal Data** list of check boxes, select **Chi-square** and **Phi and Cramer's V**. Click on **Continue** to return to the **Crosstabs** dialog box.

We recommend an additional option for computing the expected cell frequencies. This enables the user to check that the prescribed minimum requirements for the valid use of chi-square have been fulfilled. Although there has been debate about these, the practice of leading authorities has been to proscribe the use of chi-square when:

    (a)   In 2×2 tables, any of the expected frequencies are less than 5.

    (b)   In larger tables, any of the expected frequencies is less than 1 or more than 20% are less than 5.

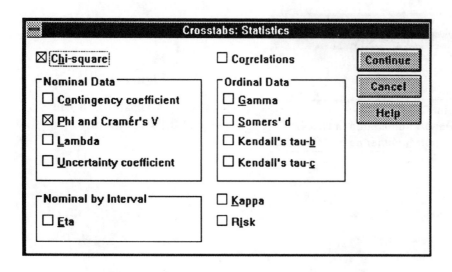

Figure 11.

The Crosstabs: Statistics dialog box

Click on **Cells** at the foot of the **Crosstabs** dialog box (Figure 10) to open the **Crosstabs: Cell Display** selection box (Figure 12). Click on the **Expected** check box in the **Counts** box. Click on **Continue** and then on **OK**.

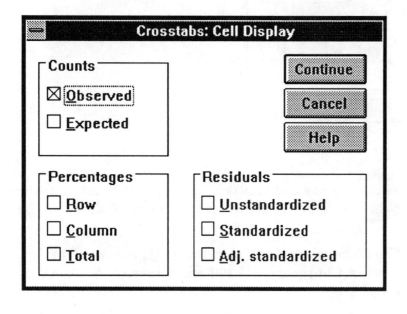

Figure 12.

The Crosstabs: Cell Display selection box

11.3.2.3 Output listing for crosstabulation and associated statistics (chi-square, phi and Cramer's V)

Output Listing 4 displays the cross-tabulation (contingency) table, with the observed and expected frequencies, as requested in the **Crosstabs: Cell Display** dialog box. None of the expected frequencies is less than 5.

Output Listing 4. A contingency table including the optional expected values (Exp Val)

```
GROUP  by  CHOICE  Children's Choice

                        CHOICE          Page 1 of 1
                 Count
                 Exp Val |Mechanic Non-mech
                         |al       anical      Row
                         |       1        2|   Total
       GROUP             ---------------------
                     1  |     30       20|      50
         Boys           |   22.5     27.5|   50.0%

                     2  |     15       35|      50
         Girls          |   22.5     27.5|   50.0%

                 Column      45       55|     100
                 Total    45.0%    55.0%   100.0%
```

Output Listing 5 shows the requested statistics.

Output Listing 5. Statistics of a contingency table

Chi-Square	Value	DF	Significance
Pearson	9.09091	1	.00257
Continuity Correction	7.91919	1	.00489
Likelihood Ratio	9.24017	1	.00237
Mantel-Haenszel test for linear association	9.00000	1	.00270

Minimum Expected Frequency -   22.500

Statistic	Value	ASE1	Val/ASE0	Approximate Significance
Phi	.30151			.00257 *1
Cramer's V	.30151			.00257 *1

*1 Pearson chi-square probability

Number of Missing Observations: 0

The first column is labelled **Chi-square**. The row labelled **Pearson** lists the conventional chi-square statistic, along with its tail probability under H_0 (labelled **Significance**). Ignore the **Likelihood Ratio** and the **Mantel-Haenszel test for linear association**.

It can be concluded that there is a significant association between the variables *group* and *choice*, as shown by the p-value (less than 0.01) for chi-square. The **phi coefficient** provides a measure of the strength of the association.

11.4 SUMMARY

1)   The degree of association between two quantitative interval variables level can be measured by a correlation coefficient. The most well-known correlation coefficient is the **Pearson** correlation.
Choose
Statistics
   Correlate
     Bivariate

2)   It is recommended that a scatterplot should **always** be requested.
Choose
Graphs
   Scatter
     Simple

3)   For ordinal data in the form of ranks, measures of association strength are provided by the **Spearman rank correlation** and **Kendall's tau-a** and **tau-b** statistics. These can be found by choosing
Statistics
   Correlate
     Bivariate

4)   Various statistics for categorial data are available in the **Crosstabs** menu, which analyses contingency tables. When the data are in the form of counts of category membership, coding variables are needed to identify the cells of the table. After preparing the SPSS data set, it is essential to indicate that the data in the column representing the cell frequencies are frequencies and not score values.
Choose
Data
   Weight Cases.
Select the appropriate variable name for the frequency data, click on the **Weight**

Cases by option, and then on > to insert the name in the **Frequency Variable** box.

To execute the cross-tabulation, choose
Statistics
  Summarize
    Crosstabs
Select the row and column variables using the **Row(s)** and **Column(s)** boxes. Choose the appropriate statistics by clicking on **Statistics** within the **Crosstabs** dialog box and then clicking on check boxes in the **Crosstabs: Statistics** selection box. It is also recommended that expected cell frequencies are selected by clicking on **Cells** within the **Crosstabs** dialog box and then clicking on the **Expected** check box.

CHAPTER 12

REGRESSION

12.1 INTRODUCTION

Much of Chapter 11 was devoted to the use of the **Pearson correlation** to measure the strength of the association between two quantitative variables, each of which has been measured on an interval scale.

But the associative coin has two sides. On the one hand, a single number can be calculated (a correlation coefficient) which expresses the **strength** of the association. On the other, however, there is a set of techniques, known as **regression methods**, which utilise the presence of an association between two variables to predict the values of one (the dependent variable) from those of another (the independent variable). It is with this predictive aspect that the present chapter is concerned.

To sum up, in **correlation**, the **degree of statistical association** between variables is expressed as a single number known as a **correlation coefficient**. In **regression**, the purpose is to **estimate** or **predict** some characteristic from a knowledge of others by constructing a **regression equation**.

12.1.1 Simple, two-variable regression

In **simple, two-variable regression**, the values of one variable (the dependent variable, y) are estimated from those of another (the independent variable, x) by a linear (straight line) equation of the general form

$$y' = b_1 (x) + b_0$$

where y' is the estimated value of y, b_1 is the slope (known as the **regression coefficient**), and b_0 is the intercept (known as the **regression constant**).

12.1.2 Multiple regression

In **multiple regression**, the values of one variable (the dependent variable y) are estimated from those of two or more other variables (the independent variables x_1, x_2, ... , x_p). This is achieved by the construction of a linear equation of the general form

$$y' = b_1 (x_1) + b_2 (x_2) + ... + b_p (x_p) + b_0$$

where the parameters b_1, b_2, ..., b_p are the partial **regression coefficients** and the intercept b_0 is the **regression constant**. This equation is known as the **multiple linear regression equation of y upon x_1 , ... , x_p** .

12.1.3 Residuals

When a regression equation is used to estimate the values of a variable y from those of one or more independent variables x, the estimates y' will usually fall short of complete accuracy. Geometrically speaking, the data points will not fall precisely upon the straight line, plane or hyperplane specified by the regression equation. The discrepancies $(y - y')$ on the predicted variable are known as **residuals**. When using regression methods, the study of the residuals is of great importance, because they form the basis for measures of the accuracy of the estimates and of the extent to which the **regression model** gives a good account of the data in question. (See Lovie, 1991, for an account of the analysis of residuals, a topic known as **regression diagnostics**.)

12.1.4 The multiple correlation coefficient

One simple (though rather limited) measure of the efficacy of regression for the prediction of y is the Pearson correlation between the true values of the target variable y and the estimates y' obtained by substituting the corresponding values of x into the regression equation. The correlation between y and y' is known as the **multiple correlation coefficient R**. Notice that the upper case is used for the multiple correlation coefficient, to distinguish it from the correlation between the target variable and any one independent variable considered separately. In simple, two-variable regression, the multiple correlation coefficient takes the **absolute** value of the Pearson correlation between the target variable and the independent variable: so if $r = -0.90$, $R = 0.90$. It can be shown algebraically that the multiple correlation coefficient cannot have a negative value.

12.2 SIMPLE REGRESSION

To illustrate the use of this technique, consider that among university authorities, there is much concern about the methods used to select students for entry. The following example concerns a study of the association between students' marks on the initial academic selection examinations and performance in their university examinations.

Given data on people's final examination marks y and their performance x on the entrance examination, a Pearson correlation can be used to measure the degree of statistical association between the former and the latter. It is also possible to use simple regression to predict examination performance at university from marks in the entrance examination. It can be shown by mathematical proof, however, that when two or more independent variables are used to predict the target variable y, the predictions will, on average, be **at least as accurate** as when any one of the same independent variables is used: in other words, the multiple correlation coefficient R must be at least as great as any single Pearson correlation r. For the moment, however, we shall be considering the simple regression of university examination performance upon the marks on one entrance examination.

12.2.1 Procedure for simple regression

12.2.1.1 Some data

In Table 1, the first score x in each (x, y) pair is a student's mark in the entrance examination *selectex*, and the second y is the same student's mark in the final university examination *finalex*.

12.2.1.2 Preparing the SPSS data set

Using the techniques described in Section 3.5, define the variables *selectex* and *finalex*, using the labelling procedure to assign the more informative names *Selection Exam* and *University Exam*. Type the data into the columns and save them to a file with a name such as **a:regress.sav**.

Table 1. Table of selection exam (x) and university exam (y) scores

x	y	x	y	x	y	x	y	x	y
49	195	62	169	58	164	54	152	55	150
60	145	56	142	52	140	63	125	49	117
46	114	41	114	49	112	48	107	55	106
43	105	48	103	37	100	48	100	40	98
39	95	41	94	45	91	47	86	53	81
41	78	37	76	34	74	46	73	44	69
42	65	43	61	40	49	44	38		

12.2.1.3 Accessing the simple regression procedure

Choose
Statistics
> **Regression**

(Figure 1) and click on **Linear** to open the **Linear Regression** dialog box (Figure 2).

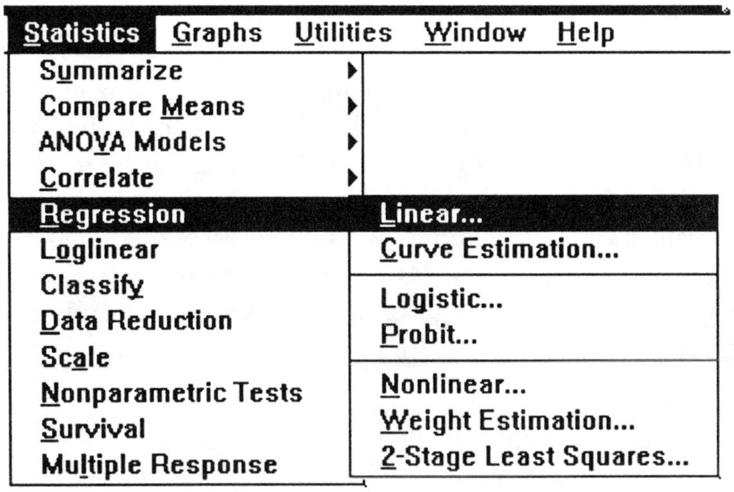

Figure 1.

Finding the Linear Regression procedure

The two variable names *selectex* and *finalex* will appear in the left-hand box. It is important to be clear about which variable is the dependent variable and which is the independent variable - in this example the dependent variable is the final university examination *finalex* and the independent variable is the selection exam *selectex*. Transfer these variable names into the appropriate boxes in the dialog box by clicking on the variable name and then on > (Figure 2).

The user is urged to request additional descriptive statistics and a residuals analysis. To obtain descriptive statistics, click on the **Statistics** button (Figure 2) to open the **Linear Regression: Statistics** dialog box (Figure 3). Click on the **Descriptives** check box and then on **Continue** to return to the **Linear Regression** dialog box.

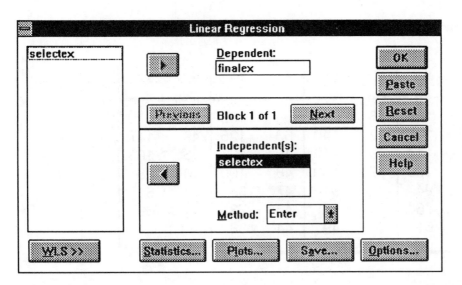

Figure 2.

The Linear Regression
dialog box

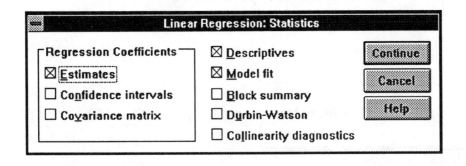

Figure 3.

The Linear Regres-
sion: Statistics dialog
box

Information about residuals is obtained by clicking on the **Plots** button (Figure 2) to open the **Linear Regression: Plots** dialog box (Figure 4). A **residual** (Section 12.1.3) is the difference between the actual value of the dependent variable and its predicted value using the regression equation. Analysis of the residuals gives a measure of how good the prediction is and whether there are any cases which are so discrepant that they might be considered as outliers and so dropped from the analysis. Click on the **Casewise plot** check box in the **Linear Regression: Plots** dialog box to obtain a listing of any exceptionally large residuals. We recommend that this is done for an initial run of the procedure. Click on **Continue** and then on **OK** to run the regression for the first time.

Once any outliers have been detected (and possibly excluded from the analysis), we recommend that the other **Standardized Residual Plots** are added by clicking on the remaining check boxes (labelled **Histogram** and **Normal probability plot**). The normal probability plot shows how well the residuals lie along a straight line (as they should do if the relationship between the dependent and the independent variable is basically a linear one).

Finally, we recommend a plot of the residuals against the predicted values. If the assumptions of linearity and homoscedasticity (homogeneity of variance) hold for the data, there should be no relationship between the predicted and residual values. SPSS creates several temporary variables (prefaced with *) during execution of a regression analysis. The appropriate ones for this plot are *zpred* and *zresid*. Click on *zresid* and then on > to the left of the **Y:** box, and on *zpred* and then on > to the left of the **X:** box. The completed box is shown in Figure 4. Click on **Continue** and then on **OK** to run the regression.

Figure 4. The Linear Regression: Plots dialog box for residuals analysis

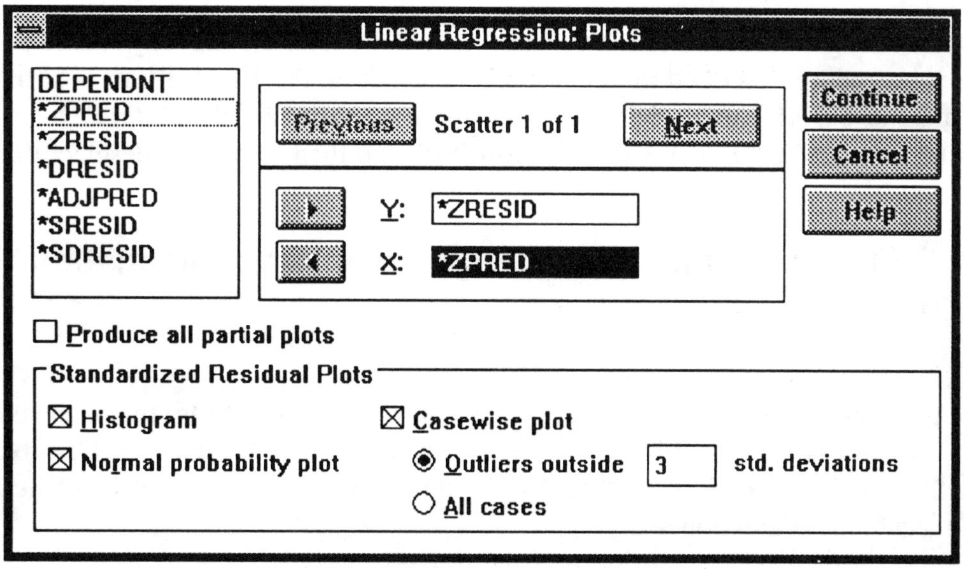

12.2.2 Output listing for simple regression

12.2.2.1 Indication of residual outliers

The **Casewise plot of standardized Residual** output (Output Listing 1) occurs after the following four items:

(1)   Means and standard deviations.
(2)   The correlation coefficient.
(3)   Multiple R and regression ANOVA.
(4)   The regression equation.

Output Listing 1. The casewise plot of standardized residual showing which outliers are greater than ± 3 standard deviations

```
Casewise Plot of Standardized Residual

Outliers = 3.     *: Selected    M: Missing

           -6.     -3.  3.    6.
   Case #   O:.......: :.......:O    FINALEX       *PRED        *RESID
        1   .           ..*        .      195     110.9517      84.0483


        1 Outliers found.
```

Output Listing 1 shows that Case 1 with a score of 195 for *finalex* is the only outlier. The next section describes how to eliminate this outlier and run the subsequent regression analysis.

12.2.2.2 Elimination of outliers

A more reliable regression analysis can be obtained by eliminating any outliers using the **Select Cases** procedure described in Section 3.9.1. Click on the **If condition is satisfied** radio button within the **Select Cases** dialog box and define the condition as *finalex ~=195.* (The symbol ~= means 'not equal to'.) Click on **Continue** and then on **OK** to deselect this case.

12.2.2.3 Output listing for simple regression after eliminating the outlier

Return to the **Linear Regression** dialog box and click on **Plots** to open the **Linear Regression: Plots** dialog box (Figure 4). Click on the remaining two check boxes to turn them on within the **Standardised Residual Plots** box (Figure 4). Click on **Continue** and then on **OK** to execute the regression analysis.

Output Listing 2 shows the descriptive statistics and the correlation coefficient.

Output Listing 2. The descriptive statistics and correlation coefficient

```
Listwise Deletion of Missing Data

              Mean   Std Dev  Label

FINALEX    102.818    32.633  University Examination
SELECTEX    47.273     7.539  Selection Exam

N of Cases =    33

Correlation, 1-tailed Sig:

             FINALEX    SELECTEX

FINALEX        1.000       .729
                 .          .000

SELECTEX        .729      1.000
                .000         .
```

Output Listing 3 contains a value for Multiple R which in the case of just one independent variable has the same absolute value as the correlation coefficient r listed in Output Listing 2. There is also an ANOVA, which is intended to test whether there really is a linear relationship between the variables by forming an F ratio of the mean square for regression to the residual mean square. In this example, the value of F is highly significant. **It should be noted, however, that only an examination of the scatterplot of the variables can ensure that the relationship between two variables is genuinely linear.**

Output Listing 3. Multiple R and the regression ANOVA

```
    * * * *   M U L T I P L E   R E G R E S S I O N   * * * *
Equation Number 1    Dependent Variable..   FINALEX  University Examination

Block Number  1.  Method:  Enter        SELECTEX


Variable(s) Entered on Step Number
   1..    SELECTEX  Selection Exam

Multiple R              .72873
R Square                .53104
Adjusted R Square       .51592
Standard Error        22.70468

Analysis of Variance
                     DF       Sum of Squares       Mean Square
Regression            1          18096.32896       18096.32896
Residual             31          15980.58013         515.50258

F =       35.10424      Signif F =  .0000
```

Output Listing 4 is the kernel of the regression analysis, because it contains the regression equation. The values of the **regression coefficient** and **constant** are given in column **B** of the table. The equation is, therefore,

Predicted Final Exam Mark = 3.15 × (*Selection Exam Mark*) - 46.30

Thus a person with a Selection Exam Mark of 60 would be predicted to score

$3.15 \times 60 - 46.30 = 142.7$ (ie 143).

Notice from the data that the person who did score 60 on the selection examination actually scored 145 on the final examination. The residual is, therefore, 145 - 143 = +2.

Output Listing 4. The regression equation and associated statistics

```
----------------- Variables in the Equation -------------------

Variable            B         SE B         Beta         T   Sig T

SELECTEX      3.154519      .532419      .728727     5.925   .0000
(Constant)  -46.304539    25.477326                 -1.817   .0788
```

The remaining parts of the listing relate to the optional residuals analysis requested from the Linear Regression: Plots *subdialog box.*

The first item is the **Casewise plot** but since we have already deselected the only outlier among the data, no plot is produced. The listing states: **No outliers found. No casewise plot produced.**

The next item is a table of statistics relating to the residuals (Output Listing 5). *PRED comprises the unstandardised predicted values, *RESID is the set of unstandardised residuals, *ZPRED contains the standardised predicted values (ie *PRED has been transformed to a scale with mean 0 and SD 1), and *ZRESID comprises the standardised residuals (ie *RESID standardised to a scale with mean 0 and SD 1).

```
Residuals Statistics:

              Min       Max      Mean    Std Dev    N
*PRED      60.9491  152.4302  102.8182   23.7805   33
*RESID    -54.4943   30.9693     .0000   22.3471   33
*ZPRED     -1.7607    2.0862     .0000    1.0000   33
*ZRESID    -2.4001    1.3640     .0000     .9843   33

Total Cases =       33
```

Output Listing 5.

Table of statistics relating to the residuals

The remaining items in the output are plots as indicated by the messages shown in Output Listing 6. To see them, it is necessary to click on the **Carousel** icon (if it is visible) or to click on the **Window** pull-down menu and select **Chart Carousel.**

```
Hi-Res Chart  # 1:Histogram of *zresid
Hi-Res Chart  # 3:Normal p-p plot of *zresid
Hi-Res Chart  # 2:Scatterplot of *zpred with *zresid
```

Output Listing 6.

Messages indicating charts available in the Chart Carousel

The histogram of *ZRESID is shown in Figure 5. The grey bars show the frequencies. The superimposed curve is the ideal normal distribution for the residuals.

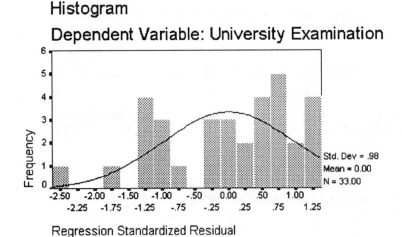

Figure 5.

The histogram of standardised residuals

The next plot is a cumulative probability plot of *ZRESID* (Figure 6). Ideally, the points should lie along the diagonal. If they do not, the residuals are not normally distributed and it may be necessary to apply a transformation to the data. (For a discussion of the rationale of transformations, see Howell, 1992, Chapter 11.)

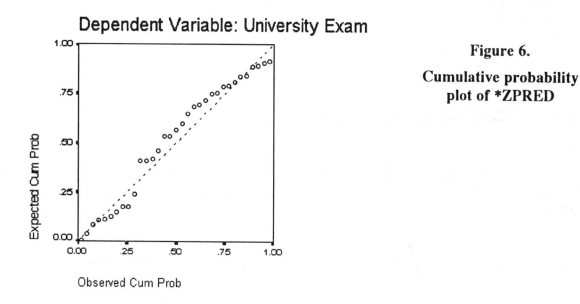

Figure 6.

Cumulative probability plot of *ZPRED*

The final plot is the scatterplot of predicted scores against residuals (Figure 7). It shows no pattern, thereby confirming that the assumptions of linearity and homogeneity of variance have been met. If the cloud of points were crescent-shaped or funnel-shaped, further screening of the data (or abandonment of the analysis) would be necessary.

Figure 7. The scatterplot of predicted scores against residuals

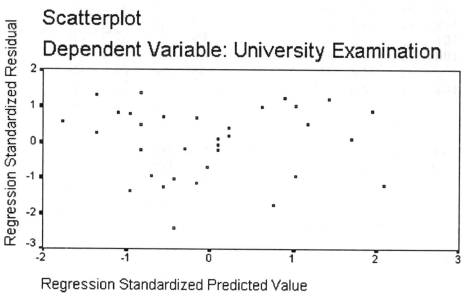

12.3 MULTIPLE REGRESSION

The process of constructing a linear equation that will predict the values of a target (dependent) variable from knowledge of specified values of a regressor (independent variable) can readily be extended to situations where we have data on two or more independent variables. The construction of a linear regression equation with two or more independent variables (or regressors) on the right hand side is known as multiple regression.

12.3.1 Some more data

Two extra variables, the subjects' ages (**A**) and their scores obtained on a relevant academic project (**P**), have been added (Table 2) to the original variables *finalex* (**F**) and *selectex* (**S**) listed in Table 1.

Table 2. An extension of Table 1, with data on two additional independent variables.

F	S	A	P	F	S	A	P
169	62	21.2	65	100	37	39.3	75
164	58	23.0	84	98	40	22.2	65
152	54	21.9	76	95	39	21.7	70
150	55	22.1	60	94	41	22.2	68
145	60	21.6	84	91	45	22.0	78
142	56	21.4	79	86	47	21.9	64
140	52	22.2	77	81	53	22.4	69
125	63	21.9	70	78	41	21.5	60
117	49	22.5	74	76	37	22.5	68
114	46	22.1	72	74	34	22.2	61
114	41	21.9	60	73	46	21.8	65
112	49	22.8	68	69	44	21.9	82
107	48	21.6	50	65	42	22.5	60
106	55	21.4	69	61	43	21.8	54
105	43	21.8	72	49	40	22.6	75
103	48	22.3	53	38	44	21.9	50

In the following discussion, we shall be concerned with two main questions:
  (1) Does the addition of more independent variables improve the accuracy of predictions of *finalex*?
  (2) Of these new variables, are some more useful than others for prediction of the dependent variable?

We shall see that the answer to the first question is 'Yes'. The second question, however, is deeply problematic, and none of the available approaches to it is entirely satisfactory.

Many years ago, Darlington (1968) drew attention to some widespread misunderstandings among users of multiple regression; in fact, he was trying to do for regression what Lewis & Burke (1949) had done some years earlier for chi-square analysis. Darlington placed special emphasis upon the thorny problem of how to say which of the independent variables in a multiple regression equation is the most 'important', or 'useful' in accounting for variability in the dependent variable. (Of more recent non-technical treatments, the most lucid we have been able to find is by Cohen & Cohen, 1983.)

There are many problems; but most of them may be summed up in a well-known apophthegm: **Correlation does not imply causation.** In a situation where everything correlates with everything else, **it is quite impossible to attribute variance in the dependent variable unequivocally to any one independent variable.** It is certainly true, for example, that the amount of damage done by a fire is strongly correlated with the number of firemen on the scene. But both variables are a direct consequence of the severity of the fire, and the correlation between them is, in this sense, an artificial one.

This fundamental dubiety is belied by considerations of some of the terms in the multiple regression equation, and by the availability of methods that have been specifically designed to evaluate the relative importance of the independent variables in the equation.

In a multiple regression equation, the coefficients of the independent variables are known as **partial regression coefficients**, meaning that they express the increase in the dependent variable that would be produced by a positive increase of one unit in the independent variable concerned, the effects of the other independent variables, both on the independent variable and the dependent variable, being supposedly held constant. Such **statistical control**, however, is no substitute for true **experimental** control, where the independent variable, having been manipulated by the experimenter, really is independent of the dependent variable.

If scores on all the variables in a multiple regression equation are standardised, the intercept of the regression equation disappears and each regression coefficient, referred to as a **beta weight**, expresses the change in the dependent variable, expressed in standard deviation units, that would be produced by a positive increment of one standard deviation in the independent variable concerned.

In this section, we shall consider two approaches to multiple regression, neither of which is entirely satisfactory. In **simultaneous** multiple regression, all the available independent variables are entered in the equation directly. In **stepwise** multiple regression, the independent variables are added to (or taken away from) the equation one at a time, the order of entry (or removal) being determined by statistical considerations. Despite the appeal of the second approach, however, there is the disconcerting fact that the addition of another 'independent' variable can completely change the apparent contributions of the other regressors to the variance of scores on the dependent variable.

12.3.2 Constructing the SPSS data set

Using the techniques described in Section 3.5, restore the original data set to the **Data Editor** window (removing the outlier), define the two new variables and type in the new data. Save the augmented SPSS data set to a file with a name such as **a:ageproj.sav**.

12.3.3 Procedure for simultaneous multiple regression

In the **Linear Regression** dialog box, transfer the variable names *selectex*, *age* and *project* into the **Independent Variables** box by highlighting them and clicking on the appropriate > button. The **Dependent Variable** box must contain the variable name *finalex*. For the **Method**, select **Enter** (for the simultaneous regression procedure) and click on **OK** to run the regression.

12.3.4 Output listing for simultaneous multiple regression

Output Listing 7 shows that the multiple correlation coefficient (**R**) is 0.77. Recalling that, when one independent variable *selectex* is used to predict *finalex*, the value of R was 0.73, we see that the answer to the question of whether adding more independent variables improves the predictive power of the regression equation is certainly 'Yes'.

Output Listing 7. The simultaneous regression of finalex upon three regressors:

selectex, age and project

```
Equation Number 1    Dependent Variable..   FINALEX   University Exam

Block Number  1.  Method: Enter      SELECTEX AGE       PROJECT

Variable(s) Entered on Step Number
    1..     PROJECT   Project Mark
    2..     AGE
    3..     SELECTEX  Entrance Exam

Multiple R            .76604
R Square              .58682
Adjusted R Square     .54255
Standard Error      22.42165

Analysis of Variance
                    DF     Sum of Squares     Mean Square
Regression           3       19992.26163      6664.08721
Residual            28       14076.45712       502.73061

F =      13.25578      Signif F =  .0000


------------------ Variables in the Equation ------------------

Variable            B         SE B         Beta        T   Sig T

SELECTEX     3.089139    .583545      .713603     5.294  .0000
AGE          1.418089   1.403718      .131831     1.010  .3210
PROJECT       .627035    .469491      .175438     1.336  .1924
(Constant) -117.713612  47.427160                -2.482  .0193
```

But what about the second question? Do both new variables contribute substantially to the predictive power of the regression equation, or is one a passenger in the equation? From column B in the section headed **Variables in the Equation**, we learn that the multiple regression equation of *finalex* upon *selectex*, *age* and *project* is:

$$finalex' = 3.08 \times (selectex) + 0.63 \times (project) + 1.42 \times (age) - 117.71$$

This, however, tells us nothing about the relative importance of the independent variables, because the **values of the partial regression coefficients reflect the original units in which the variables were measured**. From the fact that the coefficient for age is larger than that for project, therefore, one cannot conclude that age is the more important regressor.

The **beta** weights (in the column headed **Beta**) tell us rather more, because each gives the number of standard deviations change on the dependent variable that will be produced by a change of one standard deviation on the independent variable concerned. On this count, *selectex* still makes by far the greatest contribution, because a change of one standard deviation on that variable produces a change of 0.71 standard deviations on *finalex*, whereas a change of one standard deviation in *project* produces an increase of only 0.18 of a standard deviation in *finalex*. A change of one standard deviation in age produces a change of only 0.13 of a standard deviation in *finalex*. This ordering of the standardised beta weights is supported by consideration of the correlations between the dependent variable and each of the three regressors: the correlations between *finalex* and *project*, *selectex* and *age* are 0.40, 0.73 and -0.03, respectively. (These values are easily obtained by running the **bivariate correlations** procedure.) It is not surprising that the regressor with the largest beta weight also has the largest correlation with the dependent variable.

12.3.5 Procedure for stepwise multiple regression

If, in the **Linear Regression** dialog box, the choice of **Method** is **Stepwise**, rather than **Enter**, a **forward** stepwise regression will be run, whereby regressors are added to the equation one at a time. (In the **backward elimination** method, which is also available in SPSS, they are subtracted one at a time.) Selected parts of the results are shown in Output Listing 8.

The most obvious feature of the output is the multiple correlation coefficient which is given as 0.73. This is smaller than the value given for simultaneous regression of *finalex* upon *selectex*, *project* and *age* (0.77). Nevertheless, the decision of the stepwise program is that the increment in *R* with the inclusion of the variables *project* and *age* is not robust, and so those variables are dropped from the final equation.

Output Listing 8. Forward stepwise multiple regression

```
Equation Number 1    Dependent Variable..   FINALEX   University Exam

Block Number  1.  Method: Stepwise   Criteria  PIN .0500  POUT .1000
    SELECTEX AGE      PROJECT

Variable(s) Entered on Step Number
    1..     SELECTEX  Entrance Exam

Multiple R              .72919

------------------ Variables in the Equation ------------------

Variable             B        SE B       Beta        T  Sig T

SELECTEX        3.156628     .540844    .729193     5.836  .0000
(Constant)    -46.244431   25.877988              -1.787  .0840


------------- Variables not in the Equation -------------

Variable      Beta In  Partial  Min Toler      T  Sig T

AGE            .176225  .247901    .926667   1.378  .1787
PROJECT        .209240  .292409    .914528   1.647  .1104

End Block Number   1   PIN =      .050 Limits reached.
```

12.3.6 Adding another variable

Why should *selectex* be a better predictor of *finalex* than is *project*? The researcher suspects that both the university degree examination and the selection examination tap the candidate's verbal ability, as well as motivation for the material of the curriculum. Adding the candidates' verbal IQs to the regression equation, therefore, should improve the accuracy of predictions from the multiple regression equation. To test this hypothesis, the researcher obtains the verbal IQs of the same students who provided the data on the other variables. These scores are given in Table 3.

Table 3. The subject numbers and IQs of those who provided the data in Tables 1 and 2.

1	135	9	129	17	128	25	123
2	149	10	135	18	132	26	122
3	135	11	135	19	135	27	140
4	135	12	132	20	124	28	121
5	132	13	135	21	115	29	125
6	134	14	127	22	120	30	119
7	134	15	140	23	100	31	120
8	140	16	134	24	133	32	110

As an exercise, the reader may wish to add the variable *iq* to the data set and re-run both the simultaneous and the stepwise regressions. Selected parts of the results of the simultaneous regression of *finalex* upon *iq*, *age*, *projectex* and *selectex* are shown in Output Listing 9.

Output Listing 9. The simultaneous regression of finalex upon selectex, age, IQ and project

```
Equation Number 1     Dependent Variable..    FINALEX    University Exam

Block Number  1.  Method:  Enter      AGE      IQ        PROJECT  SELECTEX

Variable(s) Entered on Step Number
    1..     SELECTEX   Entrance Exam
    2..     AGE
    3..     IQ
    4..     PROJECT    Project Mark


Multiple R            .87459


------------------ Variables in the Equation ------------------

Variable              B         SE B        Beta         T  Sig T

AGE            1.231159    1.079078      .114453     1.141  .2639
IQ             1.511009     .334122      .447486     4.522  .0001
PROJECT         .500969     .361722      .140166     1.385  .1774
SELECTEX       2.494210     .467164      .576172     5.339  .0000
(Constant)  -271.728713   49.871125                 -5.449  .0000
```

It can be seen from Output Listing 9 that the addition of *iq* improves the predictive power of the regression equation: the value of multiple R is now 0.87, which is noticeably larger than it was when there were only three regressors (0.77) as listed in Output Listing 7.

Looking at the standardised **beta** weights (column labelled **Beta**), we see that a change of one standard deviation in *selectex* produces a change of 0.58 of a standard deviation in *finalex* and the same change in *iq* increases *finalex* by 0.45 of a standard deviation. These appear to be substantial contributions, in comparison with those of *project* (0.14) and *age* (0.11).

Output Listings 10 and 11 show selected parts of the output for the **forward stepwise** regression of *finalex* upon all four regressors. The first step (Output Listing 10) enters *selectex* into the equation, the second step (Output Listing 11) adds *iq* into the equation. The stepwise regression stops after it has added these variables to the equation. Notice that the final value of R is 0.85, which is close to the value of R when all four regressors are included in the regression equation (0.87). The decision of the regression procedure, therefore, is that the variables *project* and *age* do not contribute reliably to the regression equation.

Output Listing 10. The first step in the forward stepwise regression of finalex upon IQ, age, project and selectex

```
Equation Number 1    Dependent Variable..    FINALEX    University Exam

Block Number  1.  Method: Stepwise      Criteria PIN .0500 POUT .1000
   AGE       IQ        PROJECT  SELECTEX

Variable(s) Entered on Step Number
   1..    SELECTEX  Entrance Exam

Multiple R              .72919
```

```
----------------- Variables in the Equation -----------------

Variable              B        SE B       Beta        T   Sig T

SELECTEX       3.156628     .540844     .729193     5.836  .0000
(Constant)   -46.244431   25.877988               -1.787  .0840


------------- Variables not in the Equation -------------

Variable     Beta In  Partial  Min Toler       T  Sig T

AGE          .176225  .247901    .926667    1.378  .1787
IQ           .467105  .646783    .897827    4.567  .0001
PROJECT      .209240  .292409    .914528    1.647  .1104
```

Output Listing 11. The second step in the forward stepwise regression of finalex upon IQ, age, project and selectex

```
Variable(s) Entered on Step Number
   2..    IQ

Multiple R              .85300
```

```
----------------- Variables in the Equation -----------------

Variable              B        SE B       Beta        T  Sig T

IQ             1.577255     .345369     .467105     4.567  .0001
SELECTEX       2.510283     .442768     .579885     5.670  .0000
(Constant)  -219.170572   42.857219               -5.114  .0000


------------- Variables not in the Equation -------------

Variable     Beta In  Partial  Min Toler       T  Sig T

AGE          .149301  .274890    .829874    1.513  .1415
PROJECT      .169128  .308655    .840119    1.717  .0970

End Block Number   1   PIN =     .050 Limits reached.
```

12.3.7 The need for a substantive model of causation

These results highlight an important consideration for the use of multiple regression as a research tool. The addition of new regressors can radically affect the relative contributions of those variables already in the equation. To select new regressors, the researcher must be guided by a substantive theoretical rationale. A statistical model, therefore, cannot by itself yield an unequivocal interpretation of regression results: the user must also be guided by a substantive model of causation.

12.4 SUMMARY

1)   Regression generates an equation for predicting a value on a target variable from specified values of one or more other variables (the independent variables). In **simple regression**, there is only one independent variable; in **multiple regression**, there may be many.

2)   The procedure for a regression analysis is
Statistics
    Regression
and click on **Linear**. Enter the name of the dependent variable into the **Dependent:** box, and the name(s) of the independent variable(s) into the **Independent:** box. When there is only one independent variable, the **Method:** is **Enter**. When there are two or more independent variables, the recommended method is **Stepwise**.

3)   Options include selecting **Descriptives** within the **Linear Regression: Statistics** dialog box, which is obtained by clicking on **Statistics**. This causes the means and standard deviations of all the variables to be listed. It is also recommended that residuals are scrutinised by clicking on **Plots** and selecting the three options within **Standardized Residual Plots**. These provide extra information about outliers and checks for violation of the assumptions of the linear regression model. Finally a plot of ***zpred** and ***zresid** should also be included.

4)   In the listing of the output, the regression equation appears in column **B** of the section subheaded **Variables in the Equation.** In multiple regression, there may be more than one equation, in which case the final equation is the appropriate one.

5)   Any residual outliers detected by the **Casewise Plot of Standardized Residual** can be omitted by using the **Select Cases** procedure within the **Data** drop-down menu. The regression can then be run again without these cases.

CHAPTER 13

LOGLINEAR ANALYSIS

13.1 INTRODUCTION

The starting point for the analysis of nominal data is a **contingency table**, each cell of which is the **frequency of occurrence** of individuals in various combinations of categories. In an earlier chapter (Chapter 11), we described the use of the chi-square test to test for the presence of an association between qualitative variables in a **two-way** contingency table.

In a two-way contingency table, the presence (or absence) of an association between the attributes is often very apparent from inspection alone: the formal statistical analysis merely confirms (or fails to confirm) a readily discernible pattern. It is quite possible, however, to have more complex contingency tables, in which individuals are classified with respect to several qualitative variables. In such multi-way contingency tables, it is often very difficult to discern associations; and indeed, it is only too easy to misinterpret what one does see. Recent years have seen great advances in the analysis of multi-way contingency tables, and these new methods, collectively known as **loglinear analysis**, are now available in computing packages such as SPSS.

13.1.1 Comparison with ANOVA

To understand how loglinear analysis works, it may be helpful to recall some aspects of the completely randomised factorial analysis of variance, because there are some striking parallels between the two sets of techniques. In the ANOVA, it is possible to test for **main effects** and for **interactions**. Suppose that, following a three-factor experiment, all systematic sources are found to be significant. That would imply that the correct model for the experimental data must contain a term for each and every possible effect thus:

score = systematic effects* + error effects

(* 3 main effect terms + 3 two-way interaction terms + 1 three-way interaction term)

If, on the other hand, only one main effect and one of the possible two-way interactions were to prove significant, a much simpler model would account for a subject's score. This simplified model would contain, in addition to the error term, only one main effect term and one two-way interaction term thus:

score = systematic effects* + error effects

(* 1 main effect term + 1 two-way interaction term)

In the analysis of variance, the presence of an interaction often necessitates the re-interpretation of a significant main effect. Examination of the interaction may show that an experimental treatment has a strong effect at some levels (or combinations of levels) of other factors in the experiment, but no effect at other levels.

Graphs of two-way tables of means are often very illuminating: if the factor profiles are non-parallel, a two-way interaction is indicated. Graphs of three-way tables, however, are more difficult to interpret visually, because, just as graphs of two-way tables reflect the presence of main effects as well as the two-way interaction, graphs of three-way tables reflect two-way interactions as well as the three-way interaction.

There are many parallels between the foregoing considerations and the loglinear analysis of multi-way contingency tables. Just as in the context of ANOVA, it is meaningful to speak of 'main effects' and of 'interactions'. Moreover, in interpreting multi-way tables by inspection alone, it is only too easy to confuse one effect for another. Loglinear analysis, however, like ANOVA, offers methods of testing the various effects separately. As in ANOVA, the presence of an interaction often necessitates the re-interpretation of a main effect; indeed, main effects, when considered on their own, can be highly deceptive. That is why the common procedure of 'collapsing', ie combining the frequencies at all levels of some factors to exclude those factors from the classification, can produce misleading patterns in the data. As with ANOVA, a loglinear analysis tries to find the model that best accounts for the data available. It contains both main effect terms and interaction terms, so that the values in the contingency table are expressed as the sum of main effects and interaction components.

There are also important differences between loglinear and ANOVA models, however. In the ANOVA, the 'target' of the model is the **individual score** of a subject in the experiment. In loglinear analysis, the target is the **total frequency of observations in a cell**. The ANOVA model cannot predict the individual scores with perfect accuracy, because of the inevitable presence of error: errors of measurement, individual differences and experimental error. In contrast, as we shall see, it is **always** possible, by including all the possible terms in the loglinear model, to predict perfectly the cell frequencies in a contingency table. A model that contains all the possible effect terms is known as a **saturated model**. The purpose of a loglinear analysis is to see whether the cell frequencies may be adequately approximated by a model that contains **fewer** than the full set of possible treatment effects.

13.1.2 Why 'loglinear' analysis?

Recall that in the simple chi-square test of association in a two-by-two contingency table, the **expected frequencies** are obtained by **multiplying** marginal total frequencies and dividing the product by the total frequency. This is because the null hypothesis of independence of the variables implies that the probability of an individual occupying a cell of the classification is the **product** of the relevant main effect probabilities, the latter being estimated from the marginal totals. (Recall that the probability of the joint occurrence of independent events is the **product** of their separate probabilities.) Loglinear analysis exploits the fact that the logarithm (log) of a product is the **sum** of the logs of the terms in the product. Thus the **log** of the cell frequencies may be expressed as a **linear** (ie additive) function of the **logs** of the components. If one were to work directly with the cell frequencies, rather than their logs, one would require a **multiplicative** model for the data. While that is feasible, the simplicity of a summative, ANOVA-type model is lost.

13.1.3 Constructing a loglinear model

The purpose of a loglinear analysis is to construct a model such that the cell frequencies in a contingency table are accounted for in terms of a minimum number of terms. Several strategies can be followed in the construction of such a model, but the **backward hierarchical method** is perhaps the easiest to understand. The first step is to construct a saturated model for the cell frequencies, in which all the component effects are present. This model, as we have seen, will predict the cell frequencies perfectly. The next step is to remove the highest-order interaction, to determine the effect this would have upon the closeness with which the model predicts the cell frequencies. It may be that this interaction can be removed without affecting appreciably the accuracy of estimation of the target frequencies. The process of progressive elimination is continued, and each time a term is removed, a statistical test is carried out to determine whether the accuracy of prediction falls to a sufficient extent to show that the component most recently excluded should indeed be one of the components in the final model. The assessment of the goodness-of-fit at each stage of the procedure is made by means of a statistic known as the **likelihood ratio** (called **L.R. Chisq** by SPSS), which has a known distribution.

The evaluation of the final model is made by comparing the observed and expected frequencies for each cell using the likelihood ratio as described above; but it is also advisable to examine the distribution of **residuals** (the differences between the observed and expected frequencies), or more conveniently, the **standardised residuals** (the residuals expressed in standardised form) in a manner similar to that described for regression in the last chapter.

13.1.4 Small expected frequencies

Just as in the case of the chi-square test, the size of the **expected frequency** (not the observed frequency) in each cell must be adequate for the analysis to be worthwhile. Small expected frequencies can lead to a drastic loss of power.

Problems with low expected cell frequencies should not arise provided:
  (i)   There are not too many variables in comparison with the size of the
          sample.
  (ii)   There are no categories with very few cases.

Tabachnick and Fidell (1989) recommend examining the expected cell frequencies for all **two-way associations** to ensure that all **expected frequencies** are greater than 1 and that no more than 20% are less than 5.

If there is any doubt about the assumption of adequate expected cell frequencies, they can be checked out by using the **Crosstabs** procedure.

13.2 AN EXAMPLE OF A LOGLINEAR ANALYSIS

13.2.1 A three-way contingency table

In an investigation of the relationships between success on a second year university psychology statistics course and a number of possibly relevant background variables, researchers collected a body of information on a number of students, including whether or not they had taken an advanced school mathematics course and whether they had passed a data-processing examination in their first year at university. On each student's record, it was also noted whether he or she had passed the second year psychology statistics examination. (It will be noted that these yes/no variables are not true dichotomies, but artificial ones created from interval data. For present purposes, however, we shall assume that they are true qualitative variables.)

The data are presented in Table 1.

Table 1. A three-way contingency table

Advanced Maths	Yes				No			
Data Processing	Pass		Fail		Pass		Fail	
Psychology Statistics	Pass	Fail	Pass	Fail	Pass	Fail	Pass	Fail
CELL FREQUENCIES	47	10	4	10	58	17	10	20

It is useful to summarise the cell frequencies for categories of single variables as shown in Table 2.

Table 2. Summary of cell frequencies for each variable

Advanced Maths	Yes:	71	No:	105	Total: 176
Data Processing	Pass:	132	Fail:	44	Total: 176
Psych Statistics	Pass:	119	Fail:	57	Total: 176

It can be seen from Table 2 that of the 176 students in the study, 71 had taken advanced mathematics, and 105 had not. From Table 1, it can be seen that of those who had taken advanced mathematics, 57 passed first year data-processing and 14 did not, compared with 75 passes and 30 failures in the non-mathematical group. Relatively speaking, therefore, more of the mathematical group passed first year data-processing. Turning now to the statistics examination, it can be seen that of the mathematical group, the pass ratio was 51:20, compared with 68:37 in the non-mathematical group; and among those who had passed data-processing, the success ratio was 105:27, compared with 14:30 in the group that had failed data processing.

First, let us consider the (very unlikely) null hypothesis that there are **no links whatsoever** among the three variables studied: there is no tendency for those who have taken school mathematics to pass first year data-processing, no tendency for those who have passed data-processing to pass second year statistics and so on. It is a simple matter, using a pocket calculator, to use the appropriate marginal totals to obtain the expected cell frequencies in a calculation similar to that appropriate for a two-way contingency table. Since there are three dichotomous (or pseudo-dichotomous) variables, there are 8 expected cell frequencies, the values of which are shown in Table 3.

Table 3. Observed (O) and expected (E) cell frequencies for Table 1

Advanced Maths		Yes			No			
Data Processing		Pass		Fail	Pass		Fail	
Psychology Statistics		Pass Fail	Pass	Fail	Pass Fail	Pass	Fail	
Cell Freq	O	47 10	4	10	58 17	10	20	
	E	36.00 17.25	12.00	5.75	53.25 25.50	17.75	8.50	

In several cells, the observed frequencies differ markedly from the expected values, suggesting that the complete independence model gives a poor account of the data. Clearly at least some associations are present among the three variables; but where exactly are they?

A loglinear analysis on SPSS can answer that question very easily. SPSS offers a hierarchical loglinear procedure within the **loglinear** menu. This procedure begins by constructing a fully saturated model for the cell frequencies, and works backwards in the manner described above, in order to arrive at a model with a minimum number of terms. Some of these are of little interest: for example, there are fewer subjects in the advanced mathematics group than there are in the non-mathematical group, so we can expect a main effect term for this variable in the final model. Main effects are often unimportant in loglinear analysis. In the terms of ANOVA, we are seeking **interactions**, rather than **main effects**: the presence of associations among the three variables will necessitate the inclusion of interaction terms in the model.

13.2.2 Procedure for a loglinear analysis

Using the procedures described in Section 3.5, define three coding variables: *maths*, *dataproc* and *psystats*. A fourth variable, *count* will contain the cell frequencies. Type in the data and save the set in the usual way. The complete SPSS data set is shown in Figure 1.

	maths	dataproc	psystats	count
1	1	1	1	47
2	1	1	2	10
3	1	2	1	4
4	1	2	2	10
5	2	1	1	58
6	2	1	2	17
7	2	2	1	10
8	2	2	2	20

Figure 1.
The data grid
showing the SPSS
data set

It is now necessary to inform SPSS that the variable *count* contains frequencies and not simply scores. The procedure is described in Section 3.9.2.

Choose
Data
> **Weight Cases**

to open the **Weight Cases** dialog box (Chapter 3, Figure 14), and transfer the variable *count* to the **Frequency Variable** box. Click on **OK**.

If there is any doubt about whether the expected frequencies are sufficiently large, these can be checked by using the **Crosstabs** procedure (Section 11.3.2.2).

Choose
Statistics
> **Summarize**
>> **Crosstabs**

and then complete the **Crosstabs** dialog box (Figure 2) by transferring *dataproc* to the **Row(s)** box, *psystats* to the **Column(s)** box, and *maths* to the lowest box. Click on the **Cells** button to bring to the screen the **Crosstabs: Cell Display** dialog box (See Chapter 11, Figure 12). Within the **Counts** box, mark the **Expected** check box and click on **Continue**.

The **Crosstabs** procedure presents two-way contingency tables for each layer of *maths*, because that was chosen as the layering variable. The table for the first level of *maths* is shown in Output Listing 1. Provided the expected frequencies meet the criteria described in Section 13.1.4, the loglinear analysis can proceed.

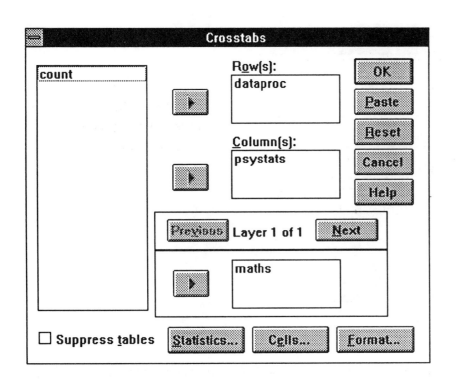

Figure 2. The completed Crosstabs dialog box

Output Listing 1. Observed and expected frequencies for a three-way contingency table

```
DATAPROC   Data Processing Exam   by   PSYSTATS   Psych Stats Exam
Controlling for..
MATHS   Advanced Maths Course   Value = 1   Yes

                       PSYSTATS         Page 1 of 1
                Count
                Exp Val |Pass       Fail
                                            Row
                            1|        2|  Total
    DATAPROC    ─────────────────────────
                    1     47        10       57
        Pass          40.9      16.1     80.3%

                    2      4        10       14
        Fail          10.1       3.9     19.7%

                Column    51        20       71
                Total  71.8%     28.2%   100.0%
```

The hierarchical loglinear procedure is executed by choosing

Statistics

    Loglinear

(See Figure 3.)

Click on **Hierarchical** to open the **Hierarchical Loglinear Analysis** dialog box (Figure 4).

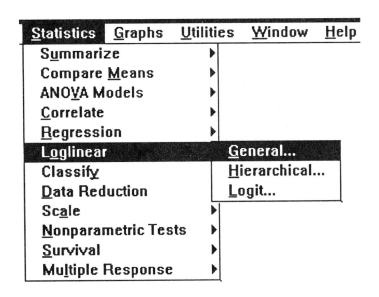

**Figure 3.
Finding the loglinear
procedure**

Figure 4. The completed Hierarchical Loglinear Analysis dialog box

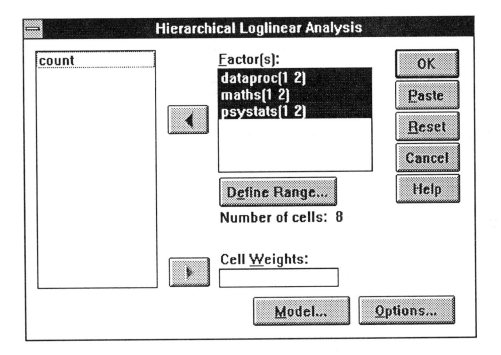

Drag the cursor down the variable names *dataproc maths psystats* to highlight them, and click on > to the left of the **Factor(s)** box to transfer these names into it. Click on **Define Range** and enter *1* into the **Minimum** box and *2* into the **Maximum** box. Click on **Continue**. The names will then appear with [1,2] after each of them (see Figure 4). Click on **Model** and within the **Model Building** box, select **Use backward elimination**. Click on **Continue**.

To execute the loglinear analysis, click on **OK**.

13.2.3 Output listing for a loglinear analysis

Output Listing 2 contains information about the data and the factors.

Output Listing 2. Basic design information

```
* * * *  H I E R A R C H I C A L   L O G   L I N E A R  * * * *
DATA   Information

      8 unweighted cases accepted.
      0 cases rejected because of out-of-range factor values.
      0 cases rejected because of missing data.
    176 weighted cases will be used in the analysis.


FACTOR Information

   Factor  Level  Label
   DATAPROC   2   Data Processing Exam
   MATHS      2   Advanced Maths Course
   PSYSTATS   2   Psych Stats Exam
```

This is followed by a table (not reproduced here) listing the counts (OBS count) for the combinations of the three factors. At this point, SPSS is fitting a **saturated model**, MATHS * DATAPROC * PSYSTATS, to the cell frequencies. The table is useful for checking the accuracy of the data transcription.

Output Listing 3 shows tests of the various possible effects. It shows that K-way and higher order effects are zero, and that the K-way effects themselves are zero. These items give the tail probabilities for the effects of specified order and (where appropriate) a statement that an effect is significant. In this example, all effects are significant up to and including the two-way level of complexity. The three-way effect, however, is not significant.

Output Listing 3. Tests of effects

Tests that K-way and higher order effects are zero.

K	DF	L.R. Chisq	Prob	Pearson Chisq	Prob	Iteration
3	1	.431	.5116	.426	.5141	3
2	4	35.310	.0000	37.077	.0000	2
1	7	110.282	.0000	123.000	.0000	0

Tests that K-way effects are zero.

K	DF	L.R. Chisq	Prob	Pearson Chisq	Prob	Iteration
1	3	74.972	.0000	85.923	.0000	0
2	3	34.879	.0000	36.651	.0000	0
3	1	.431	.5116	.426	.5141	0

Output Listing 4 shows the most interesting part of the listing:

Backward Elimination for Design 1 with generating class.

The purpose of the analysis is to find the unsaturated model that gives the best fit to the observed data. This is achieved by checking that the model currently being tested does not give a significantly worse fit than its predecessor in the hierarchy.

Recall that in the hierarchical backward elimination method, the procedure starts with the most complex model (which in the present case contains all three factors, together with all their possible interactions), and progresses down the hierarchy of complexity, eliminating each effect from the model in turn and determining which decrement in accuracy is less than the **least-significant change in the chi-square value**. At each step, such an effect would be eliminated, leaving the remaining effects for inclusion:

'The best model has generating class . . '

The procedure continues until no elimination produces a decrement with a probability greater than 0.05. The model containing the remaining effects is then adopted as 'The final model'. In this example, the final model is reached after four steps.

Output Listing 4. The main loglinear analysis

```
* * * *  H I E R A R C H I C A L   L O G   L I N E A R  * * * *

Backward Elimination (p = .050) for DESIGN 1 with generating class

   DATAPROC*MATHS*PSYSTATS

   Likelihood ratio chi square =      .00000    DF = 0  P = 1.000

- - - - - - - - - - - - - - - - - - - - - - - - - - - - - - - - - -

If Deleted Simple Effect is        DF   L.R. Chisq Change    Prob  Iter

  DATAPROC*MATHS*PSYSTATS            1                .431   .5116    3

Step 1

   The best model has generating class

       DATAPROC*MATHS
       DATAPROC*PSYSTATS
       MATHS*PSYSTATS

   Likelihood ratio chi square =      .43089    DF = 1  P =  .512
```

At Step 2, MATHS*PSYSTATS is eliminated, because it has the largest probability (.6564).

```
If Deleted Simple Effect is        DF   L.R. Chisq Change    Prob  Iter

  DATAPROC*MATHS                     1         1.029    .3104    2
  DATAPROC*PSYSTATS                  1        32.098    .0000    2
  MATHS*PSYSTATS                     1          .198    .6564    2

Step 2

   The best model has generating class

       DATAPROC*MATHS
       DATAPROC*PSYSTATS

   Likelihood ratio chi square =      .62884    DF = 2  P =  .730
```

At Step 3, DATAPROC*MATHS is eliminated, because it has the larger probability (and it is greater than the criterion level of 0.05). Having processed all the interactions, it remains for any main effect which is not part of the remaining 2-way interaction to be included. In this case, MATHS is such a variable.

```
If Deleted Simple Effect is          DF   L.R. Chisq Change    Prob  Iter

  DATAPROC*MATHS                       1               1.806   .1790    2
  DATAPROC*PSYSTATS                    1              32.875   .0000    2
Step 3

  The best model has generating class

      DATAPROC*PSYSTATS
      MATHS

  Likelihood ratio chi square =     2.43511    DF = 3  P =  .487
```

At Step 4, neither of these effects can be eliminated, because both probabilities are less than 0.05. This, therefore, is adopted as the final model.

```
If Deleted Simple Effect is          DF   L.R. Chisq Change    Prob  Iter

  DATAPROC*PSYSTATS                    1              32.875   .0000    2
  MATHS                                1               6.610   .0101    2
Step 4

  The best model has generating class

      DATAPROC*PSYSTATS
      MATHS

  Likelihood ratio chi square =     2.43511    DF = 3  P =  .487
 - - - - - - - - - - - - - - - - - - - - - - - - - - - - - - - - - - - -

The final model has generating class

    DATAPROC*PSYSTATS
    MATHS
```

The final model includes the interaction between the variables representing the data processing exam and the psychology statistics exam, plus a main effect of maths. Note that there are no interactions involving the maths variable. Thus the most interesting finding is the interaction between the two examinations.

Finally, the computer lists the table of observed frequencies and the expected frequencies **as estimated by the final model** (Output Listing 5). The final chi-square test shows that these expected frequencies do **not** differ significantly from the observed frequencies (chi-square is not significant). This Table also lists the residuals and standardised residuals.

Output Listing 5. Observed frequencies, expected frequencies and residuals estimated by the final model

```
Observed, Expected Frequencies and Residuals.

       Factor           Code      OBS count  EXP count  Residual  Std Resid


   DATAPROC          Pass
     MATHS            Yes
       PSYSTATS         Pass        47.0       42.4       4.64       .71
       PSYSTATS         Fail        10.0       10.9       -.89      -.27
     MATHS            No
       PSYSTATS         Pass        58.0       62.6      -4.64      -.59
       PSYSTATS         Fail        17.0       16.1        .89       .22

   DATAPROC          Fail
     MATHS            Yes
       PSYSTATS         Pass         4.0        5.6      -1.65      -.69
       PSYSTATS         Fail        10.0       12.1      -2.10      -.60
     MATHS            No
       PSYSTATS         Pass        10.0        8.4       1.65       .57
       PSYSTATS         Fail        20.0       17.9       2.10       .50

  - - - - - - - - - - - - - - - - - - - - - - - - - - - - - - - - - -

  Goodness-of-fit test statistics

     Likelihood ratio chi square =    2.43511    DF = 3   P =  .487
                Pearson chi square =    2.39308    DF = 3   P =  .495
```

13.2.4 Comparison with the total independence model

Notice that the expected frequencies estimated by the final model are much closer to the observed counts than those for the total independence model, whose values were listed in Table 3, and are reproduced in Table 4 for the purposes of comparison.

The reader might wish to use the loglinear procedure to check these values. After inserting the factor names and values in the **Factor(s)** box as before, click on the **Model** box. Within the **Specify model** box, select **Custom**. Enter the three factor names into the **Generating Class** box by clicking on each of *dataproc, maths* and *psystats* and > in turn. Within the **Build Term(s)** box, click on **Interaction** and select **all 3-way**. Within the **Model Building** box, click on the **Enter in single step** option. The completed dialog box is shown in Figure 5. Click on **Continue** and then on **OK**.

Table 4 contrasts the observed and expected cell frequencies under the assumptions of the 'best model' generated by the loglinear procedure with the corresponding discrepancies under the total independence model.

Figure 5. The completed Hierarchical Loglinear Analysis: Model dialog box for determining the expected frequencies assuming the total independence model

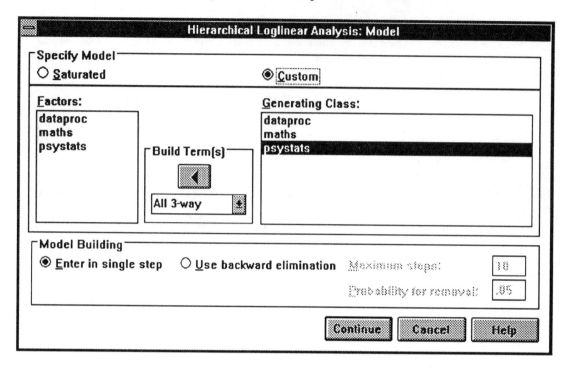

Table 4. Expected frequencies under the final loglinear model (E_{log}) and the total independence model (E_{ind})

Advanced Maths		Yes				No			
Data Processing		Pass		Fail		Pass		Fail	
Psychology Statistics		Pass	Fail	Pass	Fail	Pass	Fail	Pass	Fail
Cell Freq	O	47	10	4	10	58	17	10	20
	E_{log}	42.4	10.9	5.6	12.1	62.6	16.1	8.4	17.9
	E_{ind}	36.0	17.3	12.0	5.8	53.3	25.5	17.8	8.5

13.3 SUMMARY

1) When data are in the form of counts in the cells of a **multi-way contingency table**, loglinear analysis provides a means of constructing the model that gives the best approximation to the values of the cell frequencies.

2) The procedure for loglinear is
Statistics
   Loglinear
     Hierarchical
Click on the factor names and on > to the left of the **Factor(s)** box to transfer the factor names. Click on **Define Range** and enter the values into the **Minimum** and **Maximum** boxes. Click on **Continue**. Click on **Model** and select **Use backward elimination**. Click on **Continue** and then on **OK**.

3) If there is any doubt about whether the sizes of the expected frequencies are adequate, they can be scrutinised by using **Crosstabs** to construct the two-way crosstabulations among all the variables.

4) The output listing includes tables indicating the level of complexity of interaction at which the effects are significant, the various steps of the backward elimination of insignificant effects, and the identification of the final optimal model. The output listing concludes with a table contrasting the observed frequencies with the expected frequencies, assuming the final model.

CHAPTER 14

PREDICTION OF GROUP MEMBERSHIP: DISCRIMINANT ANALYSIS

14.1 INTRODUCTION

14.1.1 Discriminant analysis

In Section 5.2.1, the rationale of multivariate analysis of variance (MANOVA) was outlined. Essentially, the multivariate technique known as **discriminant analysis** is the obverse of MANOVA. In the MANOVA situation, you know which categories the subjects belong to and you want to explore the possibility of identifying a composite variable y which shows up differences among the groups. In other circumstances, however, one might wish to ascertain **category membership** on the basis of subjects' performance on the DVs. It would be of considerable value, for example, on the basis of records of children on a number of variables recorded during the earlier school years, to predict which children go on to further education, which secure immediate employment on leaving school, and which join the ranks of the unemployed. Discriminant analysis offers an answer to such a question.

The composite variable y obtained in MANOVA is known as a **discriminant function**, because it is a weighted sum of the DVs, with the weightings chosen such that the distributions of y for the various groups are separated to the greatest possible extent. In discriminant analysis, the very same composite variable y is constructed, so that category membership can be predicted to the greatest possible extent. Mathematically, therefore, the techniques of MANOVA and discriminant analysis have much in common. In the latter, however, the attempt is made to predict category membership using the discriminant function. There are other important differences between MANOVA and discriminant analysis (see Tabachnick & Fidell, 1989). For present purposes, however, their similarities are more notable than their differences, and it is worth noting that MANOVA computing programs can be used to perform discriminant analyses.

It is important to note that in performing a discriminant analysis on data from an experiment with two or more DVs, the former DVs now become the **independent variables**, and the group variable is now the **dependent variable**.

14.1.2 Types of discriminant analysis

There are three types of discriminant analysis (DA): **direct**, **hierarchical**, and **stepwise**. In **direct** DA, all the variables enter the equations at once; in **hierarchical** DA, they enter according to a schedule set by the researcher; and in **stepwise** DA, statistical criteria alone determine the order of entry. In most analyses, the researcher has no reason for giving some predictors higher priority than others. The third (stepwise) method, therefore, is the most generally applicable and is the only one discussed in this chapter.

14.1.3 Stepwise discriminant analysis

The statistical procedure for stepwise discriminant analysis is similar to that for multiple regression, in that the effect of the addition or removal of an IV is monitored by a statistical test and the result used as a basis for the inclusion of that IV in the final analysis. When there are only two groups, there is just one discriminant function. With more than two groups, however, there can be several functions; though it is unusual for more than the first three to be useful.

Various statistics are available for weighing up the addition or removal of variables from the analysis, but the most commonly used is **Wilks' Lambda**. The significance of the change in Lambda when a variable is entered or removed is obtained from an **F test**. At each step of adding a variable to the analysis, the variable with the largest F (**F TO ENTER**) is included. This process is repeated until there are no further variables with an F value greater than the critical minimum threshold value. At the same time, any variable which had been added earlier, but which no longer contributes to maximising the assignment of cases to the correct groups because other variables in concert have taken over its role, is removed when its F value (**F TO REMOVE**) drops below the critical maximum threshold value. These critical values are listed in Output Listing 3.

Eventually, the process of adding and subtracting variables is completed, and a summary table is listed showing which variables were added or subtracted at each step. The variables remaining in the analysis are those used in the discriminant function(s). The first table thereafter shows which functions are statistically reliable. The first function provides the best means of predicting membership of the groups: later functions may or may not contribute reliably to the prediction process. Additional tables for listing the functions and their success rate for correct prediction can be requested. Plots can also be specified.

14.2 DISCRIMINANT ANALYSIS WITH SPSS

14.2.1 A problem in vocational guidance

A school's vocational guidance officer would like to be able to help senior pupils to choose which subjects to study at university. Fortunately, some data are available from a project on the background interests and school-leaving examination results of samples of architectural, engineering and psychology students. The students also filled in a questionnaire about their extra-curricular interests, including outdoor pursuits, drawing, painting, computing, and kit construction. The problem is this. Can knowledge of the pupils' scores on a number of variables be used to predict their subject category at university? In this study, then, subject category at university (psychologists, architects or engineers) is the dependent variable, and all the other variables are the independent variables.

14.2.2 Procedure for discriminant analysis

14.2.2.1 Preparing the SPSS data set

Since the data for this example consists of the results (drawn from a research project with a very extensive data set) of 118 persons over ten variables, it would be extremely tedious for readers to prepare their own SPSS data sets. Thus the following describes how the data set would be prepared were the full data to be available.

Using the techniques described in Section 3.5, define the coding variable *sust* (full variable label: *Study Subject*), comprising three values: *1 = Architects, 2 = Psychologists, 3 = Engineers*. This is the dependent variable. Define the independent variables *sex* (which, like *sust*, is also a grouping variable), *conkit1*, *model1*, *draw1*, *paint1*, *out1*, *comp*, *vismod*, and *quals* (see Figure 2). Type in the data in the usual way.

To specify the user-missing values, follow the procedure described in Section 3.5.8. For example, since the values of the independent variable *qual* cannot be negative, an appropriate user-missing value would be a negative number, such as -9 (see Figure 1).

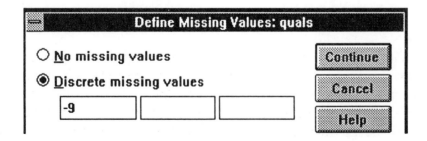

Figure 1.

Part of the Define Missing Value: quals dialog box specifying the user-missing value

Figure 2 shows the first four cases in the completed SPSS data set.

Figure 2. The first four cases in the SPSS data set

	sust	sex	conkit1	model1	draw1	paint1	out1	comp	vismod	quals
1	1	1	2	3	2	0	1	0	5	-9
2	1	1	3	2	6	2	2	0	6	10
3	1	2	5	5	6	7	0	3	4	8
4	1	1	5	6	7	1	4	3	6	-9

14.2.2.2 Finding and running discriminant analysis

Discriminant analysis is found by choosing
Statistics
    Classify

(see Figure 3). Click on **Discriminant** to open the **Discriminant Analysis** dialog box (Figure 4).

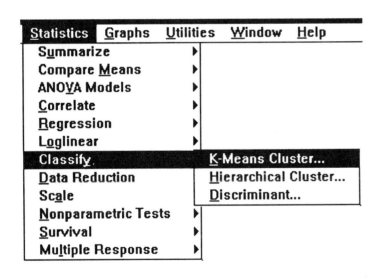

Figure 3.

Finding discriminant analysis

Select the dependent variable (here it is *sust*, the subject of study) and click on > to the left of the **Grouping Variable** box to transfer the name. Click on **Define Range** and type *1* into the **Minimum** box and *3* into the **Maximum** box. Drag the cursor down the rest of the variable names to highlight them, and click on > to the left of the **Independents** box to transfer them all. Since a hierarchical analysis is going to be used, click on **Use stepwise method**. The completed dialog box is shown in Figure 4.

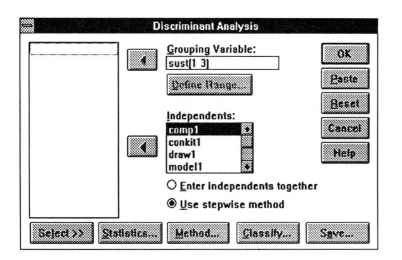

Figure 4.

The completed Discriminant Analysis dialog box

Recommended options include one-way ANOVAs for each of the variables across the three levels of the independent variable and a final summary table showing the success or failure of the analysis. To obtain the ANOVAs, click on **Statistics** and within the **Descriptives** box, select **Univariate ANOVAs**. Click on **Continue**. To obtain the success/failure table, click on **Classify** and within the **Display** box, select **Summary table**. Click on **Continue** and then on **OK**.

14.2.3 Output listing for discriminant analysis

14.2.3.1 Information about the data and the number of cases in each category of the dependent variable

The above information is shown in Output Listing 1.

Output Listing 1. Information about the data and the dependent variable

```
- - - -   D I S C R I M I N A N T   A N A L Y S I S   - - - -
On groups defined by SUST       study subject

        118 (Unweighted) cases were processed.
         10 of these were excluded from the analysis.
            0 had missing or out-of-range group codes.
           10 had at least one missing discriminating variable.
        108 (Unweighted) cases will be used in the analysis.


Number of cases by group

                 Number of cases
      SUST     Unweighted     Weighted   Label
          1         30          30.0    Architects
          2         37          37.0    Psychologists
          3         41          41.0    Engineers

      Total        108         108.0
```

14.2.3.2 Statistics

The optional **Univariate ANOVAs** selection is shown in Output Listing 2. This indicates whether there is a statistically significant difference among the dependent variable means (*sust*) for each independent variable. All these are significant except *compl* and *model1*.

Output Listing 2. Univariate ANOVAs

```
Wilks' Lambda (U-statistic) and univariate F-ratio
with 2 and 105 degrees of freedom
```

Variable	Wilks' Lambda	F	Significance
COMP1	.99997	.0013	.9987
CONKIT1	.84396	9.7064	.0001
DRAW1	.89612	6.0862	.0032
MODEL1	.96136	2.1099	.1264
OUT1	.94183	3.2427	.0430
PAINT1	.83454	10.4086	.0001
QUALS	.87670	7.3838	.0010
SEX	.76652	15.9914	.0000
VISMOD	.84351	9.7397	.0001

14.2.3.3 Selection of variables

Details of Stepwise variable selection (Output Listing 3) and Canonical Discriminant Functions (not reproduced here) are listed. Notice the values of **Minimum F to enter** is 3.84 - this critical value is the minimum value for entering variables in a stepwise analysis.

Output Listing 3. Rules for stepwise variable selection

```
Stepwise variable selection
     Selection rule:  minimize Wilks' Lambda
     Maximum number of steps...................       18
     Minimum tolerance level...................    .00100
     Minimum F to enter........................  3.84000
     Maximum F to remove.......................  2.71000
```

14.2.3.4 Entering and removing variables step-by-step

The output listing starts with a table of variables and their **F to Enter** values (not reproduced) showing that *sex* has the highest **F to Enter** value. It is, therefore, selected as the first variable to enter at Step 1 (Output Listing 4). At Step 2, the next variable with the highest **F-to-enter** value (*paint1*) is entered.

This process of entering (and possibly removing) variables one at a time continues for a further five steps until Step 7 when the criteria shown in Output Listing 3 preclude any further steps.

Output Listing 4. Entering and removing variables step-by-step

```
At step 1, SEX        was included in the analysis.

                                  Degrees of Freedom   Signif. Betw Groups
Wilks' Lambda             .76652      1    2    105.0
Equivalent F        15.99140              2    105.0     .0000


------- Variables in the Analysis after Step 1 -------


Variable  Tolerance  F to Remove   Wilks' Lambda

SEX       1.0000000     15.9914


------- Variables not in the Analysis after Step 1 -------

                      Minimum
Variable  Tolerance  Tolerance   F to Enter    Wilks' Lambda

COMP1     .7450074   .7450074     4.2028382      .7091994
CONKIT1   .9287215   .9287215     3.4285574      .7191062
DRAW1     .9950388   .9950388     6.0381945      .6867722
MODEL1    .9414225   .9414225     2.1991574      .7354177
OUT1      .9826969   .9826969     1.4938129      .7451145
PAINT1    .8832568   .8832568    10.1872805      .6409513
QUALS     .9834662   .9834662     7.6903191      .6677635
VISMOD    .9977884   .9977884     8.8257836      .6552981
```

```
At step 2, PAINT1    was included in the analysis.

                                  Degrees of Freedom   Signif. Betw Groups
Wilks' Lambda             .64095      2    2    105.0
Equivalent F        12.95175              4    208.0     .0000


------- Variables in the Analysis after Step 2 -------


Variable  Tolerance  F to Remove   Wilks' Lambda

PAINT1    .8832568    10.1873       .7665196
SEX       .8832568    15.7061       .8345440
```

Output Listing 4 (continued).

```
At step 7, COMP1    was included in the analysis.

                                 Degrees of Freedom   Signif. Betw Groups
Wilks' Lambda       .37391       7    2       105.0
Equivalent F       8.98587            14      198.0     .0000


------- Variables in the Analysis after Step 7 -------

Variable  Tolerance  F to Remove   Wilks' Lambda

COMP1     .6995932      3.8543       .4030275
CONKIT1   .8006370      4.3322       .4066375
OUT1      .8426921      3.9592       .4038200
PAINT1    .7344426     10.9168       .4563764
QUALS     .9145207     10.8321       .4557366
SEX       .5923199      7.4714       .4303510
VISMOD    .8998970      7.9591       .4340345


------- Variables not in the Analysis after Step 7 -------

                        Minimum
Variable  Tolerance    Tolerance   F to Enter   Wilks' Lambda

DRAW1     .6280746      .5205052    .9114370      .3670851
MODEL1    .7160546      .5718517    .3562813      .3712141


F level or tolerance or VIN insufficient for further computation.
```

The analysis stops at this point because none of the **F to enter** values exceeds the critical value of 3.84. Thus two variables *draw1* and *model1* are excluded from the analysis.

14.2.3.5 The summary table

The stepwise variable selection section concludes with a **Summary Table** (Output Listing 5) showing the order in which the variables were entered or removed (though in this analysis none was removed), along with values of Wilks' Lambda and the associated probability levels.

Output Listing 5. The summary table

```
                         Summary Table

           Action    Vars  Wilks'
Step  Entered Removed  in   Lambda  Sig.   Label

  1   SEX             1    .76652  .0000  sex of student
  2   PAINT1          2    .64095  .0000  Previous interest in painting
  3   QUALS           3    .53865  .0000  Total point count for highers
  4   VISMOD          4    .48073  .0000  Ability to visualise model
  5   OUT1            5    .43903  .0000  Previous interest in outdoor pursuits
  6   CONKIT1         6    .40303  .0000  Previous interest in construction kits
  7   COMP1           7    .37391  .0000  Previous interest in computing
```

14.2.3.6 Statistics of the discriminant functions

Output Listing 6 shows the percentage (**Pct**) of the variance accounted for by each discriminant function and how many of them (if any) are significant. It also shows that both functions (**Fcn**) are highly significant (see the **Sig** column on the right).

Output Listing 6. Statistics of the discriminant functions

Canonical Discriminant Functions

Fcn	Eigenvalue	Pct of Variance	Cum Pct	Canonical Corr		After Fcn	Wilks' Lambda	Chi-square	df	Sig
					:	0	.373913	100.341	14	.0000
1*	.6980	54.83	54.83	.6412	:	1	.634921	46.334	6	.0000
2*	.5750	45.17	100.00	.6042	:					

* Marks the 2 canonical discriminant functions remaining in the analysis.

14.2.3.7 Standardised coefficients and within groups correlations with discriminants

Two tables follow in the listing, the first (not reproduced here) being the standardised function coefficients, and the second (Output Listing 7) the pooled within groups correlations between the discriminating variables and the functions. It is clear from the output in Output Listing 7 that the first function is based on subjects' interests in painting, drawing, and visualising models, while the second is based on the sex of the subjects and their interest in kit construction. The asterisks mark the correlation with the higher value for each variable.

Output Listing 7. The structure matrix

Structure matrix:

Pooled within-groups correlations between discriminating variables
                                    and canonical discriminant functions
(Variables ordered by size of correlation within function)

	Func 1	Func 2
VISMOD	-.50787*	-.09751
QUALS	.42584*	-.15639
PAINT1	-.41858*	.36345
DRAW1	-.21738*	.11537
MODEL1	-.11505*	.07006
COMP1	.00603*	.00007
SEX	.19409	.69570*
CONKIT1	-.14833	-.54298*
OUT1	.19267	.24970*

* denotes largest absolute correlation between each variable and any
discriminant function.

14.2.3.8 Success of predictions of group membership

The optional selection of **Summary table** from the **Classify** options in the **Discriminant Analysis** dialog box provides an indication of the success rate for predictions of membership of the grouping variable's categories using the discriminant functions developed in the analysis (see Output Listing 8). The table indicates that the overall success rate is 72.2%.

Output Listing 8 also shows that Engineers are the most accurately classified, with 75.6% of the cases correct, Architects next with 73.3%, and Psychologists last with 67.6%. Notice that incorrectly classified Architects are more likely to be classified as Engineers than as Psychologists, and that incorrectly classified Psychologists are more likely to be classified as Engineers than as Architects!

Output Listing 8. Classification results

```
Classification results -

                          No. of    Predicted Group Membership
     Actual Group         Cases        1          2          3
  --------------------    ------    --------   --------   --------

  Group        1            30          22          2          6
  Architects                          73.3%       6.7%      20.0%

  Group        2            37           4         25          8
  Psychologists                       10.8%      67.6%      21.6%

  Group        3            41           5          5         31
  Engineers                           12.2%      12.2%      75.6%

  Percent of "grouped" cases correctly classified:  72.22%

  Classification processing summary

          118 (Unweighted) cases were processed.
            0 cases were excluded for missing or out-of-range group codes.
           10 cases had at least one missing discriminating variable.
          108 (Unweighted) cases were used for printed output.
```

14.3 SUMMARY

1) Discriminant analysis is used to predict **category membership** (the DV) from data on several other variables (the IVs). The procedure generates **discriminant functions**, which are weighted sums of IVs, in which the weightings are chosen to maximise the differences, on the new variable, among the categories.

2) The independent variables (IVs) should generally be quantitative and satisfy the usual assumption of normality of distribution, though some authorities allow qualitative binary IVs to be included.

3) The procedure for discriminant analysis is found by choosing
Statistics
  Classify
and then clicking on **Discriminant** to open the dialog box.

The grouping variable name is entered in the **Grouping Variable** box and its levels defined with the **Define Range** option. The remaining variables are entered into the **Independents** box. If the recommended stepwise method is being adopted, click on the **Use stepwise method** option. Other options include **Univariate ANOVAs** selected from the **Descriptives** box, and **Summary table**, selected from the Display box.

4) The listing includes details of which variables are included in the functions, and which functions are significant.

CHAPTER 15

THE SEARCH FOR LATENT VARIABLES: FACTOR ANALYSIS

15.1 INTRODUCTION

15.1.1 The nature of factors

Suppose that the subjects in a sample are each tested on several variables, perhaps an assortment of tests of intellectual ability, such as vocabulary, short term memory, reaction speed and so on. The correlations of performance on each test with every other test in the battery can be arranged in a rectangular array known as a **correlation matrix**, or **R-matrix**. Each row (or column) of R would contain all the correlations involving one particular test in the battery. The cells along the **principal diagonal** (running from the top left to the bottom right of the matrix) would remain empty (or contain the entry *1*), since each cell on that diagonal represents the combination of a particular test with itself; but each off-diagonal cell would be occupied by the correlation between the tests whose row and column intersect at that particular cell. The R-matrix is the starting point for several statistical procedures, but in this chapter we shall consider just one: **factor analysis.**

The presence, in the R-matrix, of clusters of sizeable correlations among subsets of the tests in the battery would suggest that the tests in a subset may be measuring the same underlying psychological dimension, or ability. If the traditional British theories in the psychology of intelligence are correct, there should be fewer (far fewer) dimensions than there are tests in the battery. The purpose of factor analysis is to discern and to quantify the dimensions supposed to underlie performance on a variety of tasks. The **factors** produced by factor analysis are mathematical entities, which can be thought of as classificatory axes, with respect to which the tests in a battery can be 'plotted'. The greater the value of a test's coordinate, or **loading**, on a factor, the more important is that factor in accounting for the correlations between that test and others in the battery.

A factor, then, has the geometric interpretation as a classificatory axis in an axial reference system with respect to which the tests in the battery are represented as points in space.

But the term **factor** also has an equivalent algebraic, or arithmetical interpretation as a linear function of the observed scores that people achieve on the tests in a battery. For example, if a battery comprises 8 tests, and each testee were also to be assigned a ninth score consisting of the sum of the 8 test scores, that ninth, artificial, score would be a **factor score**, and it would make sense to speak of correlations between the factor and the real test scores. We have seen that the loading of a test on a factor is, geometrically speaking, the coordinate of the test point on the factor axis. But that axis represents a 'factor' in the second, algebraic sense, and the loading is the correlation between the test scores and those on the factor.

In factor analysis, a major assumption is that the mathematical factors represent **latent variables** (ie psychological dimensions), the nature of which can only be guessed at by examining the nature of tests that have sizeable coordinates on any particular axis. It should perhaps be said at the outset that this claim is controversial, and there are notable psychologists who hold that the factors of factor analysis are statistical realities, but psychological fictions.

The topic of factor analysis is not elementary, and the SPSS output bristles with highly technical terms. If you are unfamiliar with factor analysis, we suggest you read the lucid texts by Kim and Mueller (1978a, 1978b) and by Tabachnick and Fidell (1989), which contain relatively painless introductions to the technical jargon.

15.1.2 Stages in a factor analysis

A factor analysis usually takes place in three stages:
- (1)   A **matrix of correlation coefficients** is generated for all the variable combinations.
- (2)   From the correlation matrix, **factors** are extracted. The most common method is called **principal factors** (often wrongly referred to as **principal components** extraction, hence the abbreviation **PC**).
- (3)   The factors (axes) are **rotated** to maximise the relationships between the variables and some of the factors. The most common method is **varimax**, a rotation method which maintains independence among the mathematical factors. Geometrically, this means that during rotation, the axes remain **orthogonal** (ie they are kept at right angles).

A fourth stage can be added at which the scores of each subject on each of the factors emerging from the analysis are calculated. It should be stressed that these **factor scores** are not the results of any actual test taken by the subjects: they are estimates of the subjects' standing on the **supposed** latent variables that have emerged as mathematical axes from the factor analysis of the data set. Factor scores are very useful, however, because they can subsequently be used as input for further statistical analysis.

It is advisable to carry out only Stage 1 initially, in order to be able to inspect the correlation coefficients in the correlation matrix R. Since the purpose of the analysis is to link variables together into factors, those variables must be related to one another and therefore have correlation coefficients larger than about 0.3. Should any variables show no substantial correlation with any of the others, they would be removed from R in subsequent analysis. It is also advisable to check that the correlation matrix does not possess the highly undesirable properties of **multicollinearity** and **singularity**. The former is the condition where the variables are very highly (though imperfectly) correlated; the latter arises when some of the variables are exact linear functions of others in the battery, as when the variable C is constructed by adding together the subjects' scores on variables A and B. Should either multicollinearity or singularity be present, it would be necessary to drop some of the variables from the analysis.

15.1.3   The extraction of factors

The factors (or axes) in a factor analysis are **extracted** (or, pursuing the geometric analogy, **constructed**) one at a time, the process being repeated until it is possible, from the loadings of the tests on the factors so far extracted, to generate good approximations to the correlations in the original R matrix. Factor analysis tells us how many factors (or axes) are necessary to achieve a reconstruction of R that is sufficiently good to account satisfactorily for the correlations it contains.

15.1.4   The rationale of rotation

If we think of the tests in the battery and the origin of the axis (factor) set as stationary points and rotate the axes around the origin, the values of all the loadings will change. Nevertheless, the new set of loadings on the axes, *whatever their new position*, can still be used to produce exactly the same estimates of the correlations in the R-matrix. In this sense, the position of the axes is quite arbitrary: the factor matrix (or **F-matrix**) only tells us *how many* axes are necessary to classify the data adequately: it does not thereby establish that the initial position of the axes is the appropriate one.

In **rotation**, the factor axes are rotated around the fixed origin until the loadings meet a certain criterion. The set of loadings that satisfies the criterion is known as the **rotated factor matrix**. The purpose of any rotation is to achieve a configuration of loadings having the qualities collectively known as **simple structure** which, loosely conceived, is the set of loadings that shows the maximum number of tests loading on the minimum number of factors. The idea is that the fewer the factors that are involved in accounting for the correlations among a group of tests, the easier it is to invest those factors with psychological meaning. In fact, simple structure is an ideal never achieved in practice, partly because the concept, in its original form, is actually rather vague and embodies contradictory properties. Modern computing packages such as SPSS offer a selection of rotation methods, each based upon a different (but reasonable) interpretation of simple structure. The most commonly used method of rotation is known as **varimax**.

15.2 A FACTOR ANALYSIS OF DATA ON SEVEN VARIABLES

Suppose a researcher has available the scores, on seven variables, of 120 applicants for a place on a course on cartography. In order to identify the psychological dimensions tapped by the seven variables, it is decided to carry out a factor analysis on the correlation matrix. The variable set comprises the following tests: **Mapping; Engineering; Spatial ability; Mathematics; English; Art; Intelligence.** Section 15.2.1 outlines the procedure for a factor analysis using the scores directly. Sometimes, however, it is convenient to use previously computed correlations in the form of a correlation matrix as the input for a factor analysis; the procedure for this is given in Section 15.2.3.

15.2.1 Procedure for factor analysis with raw scores

15.2.1.1 Preparing the SPSS data set

Using the techniques described in Section 3.5, define the seven variables *artwork, engineer, english, intellig, mapping, maths* and *spacerel,* using the variable labels procedure to assign the fuller labels *Mapping, Engineering, Spatial Ability* and so on to the rather cryptic variable names.

Each of these variables will comprise the raw scores that the 120 applicants achieved on that particular test. Note that there are no grouping variables in this data set: this is a purely correlational (as opposed to experimental) study. Inasmuch as there can be said to be an 'independent' variable, it is one whose existence must be inferred from whatever patterns may exist in the correlation matrix. It is the *raison d'être* of factor analysis to make such an inference credible.

Type in the data and save the SPSS data set in the usual way.

15.2.1.2 Running the factor analysis

Find factor analysis by choosing
Statistics
    Data Reduction

(Figure 1). Click on **Factor** to open the **Factor** dialog box (Figure 2).

Highlight all the variable names in the **Factor** dialog box and click on > to transfer them to the **Variables** box.

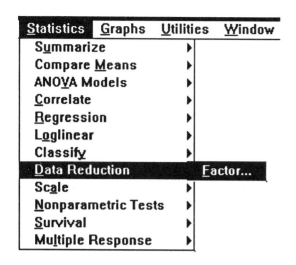

Figure 1.

Finding the factor analysis procedure

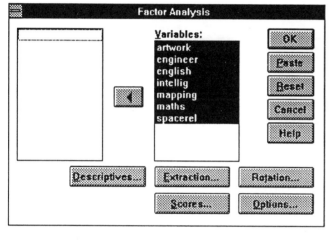

Figure 2.

The completed Factor Analysis dialog box

It only remains to select some options which regulate the manner in which the analysis takes place and produce some extra items of output. Click on the **Descriptives** button to open the **Factor Analysis: Descriptives** dialog box (Figure 3). Click on the following check boxes: **Coefficients, Determinant, KMO and Bartlett's test of sphericity,** and **Reproduced.** (**KMO** is the **Kaiser-Meyer-Olkin measure of sampling adequacy,** explained later in Section 15.2.2.) This will produce a range of matrices and diagnostics indicating the adequacy of the factor analysis. Click on **Continue** to return to the **Factor Analysis** dialog box.

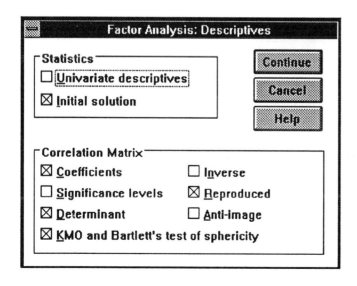

Figure 3.

The Factor Analysis: Descriptives dialog box

Another option is a special graph called a **scree plot,** which shows the variance (expressed as an **eigenvalue**) associated with each factor. Click on the **Extraction** button in the **Factor Analysis** dialog box to open the **Factor Analysis: Extraction** dialog box (Figure 4). Click on the **Scree plot** check box. Click on **Continue** to return to the **Factor Analysis** dialog box.

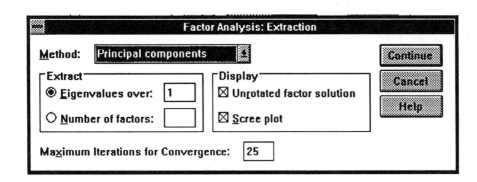

Figure 4.

The Factor Analysis: Extraction dialog box

To obtain the rotated F-matrix, click on the **Rotation** button in the **Factor Analysis** dialog box to obtain the **Factor Analysis: Rotation** dialog box (Figure 5). In the **Method** box, mark the **Varimax** radio button. Click on **Continue** to return to the **Factor Analysis** dialog box.

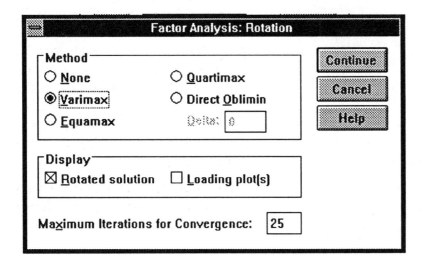

Figure 5.

The Factor Analysis: Rotation dialog box

Finally, to make the F-matrix easier to interpret, it is possible to suppress small factor loadings. Click on the **Options** button in the **Factor Analysis** dialog box to obtain the **Factor Analysis: Options** dialog box (Figure 6). In the box labelled **Coefficient Display Format,** click on the **Suppress absolute values less than:** check box and type the value *0.50* into the text box. This will have the effect of removing all loadings less than 0.5 from the F-matrix. Click on **Continue** and then on **OK** to execute the factor analysis.

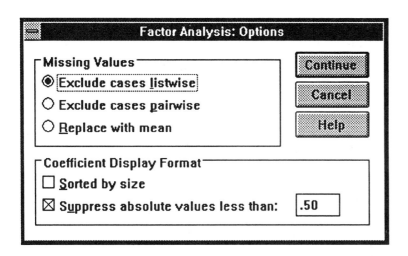

Figure 6.

The Factor Analysis: Options dialog box

15.2.2 Output listing for factor analysis

15.2.2.1 The correlation matrix

A correlation matrix is *square*, that is, there are as many rows as there are columns. The diagonal of cells running from top left to bottom right is known as the **principal diagonal** of the matrix. Since the variables are labelled in the same order in the rows and columns of **R,** each of the cells along the principal diagonal contains the correlation of one of the variables with itself (i.e. *1*). The correlations in the off-diagonal cells are the same above and below the principal diagonal (the correlation of *maths* with *english* is the same as that of *english* with *maths*). A **triangular matrix** is that part of a square matrix comprising the entries along the principal diagonal and the off-diagonal entries either above or below the diagonal: the **upper triangular matrix** comprises the principal diagonal plus the entries above; the **lower triangular matrix** comprises the principal diagonal plus the entries below. Either of the triangular versions of **R** contains all the information in the square matrix.

The **correlation matrix** derived from all the variables (in lower triangular form), together with the value of its **determinant** is shown in Output Listing 1. Provided the determinant is larger than 0.00001, the matrix can be assumed not to suffer from multicollinearity or singularity.

Output Listing 1. The correlation matrix

```
Correlation Matrix:

          MAPPING   ENGINEER   SPACEREL    MATHS    ENGLISH   ARTWORK   INTELLIG

MAPPING   1.00000
ENGINEER   .38230   1.00000
SPACEREL   .65020    .40830    1.00000
MATHS      .51750    .65560     .44190   1.00000
ENGLISH    .23840    .35870     .15540    .41170   1.00000
ARTWORK    .54320    .35300     .72220    .23040    .19900   1.00000
INTELLIG   .45540    .62200     .54440    .65720    .54350    .35550   1.00000

Determinant of Correlation Matrix =       .0272545
```

15.2.2.2 Measure of sampling adequacy and Bartlett's test of sphericity

The next item is the **Kaiser-Meyer-Olkin (KMO) measure of sampling adequacy** (which should be greater than about 0.5 for a satisfactory factor analysis to proceed) and the **Bartlett test of sphericity**. If the Bartlett test is **not** significant (ie its associated probability is greater than 0.05), then there is the danger that the correlation matrix is an identity matrix (ie the diagonal elements are 1 and the off-diagonal elements are 0) and is therefore unsuitable for further analysis. In the present example, we are reassured by the following statements in the output listing:

```
Kaiser-Meyer-Olkin Measure of Sampling Adequacy =  .75160

Bartlett Test of Sphericity = 417.29363, Significance =     .00000
```

15.2.2.3 A table of initial statistics for principal components analysis

Output Listing 2, to the right of the column of asterisks, tabulates factors, their eigenvalues, the percent of variance attributable to each factor, and the cumulative variance for the factor and the previous factors. The program subsequently drops any factors with an eigenvalue of less than 1. (An **eigenvalue** is a measure of standardised variance with a mean of 0 and a standard deviation of 1. Because the variance that each standardised variable contributes to a principal components extraction is 1, a component with an eigenvalue of less than 1 is less important than an observed variable, and can therefore be ignored.)

Notice that the first factor accounts for 53.5% of the variance and the second factor for the next 17.8% of the variance. The remaining factors are insignificant.

Output Listing 2. Initial statistics from the analysis

Initial Statistics:

Variable	Communality	*	Factor	Eigenvalue	Pct of Var	Cum Pct
MAPPING	1.00000	*	1	3.74728	53.5	53.5
ENGINEER	1.00000	*	2	1.24626	17.8	71.3
SPACEREL	1.00000	*	3	.69019	9.9	81.2
MATHS	1.00000	*	4	.51560	7.4	88.6
ENGLISH	1.00000	*	5	.37528	5.4	93.9
ARTWORK	1.00000	*	6	.25194	3.6	97.5
INTELLIG	1.00000	*	7	.17345	2.5	100.0

15.2.2.4 The unrotated factor matrix

Output Listing 3 shows the loadings of the seven tests on the two factors extracted. When the factors are **orthogonal** (ie uncorrelated with each other), these factor loadings are the correlation coefficients between the variables and the factors. Thus the higher the absolute value of the loading (which can never exceed a maximum of 1), the more the factor contributes to the variable.

Note that the gaps in the Table represent factor loadings with values less than 0.5, because the option of suppressing coefficients below a stipulated level (we selected 0.5) was taken in order to make the table easier to read.

```
Factor Matrix:
                Factor  1      Factor  2
    INTELLIG     .82647
    SPACEREL     .78187
    MATHS        .77899
    MAPPING      .75007
    ENGINEER     .74840
    ARTWORK      .66104         -.57307

    ENGLISH      .53515          .53830
```

Output Listing 3.

The unrotated factor matrix

15.2.2.5 A table of final statistics

Output Listing 4 contains the **communalities**, which show how much of the variance in the variables has been accounted for by the two factors that have been extracted: for example, nearly 85% of the variance in Space Relations is accounted for, whereas only 57% of the variance in English is accounted for. The right side shows the two factors and their associated variances.

Output Listing 4. Some final statistics from the analysis

```
Final Statistics:
```

Variable	Communality	*	Factor	Eigenvalue	Pct of Var	Cum Pct
MAPPING	.67226	*	1	3.74728	53.5	53.5
ENGINEER	.64117	*	2	1.24626	17.8	71.3
SPACEREL	.84794	*				
MATHS	.72105	*				
ENGLISH	.57615	*				
ARTWORK	.76538	*				
INTELLIG	.76957	*				

15.2.2.6 Reproduced correlation matrix and residuals

Output Listing 5 shows the **reproduced correlation matrix** of coefficients, computed from the extracted factors. The elements of this matrix are subtracted from those of the original correlation matrix to produce a matrix of **residuals**, the properties of which indicate the adequacy of the factor model.

This table lists both the correlations (the values in the columns below the asterisks) and the residuals (the values in the columns above the asterisks). A good factor model should be a good fit; the sentence at the foot of Output Listing 5 states the number and proportion of residuals (ie the differences) that are greater than 0.05. Sometimes what appears to be an unsatisfactory factor analysis can be saved by dropping a variable that correlates too highly with the others. A new analysis without the offending variable can easily be performed by returning to the **Factor Analysis** dialog box and removing the unwanted variable (eg *artwork*) from the list of variables.

Output Listing 5. A reproduction of R from the loadings in the F matrix, and residuals

Reproduced Correlation Matrix:

	MAPPING	ENGINEER	SPACEREL	MATHS	ENGLISH
MAPPING	.67226*	-.08477	-.09733	.04512	.01525
ENGINEER	.46707	.64117*	-.03835	-.02363	-.19508
SPACEREL	.74753	.44665	.84794*	-.00276	-.00117
MATHS	.47238	.67923	.44466	.72105*	-.18711
ENGLISH	.22315	.55378	.15657	.59881	.57615*
ARTWORK	.68559	.33156	.79561	.32127	.04528
INTELLIG	.52251	.70228	.50311	.74322	.60062

	ARTWORK	INTELLIG
MAPPING	-.14239	-.06711
ENGINEER	.02144	-.08028
SPACEREL	-.07341	.04129
MATHS	-.09087	-.08602
ENGLISH	.15372	-.05712
ARTWORK	.76538*	-.02228
INTELLIG	.37778	.76957*

The lower left triangle contains the reproduced correlation matrix; the diagonal, reproduced communalities; and the upper right triangle residuals between the observed correlations and the reproduced correlations.

There are 12 (57.0%) residuals (above diagonal) with absolute values > 0.05.

15.2.2.7 The rotated factor matrix

Output Listing 6 shows the effect of trying to simplify the previous Factor Matrix by minimising the number of factors on which variables have high loadings. *Space Relations*, *Artwork*, and *Mapping* are now loaded substantially only on Factor 2, whereas *Maths*, *English*, and *Engineering* are now loaded only on Factor 1, the matrix is much easier to interpret psychologically. Compare this table with the unrotated matrix in Output Listing 3. Again, loadings with a value of less than 0.5 have been suppressed.

```
Rotated Factor Matrix:
                 Factor  1      Factor  2
INTELLIG          .80332
MATHS             .79881
ENGLISH           .75864
ENGINEER          .74003

SPACEREL                         .89017
ARTWORK                          .87039
MAPPING                          .75530
```

Output Listing 6.

The rotated factor matrix

15.2.2.8 Factor transformation matrix

This matrix, not reproduced here, specifies the rotation applied to the factors, and for our purposes can be ignored.

15.2.2.9 Scree plot

This optional plot (Figure 7) graphs the eigenvalues of all the factors. To see it on the screen, it is necessary to click on the **Carousel** icon at the foot of the screen or to click on the **Windows** drop-down menu and select **Chart Carousel**. The plot is useful for deciding how many factors to retain. The point of interest is where the curve connecting the asterisks starts to flatten out. This region of the curve has been likened to the rubble or scree on a mountain side. It can be seen that the curve begins to flatten out between the second and third factors. Note also that Factor 3 has an eigenvalue of less than 1, so only two factors have been retained.

Figure 7. The factor scree plot

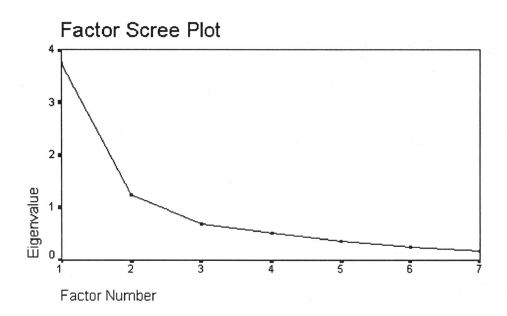

In the event of more factors remaining in an analysis than are desired, the user can return to the original **Factor Analysis** dialog box and alter the specifications. Within the **Factor Analysis: Extraction** dialog box (Figure 4), specify how many factors are to be retained, and re-run the analysis.

15.2.3 Using a correlation matrix as input for factor analysis

Sometimes it may be more convenient to use correlations rather than raw scores as the input for a factor analysis. Unfortunately this cannot be done by using the dialog box interface: instead the user has to resort to **SPSS Command Syntax**. There are two stages:

    (1)   Preparing the correlation matrix.
    (2)   Preparing the factor analysis command.

15.2.3.1 Preparation of the correlation matrix

Choose
File
    New

(Figure 8). Click on **SPSS Syntax** to open the syntax window (Figure 9).

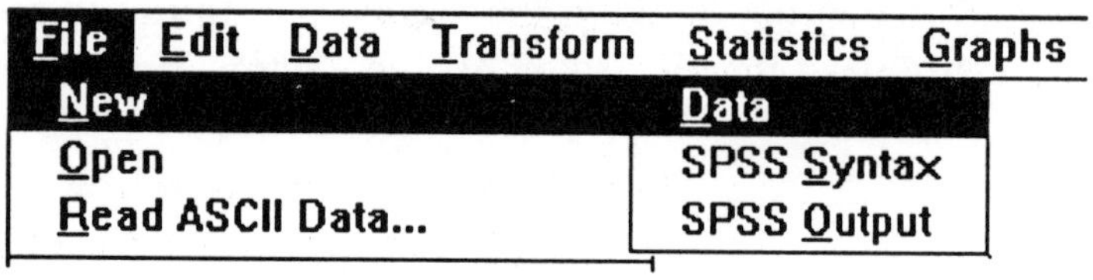

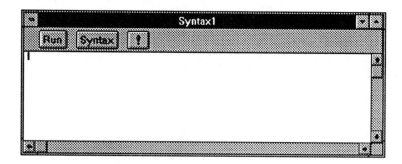

Figure 8.

Finding the syntax window

Figure 9.

The syntax window

The form of the syntax will be familiar to readers who have used SPSS/PC+ (see **SPSS/PC+ Made Simple, Kinnear & Gray, 1992)**. It consists of a series of **commands**, some relating to the data (the **data commands**), others to statistical procedures. A command can have several **subcommands**; but it must always finish with a full stop (.).

Type **Matrix data** in the syntax window and then click on the **Syntax** box to open the **Matrix Data Syntax** help window (Figure 10).

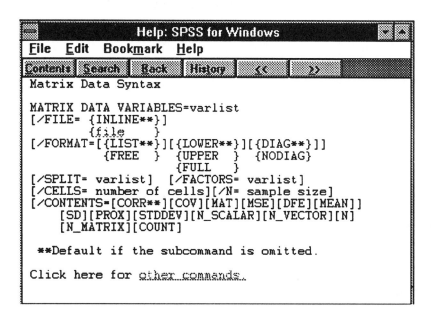

Figure 10.

The Matrix Data Syntax help window

The user can then inspect the syntax and return to the syntax window to type in the relevant parts of the **Matrix Data** command together with the data, or can click on the **Edit** menu of the help window and select **Annotate**. When the **Annotate** window appears, click on **Paste** to copy the contents of the help window to it as shown in Figure 11.

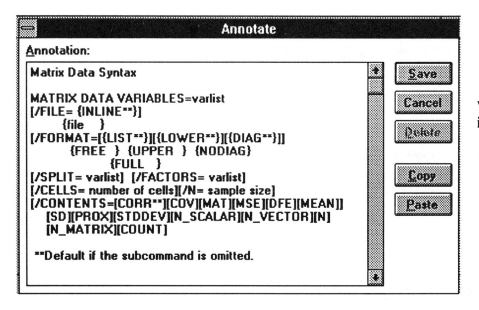

Figure 11.

The Annotate window after pasting in the contents of the Matrix Data Syntax help window

The command can then be amended by deleting all the subcommands (they are in square brackets and each begins with /) and entering the variable names in place of *varlist* (see Figure 12). Notice the variable *ROWTYPE_* which is a special string variable used to identify the type of data for each record. Thus *CORR* indicates a record of correlation coefficients, *N* is a record of counts (with a value for each of the experimental variables). The default structure of a correlation matrix is a lower triangular matrix. If an upper triangular or rectangular matrix is to be used, an additional /*FORMAT* subcommand is required. The value of *N* is not needed for a factor analysis but it is needed for tests of significance and for assessing the sampling adequacy of the data. The correlation matrix and value of *N* are then entered (preceded in each row with *CORR* or *N*, as appropriate) between the usual *BEGIN DATA* and *END DATA* commands. The full stops after *BEGIN DATA* and *END DATA* (and after the variable list) **must not be omitted**. (See ***SPSS/PC+ Made Simple, Kinnear & Gray, 1992***; Chapter 2, Section 2.4.1.)

Figure 12. The matrix data command and data in the syntax window

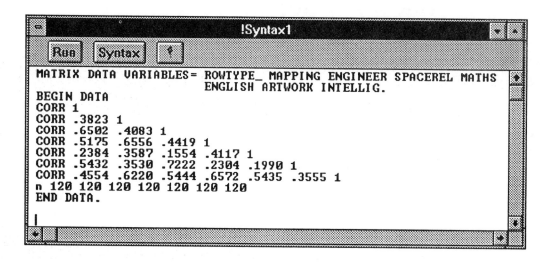

When all is complete, click on **Copy** to copy the command to the Clipboard. From there, the command can be pasted into the syntax window using the **Paste** option in the **Edit** menu.

Syntax commands are run by highlighting them with the cursor and then clicking on the **Run** button near the top of the syntax window. Run the **Matrix Data** commands by dragging the cursor over all the syntax in Figure 12, and then clicking on **Run**. If all is well, no error messages should appear in the **Output** window. The matrix of correlations and the vector of counts can be inspected in the **Data Editor** window by clicking on the **Window** menu and selecting **Newdata**. Part of the **Data Editor** window is shown in Figure 13.

Figure 13. Part of the data set in the Data Editor window after running the Matrix Data commands

	rowtype_	varname	mapping	engineer	spacerel
1	N		120.0000	120.0000	120.0000
2	CORR	MAPPING	1.0000	.3823	.6502
3	CORR	ENGINEER	.3823	1.0000	.4083
4	CORR	SPACEREL	.6502	.4083	1.0000

15.2.3.2 Preparation of the factor analysis command

The factor analysis must also be executed from a command in the syntax window because a special subcommand (not available in the **Factor Analysis** dialog box) is needed to read a correlation matrix. Return to the syntax window and type **Factor** on the next line after *END DATA* . Click on **Syntax** to open the **Factor Syntax Help** window. The same command preparation procedure is used as in the previous subsection, either by preparing the command in the **Annotate** window or by typing directly in the syntax window. The completed command is shown in Figure 14.

Figure 14. The FACTOR command in the syntax window

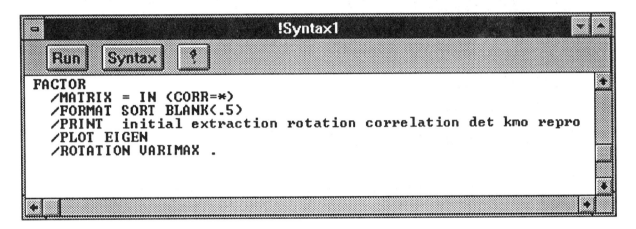

Notice the identification of the source of the matrix in the */MATRIX =IN* subcommand is given as (*CORR=**). This shows that it is a correlation matrix (and not, say, a factor matrix), and that it is in the current data file (represented by *) as shown in the **Data Editor** window. The */FORMAT* option is the same as that selected in the **Options** dialog box, the */PRINT* options are those selected in the **Descriptives** dialog box, the */PLOT* option is that selected in the **Extraction** dialog box, and the */ROTATION* option is also that in the **Rotation** dialog box.

Run the **Factor** command by highlighting the whole command with the cursor and then clicking on the **Run** button. The output listing for the factor analysis will be identical to that previously described.

15.3 SUMMARY

1)   **Factor analysis** is a set of techniques designed to account for the correlations among a set of variables in terms of relatively few underlying dimensions, or **factors.**

2)   Several different kinds of factor analysis have been devised. The most common is the **principal factors** method (which SPSS terms **principal components** (PC)).

3)   The relationships between the variables and **some** of the factors are maximised by a process called **rotation**. The most common method of rotation is **varimax.**

4)   To run a factor analysis from raw data, choose
        Statistics
          Data Reduction
        and click on **Factor**. Select the variables to be used in the analysis by dragging the cursor down the list of variable names in the **Factor Analysis** dialog box and clicking on > to transfer them to the **Variables** box.

5)   Options available in the **Descriptives, Extraction, Rotation,** and **Options** dialog boxes include the plotting of the **scree slope** showing the variance accounted for by each factor, suppressing factor loadings with a value of less than a defined number (**0.5** is recommended), selecting the method of factor rotation (**varimax** is recommended), and printing various matrices and statistics (the **correlation matrix** and its **determinant, KMO** and **Bartlett's test of sphericity,** and the **reproduced correlation matrix** are recommended).

6)   If the data are in the form of a correlation matrix rather than raw scores, the command syntax must be used instead of the dialog boxes.

EXERCISES

EXERCISE 1
SOME BASIC WINDOWS OPERATIONS

BEFORE YOU START

Before you begin the first exercise, there are one or two preliminaries which require your attention.

Know the material of Chapter 1

An essential prerequisite is a knowledge of the material in Chapter 1. If you are already an experienced computer user, however, you might well omit the elementary outline of computer basics that Chapter 1 contains.

Read Chapter 2

Even if you already have some experience of computing, we strongly recommend that you study Chapter 2 closely before proceeding with this practical.

Arrange access to a network

We assume that most of our readers will be users of a network, rather than owners (or exclusive users) of a PC. Assuming you have access to a network, there may be an identification, or logging in, procedure. If so, make sure you have organised your number and password.

Have two floppy disks with you

If you have access to a PC only through a network, you will probably be unable to save material to files on your PC's (or the file server's) hard disk. You must then use floppy disks for all your storage. In view of our dire warnings in Chapter 1 about disk corruption and rising blood pressure, we urge you to have available two floppy disks and to back up important files with duplicates on the second disk.

IF YOU HAVE NOT USED A COMPUTER BEFORE

If you are already an experienced user of a PC, you can ignore this section and pass on to the next.

Learn to find your way around the keyboard

If you are a newcomer to computing (and a non-typist), a major obstacle to progress can be unfamiliarity with the PC keyboard. To overcome this difficulty, turn to Section 1.3 and systematically work through the keys described, identifying each on the real keyboard from the illustration or the description. It may be worth repeating this exercise when beginning the next two or three sessions.

Boot up the machine if necessary

The details of using a computer in a network vary enormously. If your machine is not already up and running, first establish whether a special booting-up disk is to be inserted in the disk drive. Now turn on the power, remembering that there may also be a crucial switch at the end of the bench.

GETTING INTO WINDOWS

As we explained in Chapter 1, you may or may not be transferred directly to **Windows** on booting up the machine: a menu may appear on the screen, or the DOS prompt, to which you must respond by typing **win** and pressing ↵.

The Program Manager window: look at the pointer

As the first window, the **Program Manager**, appears, watch out for the hour-glass and wait for it to disappear before experimenting with the mouse pointer.

The parts of a window

You have already read the descriptions in Section 2.2 of the various parts of a window. Now look for the various features in the display before you. Do not be surprised if, at first, things look very different from the illustration in Figure 1 (p.14). Much depends on which applications are loaded into your computer. Moreover, **Windows** offers the user a very tailorable environment, and windows may be sized, shaped and positioned in an infinite variety of ways.

Title bar

The **title bar** is always the top structure in a window.

Menu bar

Notice the white **menu bar**, just underneath the **title bar**. With the mouse, click on the **File** caption and obtain the **File** drop-down menu. Having noted the choices it offers, remove it by clicking with the mouse on any point outside the menu boundaries.

Control-Menu box

At the left-hand end of the title bar is the **Control-Menu** box, consisting of a small square containing a horizontal bar. This is used to close a window.

Maximise and Minimise buttons

Identify the **Maximise** and **Minimise** buttons (see Figure 1 and read the description in Section 2.2.2).

Reducing a window to an icon

Click on the **Minimise** button. The effect is dramatic: the **Program Manager** is now a tiny icon in the bottom left corner of the screen, which now appears as a huge area known as the **desktop**. Restore the **Program Manager** window by double-clicking on the icon. At the level of the title bar, in a square to the right of the one containing the **Minimise** button, are two arrows: the upper arrow, the **Maximise** button, has the effect of making the window occupy the entire screen; the lower button restores the window to its original size.

Click-and-drag operations

Notice what happens when the screen pointer touches a border or corner of a window: the pointer changes from a diagonally upward-pointing single arrow to a double-headed arrow. Only when the double-headed arrow appears, can the window by re-sized by clicking-and-dragging on the border (or corner) with the mouse.

Open and close the Clipboard Viewer window

Notice that, in addition to the **File Manager**, there are other windows, one of which has the caption **Accessories** in its title bar. In the **Accessories** window, is the icon of the **Clipboard Viewer**. Double-click on this to open the **Clipboard** window. Explore this window, comparing it with that of the **Program Manager**. Close it by clicking on the **Control-Menu** box.

THE FILE MANAGER WINDOW

Within the **Program Manager** window, is the window of the **Main** group of applications. The **File Manager** icon is a drawing of a filing cabinet. Double-click on this to bring to the screen the **File Manager** window. You will see the directories (arranged in a **directory tree**) on the left. One of these, probably **spsswin**, will be highlighted.

The path name of the SPSSWIN directory

Notice the path name in the title bar: C:\SPSSWIN*.*. These terms are explained in Section 2.3.1. On the right of the directory tree are icons of all the files that directory contains. See what happens to the path name when you click on another directory. Notice also that all the file icons change, since the new directory contains different files.

Format two disks

Read Section 2.3.2 carefully and follow the instructions for formatting your two floppy disks, noting carefully the features of the **Format Disk** dialog box (Figure 3, p.19) and of the confirmation dialogs that appear at various stages in the proceedings.

Copying a file to a floppy disk

Following the instructions in Section 2.3.2.4, copy the file **bank.sav** on to one of your floppy disks. Return to the **File Manager** window, and by clicking on the drive **a:** icon, confirm that your disk does indeed contain the file **bank.sav**.

Deleting a file from a floppy disk

Following the instructions in Section 2.3.2.5, delete the file **bank.sav** from your floppy disk. Return to the **File Manager** window, and by clicking on the drive **a:** icon, confirm that your disk no longer contains the file **bank.sav**.

FINISHING THE SESSION

Close the **File Manager** window by clicking on the **Control-Menu** box and (if this is appropriate on your network) leave Windows by clicking on the **Control-Menu** box of the **Program Manager**.

EXERCISE 2
DESCRIBING AND SAVING DATA

BEFORE YOU START

We urge you to read Chapter 3 carefully before working through this practical exercise. Bring your two floppy disks to the session with you, because you will be asked to construct a data set which will be used again in subsequent practical sessions.

GETTING INTO SPSS

Using the procedures described in Section 3.5, bring to the screen the SPSS **Data Editor** window. As the window is forming on the screen, note that the pointer changes to an hour-glass, indicating that something is happening. Note also that a series of messages appears in the **Status Bar**, which runs along the lower border of the SPSS application window. When the statement: 'SPSS Processor is ready' appears, the **Data Editor** is ready to receive your instructions. Move the screen pointer around, noticing how it changes shape when in different areas of the **Data Editor** window.

THE PROJECT

An investigation of the effects of a drug upon performance

The data we are going to explore in this exercise might have been produced by the following project. A team of investigators has good reason to believe that a small dosage of a certain drug increases the speed with which people can make decisions. They decide to try to confirm this by carrying out an experiment in which the decision times of 14 people who have ingested the drug are compared with those of a control group of 14 other people who have performed the task under a placebo condition. The experimenters expect that the decision times of the experimental group will tend to be shorter than those of the placebo group. The results are shown in Table 1.

Table 1. Decision times of the experimental and placebo groups in the drug experiment

	DRUG GROUP				PLACEBO GROUP		
Subject	Time	Subject	Time		Subject	Time	Subject	Time
1	471	2	494		15	446	16	749
3	386	4	323		17	599	18	460
5	660	6	406		19	390	20	477
7	345	8	425		21	556	22	440
9	421	10	407		23	471	24	501
11	386	12	550		25	492	26	392
13	470	14	393		27	578	28	398

Constructing the SPSS data set

Construct the data set along the lines described in Section 3.5. The first column in the grid will represent the grouping variable (ie the type of treatment - drug or placebo) and we shall name it *group*. The second column will represent all the subjects' scores on the dependent variable and will be named *score*. Notice that this column will include the scores for **both** treatments; the first column, which represents the type of treatment, will be used by the computer to distinguish whether a score in the second column belongs to the drug group or to the placebo group. The correct form of the SPSS data set is shown in Table 2.

Table 2. The SPSS data set

group	score
1	471
1	494
1	386
.	.
1	393
2	446
2	749
.	.
2	398

In Table 2, notice that the value of *group* changes from *1* to *2* from subject 15 onwards, signifying that their scores were obtained under different conditions from those of subjects 1 to 14: the value *1* represents the drug condition; the value *2* represents the placebo condition. Define the variables *group* and *score*, and enter the data of Table 2 into the **Data Editor** grid in the manner described in Section 3.5.4. Use the labelling procedure to assign the value labels *drug* and *placebo* to the code numbers *1*, and *2*, respectively. When the data have been entered, save them to a file with a name such as **explore.sav**, from which they can be recalled at a later session.

Exploring the data

The first step is always to examine the data set to see whether it has any odd features.

Means and standard deviations

We shall want a table of means and standard deviations, together with indicators of distribution shape such as stem-and-leaf displays and boxplots. The statistics for the subgroups are most easily obtained with the **Means** procedure, and the plots from the **Explore** procedure. Follow the instructions in Section 4.3.3.3, remembering that the dependent variable name is *score* and the independent variable name is *group*.

• **Write down the values of the means and standard deviations. Are the standard deviations similar in value?**

Note that the **Means** procedure requires the presence of a grouping variable in the data set. To obtain the mean and standard deviation of a set of ungrouped data, use the **Descriptives** procedure.

Graphical displays of the data

To draw the plots, proceed as described in Section 4.3.3.4. The output listing begins with the stem-and-leaf displays for the two groups. The boxplots are then drawn in the **Chart Carousel**. They can be brought to the screen either by clicking on the **Carousel** icon or by clicking on the **Window** drop-down menu and selecting **Chart**. Further details about the boxplots are given in Section 4.3.3.4. When there is a marked discrepancy between the mean and median of a set of scores, it may be because the distribution is skewed or otherwise asymmetrical. Atypical scores, or **outliers** can also pull the value of the mean away from that of the median.

Printing the listing

If you want to print out the listing, follow the procedure described in Section 3.8. The precise details will depend upon your local set-up.

EXERCISE 3
COMPARING THE AVERAGES OF TWO INDEPENDENT SAMPLES

BEFORE YOU START

Before proceeding with this exercise, we suggest you read Chapter 6 carefully. This exercise concerns the **independent samples t-test** described in Section 6.2.4; the next will be concerned with the **paired samples t-test**, which is described in Section 6.2.3.

The data from Exercise 2 will be used again for the present exercise. In that experiment, the subjects were randomly assigned to either the Drug or the Placebo condition. Their scores, therefore, are two independent samples of interval data. Provided the distributions of the scores are appropriate, the independent samples t-test can be used to test the null hypothesis of no difference (in the population) between the means of the Drug and Placebo groups.

The **t-test** is an example of a **parametric** test: that is, it makes certain assumptions about the populations from which the samples have supposedly been drawn. It is assumed, for example, that the populations are normal, and that they have the same variance. When a data set is examined (by the methods of Chapter 4), it is often quite clear that neither the assumption of normality of distribution nor that of homogeneity of variance is tenable. This can mean that the **tail probability**, or **p-value**, given in the t-test output is misleading. One solution to this problem is to use a **nonparametric** test, a method which makes fewer assumptions about the population distributions. Later in this exercise, we shall use a nonparametric text, the **Mann-Whitney**, to compare the medians of the Drug and Placebo groups.

THE INDEPENDENT SAMPLES T-TEST

If you worked through Exercise 2 and stored the data to a file on floppy disk, they can easily be restored to SPSS by using the **Open** procedure. Otherwise, the data of Exercise 2 must be typed into the **Data Editor** grid as described in Exercise 2 and then saved.

Exploring the data

Before any formal statistical tests are carried out, it is essential to explore the data distributions. **Outliers** can also be detected at this stage. In this case, however, the data have already been thoroughly explored. In the previous exercise, it was found that both samples had practically identical variances (ie their standard deviations had very similar values) and the various plots (boxplots and stem-and-leaf displays) indicated that the distributions were such as to permit the use of a parametric test. The only untoward finding was that one of the subjects in the Placebo group had a score of *749*, which is highly atypical of the group as a whole.

Procedure for an independent samples t-test

Full details of the procedure for the independent samples t test are given in Section 6.2.4. Run the procedure as described in that section.

Output listing for the independent samples t-test

Guidance on how to interpret the listing is given in Section 6.2.4. We suggest you study that section and try to answer the following questions.

- Write down the value of t and its tail probability. Is the p-value evidence against the null hypothesis? Remember that if the result is sufficiently unlikely (ie $p < 0.05$) under the null hypothesis, it is regarded as evidence against the null hypothesis and hence in favour of the experimental hypothesis. Write down your interpretation of the result of the test: has the t-test confirmed the pattern shown by the means of the two groups?

A NONPARAMETRIC TEST: THE MANN-WHITNEY

When there are serious violations of the distribution assumptions of the t test, a nonparametric test should be considered. When there are two independent samples of scores, the **Mann-Whitney** test can be used to compare the medians of the two groups. It should be noted, however, that whereas in the parametric test the null hypothesis stated that the two population means are equal, the nonparametric test concerns **medians**, not means: in the **Mann-Whitney** test, the null hypothesis states that the population medians are equal.

Procedure for the Mann-Whitney test

The **Mann-Whitney** test procedure is fully described in Section 6.3.2. Run the procedure as described in that section.

Output listing for the Mann-Whitney test

The listing gives the values of the statistics U and W (the W statistic belongs to a test by Wilcoxon which is the exact equivalent of the Mann-Whitney), followed by an exact 2-tailed probability value, and then a standard normal deviate score Z and a 2-tailed probability value corrected for ties. If this p-value is less than 0.05, the null hypothesis can be rejected and the groups declared to differ significantly.

- Write down the results of the Mann-Whitney test, including the value of U and its p-value. State whether the result is significant and whether the Mann-Whitney test confirms the result of the t-test. In what circumstances would you expect the p-values of U and t to differ?

EXERCISE 4
COMPARING THE AVERAGES OF TWO SAMPLES: PAIRED DATA

BEFORE YOU START

The methods described in the previous exercise, (the **independent samples t-test** and the **Mann-Whitney** test), are appropriate for data from a between subjects experiment, that is, one with independent samples of subjects in the two groups. Suppose, however, that the data had come from an experiment in which the same subjects had been tested under both the experimental and control conditions. Such a within subjects experiment would yield a set of paired (or related) data. In this exercise, we shall consider some methods for comparing the averages of the scores obtained under the experimental and control conditions when we have a set of paired data (SPSS calls this **paired samples**), rather than independent samples. Before proceeding with this exercise, the reader should review the material in Sections 6.2.2 and 6.2.3.

THE PAIRED SAMPLES AT-TEST

An experiment on hemispherical specialisation

In an experiment investigating the relative ease with which words presented in the left and right visual fields are recognised, subjects were instructed to fixate a spot in the centre of the field. They were told that, after a short interval, a word would appear to the left or the right of the spot and they were to press a key as soon as they recognised it. In the trials that followed, each word was presented an equal number of times in each field, though the order of presentation of the words was, of course, randomised. From the results, a table of median decision times was constructed from the subjects' reactions to presentations of 40 words in each of the two visual field (Table 1).

Table 1. Median decision times for words presented to the right and left visual fields

Subject	Right visual field	Left visual field
1	323	324
2	493	512
3	502	503
4	376	385
5	428	453
6	343	345
7	523	543
8	439	442
9	682	683
10	703	998
11	598	600
12	456	462
13	653	704
14	652	653

Do these data support the experimental hypothesis that there is a difference between the response times for words in the left and right visual fields?

Rationale of the paired samples t-test

In the **paired samples t-test**, the strategy is to subtract (consistently) either the first or the second member of each pair of scores from the other, producing a single column of difference scores. If there is, in the population, no difference between the mean scores for the right and left visual fields, the mean difference will also be zero. The null hypothesis to be tested states that our 14 difference scores are a sample from a population with a mean of zero and a variance which can be estimated from the difference scores in the sample. If we can assume that the population of differences is normally distributed, the null hypothesis can be tested with the statistic t, where

$$t = \frac{\text{mean difference}}{\text{standard error of the difference}}$$

and

$$\text{standard error of the difference} = \frac{\text{standard deviation of the differences}}{\sqrt{n}}$$

If there are n pairs of data (ie n subjects), this t statistic has (n-1) degrees of freedom. In the present example, df = 13. The **one-sample t-test** presupposes that the difference scores are normally distributed. Should it turn out from preliminary inspection of the data, that the differences are far from being normally distributed, or that there are huge outliers, the user should beware of the t-test, especially with a small data set, such as the present one, and should consider using a test that makes fewer assumptions about the data. For sets of paired data showing contraindications against the use of the related t-test, there are two nonparametric tests, neither of which assumes normality of the population distribution; both, moreover, are robust to the influence of outliers. These tests are:

(1) The **Wilcoxon matched pairs test**.
(2) The **Sign test**.

The latter is the more resistant to the leverage exerted by outliers; but, provided there are no outliers, the Wilcoxon is the more powerful test. (On the other hand, there are those who would say that if the data are good enough for the Wilcoxon, they are good enough for the paired samples t-test.)

Before proceeding with this exercise, we strongly urge you to read Section 6.2.3, which describes the procedure for a paired samples t-test.

Preparing the SPSS data set

In the data set for the independent samples t-test, one of the variables must be a grouping variable, showing which subjects performed under which conditions. With the paired samples t-test, however, there was only one group and so no coding variable need be constructed. Define two variables: *rvf* (*Right Visual Field*), and *lvf* (*Left Visual Field*) and enter the data in the usual way, as described in Section 3.5. The two columns *rvf* and *lvf* are sufficient for SPSS to run a paired samples t-test. As always, however, it is wise to explore the data, rather than pressing ahead with the formal test automatically. Since the null hypothesis concerns only the population of differences (rather than the separate *rvf* and *lvf* populations), we first calculate the differences and see how those are distributed. It is a very simple matter to obtain the differences by using the **Compute** procedure (Section 4.4.2) to create a new variable, *diffs*, containing the (*rvf* - *lvf*) difference for each subject.

Exploring the data

To list the values within *diffs*, click on
Statistics
  Summarize
    List Cases
to open the **List Cases** dialog box. Click on *diffs* and then on > to paste the name into the **Variable(s)** box. Click on **OK**.

From inspection of the column of differences, it is quite clear that there is a glaring outlier. It is instructive to ascertain the effect of its presence upon the results of the t-test, in comparison with the nonparametric **Wilcoxon** and **Sign** tests. Although, in the paired samples t-test, the interest centres on the column of differences rather than the original scores, it is nevertheless of interest to see the scatterplot of *rvf* against *lvf*, which, ideally, should show an elliptical cloud of points indicating a bivariate normal distribution. Use the procedure in Section 6.2.3 to obtain a scatterplot of *lvf* against *rvf* and notice how the outlier shows up dramatically.

Running the paired samples t-test
Run the **paired samples t-test** by following the procedure described in Section 6.2.3.

Output listing for the paired samples t-test
From the details given in the t-test listing, it is clear that there are contraindications against the use of the paired samples t-test for the data in the present experiment. There is marked discrepancy between the standard deviations of the scores obtained under the *rvf* and *lvf* conditions. This arises from the presence of an outlier, which showed up dramatically in the scatterplot.

- **From the listing, write down the value of *t* and its p-value. Is *t* significant? Write down, in terms of the research hypothesis, the meaning of this result.**

What has happened here? You should find the t-test result paradoxical to say the least. Each of the fourteen pairs of data (one pair from each subject) shows a difference in the same direction: the *rvf* time is always lower than the *lvf* time. Moreover, in the case of the outlying pair of scores, the difference is even greater. Surely this should strengthen the evidence against the null hypothesis? Yet, in fact, the t-test does not show significance. This is because the outlier has exerted more leverage upon the denominator of the t statistic than it has upon the numerator, thus reducing the value of t (see Section 6.2.3).

NONPARAMETRIC ALTERNATIVES TO THE PAIRED SAMPLES T-TEST

The Wilcoxon matched pairs test
Now carry out the **Wilcoxon matched pairs** test, following the procedure described in Section 6.3.2.

- **Write down the value of the statistic and its p-value. Compare the p-value with that for the t-test. Relate the result of the Wilcoxon test to the experimental hypothesis.**

The Sign test
This test is based very simply on how many positive and negative differences there are between pairs of data, assuming that the value of one variable is consistently subtracted from the value of the other. It is a straightforward application of the binomial model to paired data, such as the results of the visual field experiment above. To merely record the signs (rather than the magnitudes) of the differences between the times for the left and right visual fields is certainly to lose a considerable amount of information. Indeed, when paired data show no contraindications, the related t-test is preferable to the Sign test, for to use the latter in such circumstances would be to make a needless sacrifice of power. The great advantage of the Sign test, however, is its robustness to the influence of outliers; moreover, there are no requirements about bivariate normality in the original paired data.

The procedure is very similar to that for the Wilcoxon test except that within the **Test Type** box, the **Wilcoxon** check box should be clicked off and the **Sign** check box clicked on. Click on **OK** to run the procedure.

- **Write down the results of the Sign test, including the p-value. Is the result significant? Compare this with the result of the paired samples t-test and explain any discrepancy.**

You may have noticed that the p-value for the **Sign** test is even smaller than that for the **Wilcoxon** test. This is because, although the Wilcoxon test is less sensitive to the presence of outliers than is the t-test, it is still affected by them to some extent.

ELIMINATING THE OUTLIERS

When there are contraindications for the **paired samples t-test**, the use of a nonparametric test is not the only alternative available. Another approach is to consider the possibility of eliminating some of the data. In the present set of paired data, there is one (*lvf-rvf*) difference which is much larger than all the others. This may have arisen because subject 10 has special difficulty in recognising words in the left visual field. At any rate, that subject's performance is quite atypical of this sample of participants and certainly calls into question the claim that he or she was drawn from the same population as the others. It is instructive to reanalyse the data after excluding the scores of Subject 10. This is done by using the **Select Cases** procedure (Section 3.9.1). Follow the procedure described in that section to eliminate the data from subject 10. (Hint: give the instruction to select cases if *rvf* is *not equal* to 703.)

Now re-run the **paired samples t-test**, the **Wilcoxon** and the **Sign** test on the reduced data set. Examine the new listings.

- **Write down the value of t and its tail probability. Write down your interpretation of this new result. Similarly give the statistics and their p-values for the Sign and Wilcoxon tests, commenting on the relative sizes of the p-values.**

Appendix to Exercise 4

SOME NOTES ON ONE-SAMPLE TESTS

So far, we have been concerned with tests of the null hypothesis that, in the population, there is no difference between the averages of two correlated samples of data. There can arise, however, situations where one has a single sample of scores and wishes to test the null hypothesis that the sample has been drawn from a population with a specified mean, which may be other than zero.

The one-sample t-test

Suppose it is known that, over the years, the mean performance on a spelling test of children in a particular class at school is 51. One year, however, following the introduction of a new teaching method, it is hoped that a higher level of performance will be achieved. At the end of the year, it is found that the mean of the children's spelling scores is 60. Is this improvement significant?

The null hypothesis that the population mean has value 51 can be tested by defining (in the **Data Editor** grid) the variable *scores*, containing the children's marks. Now use the **Compute** procedure to define another variable *mean*, containing the constant value *51*. Run the **paired samples t-test** in the usual way to make the required one-sample test.

As an exercise, use the **t-test** to test the hypothesis that the column *diffs* contains a sample of scores from a population whose mean is zero. (This has already been done by the paired samples t-test procedure; but now define the variable *hyp* (hypothesis) and enter 14 zero values. Proceed as described above.)

The binomial test

So far the binomial model has been considered only in the context of the **Sign** test for a difference between the medians of correlated columns of paired data. The question also arises as to whether there is reason to reject the null hypothesis of chance performance. Suppose, for example, that a child is presented with a series of 20 pairs of objects, one member of each of which contains a reward. Sometimes the child makes the correct choice; but is this just good luck, or has the rule really been understood?

There are two ways of entering the data for the binomial test:

Method 1. You can decide upon a code for right and wrong guesses (eg 1 for a correct answer, 0 for a wrong one), and enter the person's performance as a series such as:

1 1 0 1 1 1 1 0 0 0 1 1 1 0 1 1 1 1 1 1

If we assume that there were only two choices for each question (ie the probability of a correct guess is ½ each time), the procedure for the first method is as follows:

Define the variable *guesses*, containing the above sequence of code numbers representing the subject's performance. Next, choose

Statistics
  Nonparametric Tests
    Binomial

to open the **Binomial Test** dialog box. Click on *guesses* and on > to transfer the name to the **Test Variable** box. Click on **OK** to run the procedure.

Method 2. Alternatively, the data can be entered as the numbers of correct and incorrect answers produced (in the current example, the child got 15 choices right and 5 wrong in a sequence of 20 trials). The **Weight Cases** procedure (see Section 3.9.2) instructs SPSS to treat the values *15* and *5* as frequencies rather than as scores.

As an exercise, try both methods to assess the child's performance.

So far, the binomial test has assumed the default value of 0.5 for the proportion of cases expected in the first category (ie the probability p of a case falling into the first category). In most experimental situations (and multiple-choice examinations), however, there are more than two choices at each trial. We need to be able to cope with situations where p is not 0.5. This is easily dealt with by changing the value of **Test Proportion** in the **Binomial Test** dialog box to whatever value is required. If there were four choices for each question, for example, the value would be 0.25.

EXERCISE 5
THE ANALYSIS OF NOMINAL DATA:
THE CHI-SQUARE TEST

BEFORE YOU START

Before you proceed with this practical, we strongly recommend that you read Chapters 5 and 11 (especially Section 11.3.2). Basically there are two applications of chi-square tests to the analysis of nominal data:

    (1)   For **goodness-of-fit** (when one variable is being studied).
    (2)   For the presence of an **association** between two variables.

THE CHI-SQUARE TEST OF GOODNESS-OF-FIT

Some nominal data on one qualitative variable

Suppose that a researcher, interested in children's preferences, suspects a spatial response bias towards the right hand side. Thirty children enter a room containing three identically-marked doors: one to the right; another to the left; and a third straight ahead. They are told they can go through any of the three doors. Their choices are shown in Table 1.

Table 1. The choices of one of three exit doors by thirty children

Left	DOOR Middle	Right
5	8	17

It looks as if there is indeed a preference for the rightmost door, at least among the children sampled. Had the children been choosing at random, we should have expected about 10 in each category: that is, the theoretical, or expected distribution (E), of the tallies is a **uniform** one. The observed frequencies (O), on the other hand, have a distribution which is far from uniform.

Pearson's chi-square test can be used to test the goodness-of-fit of the expected to the observed distribution. Its rationale is lucidly discussed in any good statistics textbook (eg Howell, 1992). Here, we shall merely describe the SPSS procedure.

Procedure for the chi-square test of goodness-of-fit

Preparing the SPSS data set
Define the variable *position* for the three positional categories and a second variable *freq* for the numbers of children in the different categories. Use the **Labels** procedure to assign the code numbers *1*, *2* and *3* to the *position* categories *Left*, *Centre* and *Right*, respectively.

Run the Weight Cases procedure
To ensure that SPSS treats the entries in *freq* as frequencies rather than scores, follow the procedure described in Section 3.9.2.

Finding the dialog box
Choose
Statistics
  Nonparametric Tests
    Chi-Square
to open the **Chi-Square Test** dialog box. Click on *position* (not on *freq*) and on > to transfer *position* to the **Test Variable List** box. Click on OK to run the test.

• Write down the value of the chi-square statistic and its p-value. Does the test show significance, ie is the p-value sufficiently small to constitute evidence against the null hypothesis? Write down the implications for the experimenter's research hypothesis.

Running the goodness-of-fit test on a set of raw data
When the researcher carried out the experiment, the door that each child chose was noted at the time. In terms of the code numbers, their choices might have been:
1 1 3 2 1 1 3 3 . . . and so on.
If the user defines the variable *position*, and enters the 30 (coded) choices that the children made, the chi-square test is then run directly: there is no weighting of cases.

THE CHI-SQUARE TEST OF ASSOCIATION BETWEEN TWO QUALITATIVE VARIABLES

The reader should study Section 11.3.2 before doing this part of the exercise.

An experiment on children's choices

Suppose that a researcher, having watched a number of children enter a room and recorded each child's choice between two objects, wants to know whether there is a tendency for boys and girls to choose different objects. This question concerns two variables: *gender* and *choice*. In statistical terms, the researcher is asking whether they are associated: do more girls than boys choose object A and more boys than girls choose object B? Suppose that the children's choices are as in Table 2.

Table 2. Choices by 50 children of one of two objects

	BOYS	GIRLS
OBJECT A	20	5
OBJECT B	6	19

Procedure for the chi-square test of association between two variables

The use of the **Crosstabs** procedure is fully described in Sections 11.3.2.1 and 11.3.2.2. We recommend the inclusion of the option for obtaining the expected frequencies. This will enable you to check for the presence of cells with unacceptably low expected frequencies (see Section 11.3.2.2 for details).

Output listing for the chi-square test of association

The listing is discussed in Section 11.3.2.3. First, a crosstabulation table is listed showing the observed and expected frequencies in each cell, along with row and column totals. Second, a table of various chi-square statistics, together with their associated significance levels, is listed.

- **Write down the value of the Pearson chi-square and its associated tail probability (p-value). Is it significant? In terms of the experimental hypothesis, what has this test shown?**

EXERCISE 6
ONE-FACTOR ANALYSIS OF VARIANCE

BEFORE YOU START

We suggest that you review the material in Chapter 7 before working through this practical exercise.

THE EXERCISE

The purpose of this exercise

In one-factor ANOVA, the **F ratio** compares the spread among the treatment means with the (supposedly uniform) spread of the scores within groups about their group means. The purpose of this exercise is to help clarify the rationale of the F ratio by showing how its value is affected by various manipulations of some (or all) of the data. Before proceeding with this exercise, we ask you to suppose that a one-factor ANOVA has been carried out upon a set of data and yields an F value of, say, *7.23*. Now suppose we were to multiply every score in the experimental results by a constant, say 10. What would happen to the value of F: would it still be *7.23*? Or would it increase? Or decrease?

We also invite you to speculate upon the effect that adding a constant (say 10) to all the scores in just one of the groups would have upon F: suppose, for example, we were to add 10 to all the scores in the group with the largest mean. Would F stay the same, increase or decrease in value? Would the effect be the same if the constant were added to the scores of the group with the smallest mean?

As a first approach to answering these questions, we shall carry out a **one-factor** ANOVA on a set of data. Then we shall see what happens to the value of F when the data are transformed as described in the previous paragraphs.

Some data from a completely randomised experiment

Suppose a researcher is interested in how well non-Chinese-speaking students can learn Chinese characters using different kinds of mnemonic. Independent groups of participants are tested under three conditions: *No Mnemonic*, *Mnemonic 1* and *Mnemonic 2*. The dependent variable is the number of Chinese characters that are correctly recalled. The data are shown in Table 1.

Table 1. Results of a completely randomised experiment on the effects upon recall of logographic characters of different mnemonic systems

No Mnemonic (scores of 10 control subjects)	4 6 4 3 5 7 10 4 9 11
Mnemonic 1 (scores of 10 subjects trained in Mnemonic 1)	11 9 16 10 12 17 18 16 8 11
Mnemonic 2 (scores of 10 subjects trained in Mnemonic 2)	21 16 15 16 18 11 9 12 19 20

Construction of the SPSS data set

Recast the data of Table 1 into a form suitable for analysis by SPSS by following the procedure described in Chapter 3. Save the data set: we shall be using it again in the next exercise.

Exploring the data

As always, we recommend a preliminary exploration of the data set before any formal testing is carried out, in case there are contraindications for the use of the ANOVA. As in Exercise 2, use the **Means** procedure for descriptive statistics and **Explore** for checks on the distributions of the scores within the groups. (**Explore** inundates the user with a surfeit of statistics: the **Means** procedure is therefore preferred.)

- **Examine the output listing for the Means procedure. Do the means appear to differ? Are the standard deviations similar in value?**

The output listing for the **Explore** procedure begins with the stem-and-leaf displays for the three groups. It then plots the boxplots in the **Chart Carousel**: they can be seen on the screen by clicking on the **Carousel** icon or clicking on the **Window** drop-down menu and selecting **Chart**. Further details about the boxplots are given in Section 4.3.3.4.

- **Do the boxplots suggest any anomalies in the distributions of the data in any of the three groups? Write a statement assessing the suitability of the data for ANOVA.**

Procedure for the one-way analysis of variance (ANOVA)

The procedure for the one-way ANOVA is described in detail in Section 7.2.2.

Output listing for the one-way ANOVA

- **Write down the value of F and its associated p-value. Is F significant? What are the implications of this result for the experimental hypothesis?**

REANALYSIS OF TRANSFORMED DATA SETS

In this section, we return to the question of the effects upon the ANOVA statistics of subjecting the data (or sections of the data) to such operations as multiplying every score by a constant.

Multiplying every score by a constant

We recommend that whenever you have occasion to transform the values of a variable in the SPSS data set, you should construct a new target variable, rather than change (perhaps irreversibly) the original data. Use the **Compute** procedure (Section 4.4.2) to multiply each value in the data set by a factor of 10. Follow the instructions in that section, choosing, for the target variable, a mnemonic name such as *allbyten*. Now change the **One-way ANOVA** dialog box so that the dependent variable is *allbyten* instead of *score* and click on **OK** to run the analysis.

Output listing for the one-way ANOVA

- **Write down the value of F and its associated p-value. Is F significant? What are the implications of this result for the experimental hypothesis?**

In the output listing, you will see that both the between groups and within groups variance estimates have increased by a factor of 100. This is not at all surprising, since it is easy to show algebraically that when each of a set of scores is multiplied by a constant, the new variance is the old variance times the square of the constant. Since the factors of 100 in the numerator and denominator of the F ratio cancel out, the value of the F ratio remains unchanged.

Adding a constant to the scores in only one group

This time, we want a target variable which contains, for two of the three groups, the original scores; but to the values of the Mnemonic 2 group has been added a constant of +10. First, make a copy of the values in *score* to a new variable *g3plus10* in the **Data Editor** grid using the technique described in Section 3.5.5. Second, use the **Compute** procedure to add the value *+10* to the values in this new variable when the grouping variable has the value *3*. In the **Compute** dialog box, type *g3plus10* into the **Target Variable** box, transfer it to the **Numeric Expression** box and add *+10* after the variable name. Click on **If** to open the **Compute Variable: If Cases** dialog box. Transfer the name *group* into the box and add the expression *=3*. Click on **Continue** and then on **OK** to run the procedure. In the **Data Editor** grid, check that the values in *g3plus10* for the third group have changed but the rest have their original values.

Now re-run the **one-way ANOVA**, using *g3plus10* as the dependent variable.

Output listing for the one-way ANOVA

- **Write down the value of F and its associated p-value. Is F significant? What are the implications of this result for the experimental hypothesis?**

You will see that the effect of adding a constant of *10* to all scores in the *Mnemonic 2* group has no effect at all upon the within groups variance estimate, which is not surprising, since adding the same constant to all the scores in a set has no effect upon the spread of the scores - it merely shifts the mean. The between groups mean square, however, computed from the values of the treatment means alone, has increased its value considerably. The within groups mean square, on the other hand, is the average of the variance estimates of the scores within groups and is quite independent of the spread among the group means. Consequently, it is quite possible to change the value of the former without affecting that of the latter and vice-versa. The effect of increasing the mean of the third group is to increase the spread of the three treatment means and hence the value of the numerator of the F ratio.

EXERCISE 7

ONE-WAY ANOVA AND THE TUKEY TEST FOR PAIRWISE MULTIPLE COMPARISONS

BEFORE YOU START

Before you proceed with this practical exercise, we recommend that you read Sections 7.1 and 7.2.3.3. In Section 7.1, it was pointed out that if **pairwise t-tests** are used to make comparisons among an array of treatment means, the probability of at least one test showing significance, even when the ANOVA null hypothesis is true (ie all treatment means have the same value in the population), can be considerably greater than the significance level (say, 0.05) set for each test. In other words, while the type I error rate **per comparison** may be set at 0.05, the type I error rate for the whole family of comparisons (the **per family** type I error rate) can be much greater. The purpose of this exercise is to make pairwise comparisons among an array of treatment means, while at the same time controlling the **per family** type I error rate.

In this context, it makes a considerable difference whether the comparisons are planned or unplanned. For the purposes of this exercise, we shall assume that the desired comparisons are unplanned. In other words, we are looking for a data-snooping technique to make unplanned pairwise comparisons among an array of treatment means, while at the same time controlling the **per family** type 1 error rate. The method we shall use is **Tukey's Honestly Significant Difference test (HSD)**. While many other tests are used to make multiple pairwise comparisons, the HSD test is known to be especially effective in controlling the **per family** type I error rate. The use of the HSD test will be illustrated with the same data that we used in Exercise 6. For the purposes of comparison, we shall also look at some other procedures for unplanned pairwise multiple comparisons.

PROCEDURES FOR UNPLANNED MULTIPLE COMPARISONS

With data from a completely randomised experiment, it is a simple matter to run various multiple comparisons procedures with SPSS, because these can be requested from the **One-way ANOVA** dialog box.

Specifying multiple comparisons procedures with the one-way ANOVA

Restore the data from Exercise 6 by following the usual procedure. Proceed as for the **one-way ANOVA**, but this time click on the **Post-hoc** button to bring to the screen the **One-Way ANOVA: Post Hoc Multiple Comparisons** dialog box. Mark the check boxes for all the options offered: **Least Significant Difference**, **Bonferroni** and so on. Click on **Continue** and then on **OK** to run the ANOVA and the multiple comparisons procedures.

Output listing for unplanned multiple comparisons procedures

Study the output listing for the various multiple comparisons tests, noting their presentations of the results and comparing their decisions about which differences are significant.

- **Construct your own table comparing the decisions of the various post-hoc procedures.**

EXERCISE 8
FACTORIAL ANALYSIS OF VARIANCE
(BETWEEN SUBJECTS EXPERIMENTS)

BEFORE YOU START

Before proceeding with this practical, please read Chapter 8. The following exercise assumes a knowledge of the standard **factorial** ANOVA terminology.

THE TWO-WAY ANALYSIS OF VARIANCE

An experiment on the memories of chess players

'Must have a marvellous memory!'. This is something often said of a good chess player; but do good chess players necessarily have better memories than those who are mediocre? To find out, a psychologist tested chess players at three levels of proficiency on their ability to reconstruct board positions they had just been shown. Some of the positions used were from real games selected from tournaments; but others were merely random placings of the same pieces. The psychologist predicted that whereas the better players would show superior reconstructions of real board positions, this superiority would disappear when they tried to reproduce random placements. The dependent variable in this experiment was a subject's *score* on reconstruction. There were two independent variables (factors):

(1) Competence (3 levels: Novice, Average, Good).
(2) Position (2 levels: Real, Random).

An important feature of the design of this experiment was that a different sample of subjects performed under each of the six treatment combinations: that is, each group of players at a given level was subdivided into those reconstructing *Real* positions and those reconstructing *Random* positions.

What the psychologist is predicting is that, when performance is averaged over *Random* and *Real* positions, the better players will achieve higher performance means; but this will turn out to be because of their superior recall of *Real* board positions only, and the beginners will be just as good at reconstructing *Random* positions. The **two-factor ANOVA**, therefore, should show a significant interaction between the factors of *Competence* and *Position*, as well as (possibly) a main effect of *Competence*. The latter might be expected to arise because the better players' much superior performance in reconstructing real board positions pulls up the mean value of their performance over both *Real* and *Random* positions, even though they may not excel beginners on the *Random* task.

The results of the experiment are shown in Table 1.

Table 1. Results of the experiment on the reconstruction of positions by chess players

	CHESS COMPETENCE		
	Novice	Average	Good
TYPE OF PROBLEM Real	38 39 42 40 40	65 58 70 61 62	88 97 79 89 89
Random	50 53 40 41 36	50 40 43 37 38	41 40 50 42 41

Procedure for the two-factor between subjects experiment

Before proceeding further, we strongly recommend you to study Section 8.2.

Constructing the SPSS data set

Recast the data of Table 1 into a form suitable for entry into SPSS along the lines of the description in Section 8.2.1. You will need two coding variables, *compet* and *position*, and one dependent variable *score*. As always, save the data set.

Exploring the data

Before proceeding with the ANOVA, it is important to explore the data to check for contraindications, such as heterogeneity of variance. Since the samples are small, stem-and-leaf displays or boxplots of the data in the six cells of the experiment are unlikely to be illuminating. We suggest, therefore, that you construct a table of means to include the cell means and the marginal means (ie row means and column means) by using the **Means** procedure twice, the first time including both *compet* and *position* in the **Independent List** box, the second time **layering** both the independent variables (see Section 8.2.3.2). The first operation obtains the marginal means, the second obtains the cell means. You should now have a table of cell means, and also the row and column means.

- **From inspection of the marginal means, are there any indications of main effects? Do the cell means give any indication of an interaction?**

Procedure for the two-way ANOVA

Follow the description in Sections 8.2.1 and 8.2.2.

Output listing for the two-way ANOVA

The ANOVA summary table gives F ratios for the main effects of *compet* and *position* and also for the interaction between the two factors.

- **Write down the values of *F* (and the associated p-values) for the main effect and interaction terms. Do these results confirm your predictions from inspection of the output from the Means procedure? Relate these results to the experimental hypothesis**

about the memory of chess players.

Obtaining a graph of the cell means

Follow the procedure in Section 8.2.3.3. Inspect the graph and interpret the results of the ANOVA tests accordingly.

Unplanned multiple comparisons among the marginal and cell means

Follow up the main ANOVA with unplanned pairwise comparisons among the marginal and cell means, as described in Section 8.2.3.4.

EXERCISE 9
WITHIN-SUBJECTS (REPEATED MEASURES) EXPERIMENTS

BEFORE YOU START

Before proceeding with this exercise, we suggest you study Chapter 9.

ANALYSIS OF DATA FROM A ONE-FACTOR WITHIN SUBJECTS EXPERIMENT

A comparison of the efficacy of statistical packages

Imagine an experiment which measures the time taken for ten subjects to perform an analysis using three statistical computer packages Pack1, Pack2 and Pack3. During the course of the experiment, each subject uses every package and the order of use is systematically varied across subjects. The results are shown in Table 1.

Table 1. Table of times taken by participants to carry out an analysis with different computing packages

	Pack1	Pack2	Pack3		Pack1	Pack2	Pack3
S1	12	15	18	S6	10	12	14
S2	18	21	19	S7	18	17	21
S3	15	16	15	S8	18	17	21
S4	21	26	32	S9	23	27	30
S5	19	23	22	S10	17	25	21

Preparing the SPSS data set

Prepare the SPSS data set as described in Section 9.4.2. Since there is just one group of subjects, there is no grouping variable.

Running the repeated measures ANOVA procedure
Proceed as described in Section 9.4.3.

Exploring the data
Using the methods described in Chapter 4, examine the distributions of the scores within the samples and obtain their means and standard deviations.

Procedure for the repeated measures ANOVA
Follow the procedure described in Section 9.4.3 .

Output listing for the repeated measures ANOVA
Section 9.4.4 offers some guidelines for the interpretation of the output listing. The most important item is the univariate ANOVA summary table for the *package* factor.

- **What is the value of the F ratio and its associated p-value (tail probability) for *package*?
  Is *F* significant? What are the implications for the experimental hypothesis?**

At this point, however, we must issue a word of warning. In Chapter 9, attention was drawn to the fact that the model for repeated measures ANOVA makes an important assumption, over and above the usual requirements of homogeneity of variance and normality of distribution. This is the assumption of **homogeneity of covariance**. Often (indeed, usually) the data sets yielded by psychological repeated measures experiments show marked heterogeneity of covariance. If there is heterogeneity of covariance, the true p-value may be somewhat higher than that given in the ANOVA summary table. If, therefore, the p-value is very small, say, less than 0.01, it is safe enough to say that we have evidence against the null hypothesis. If, however, the p-value is just under 0.05, we need to look at the result more carefully, and consider the possibility of a **conservative F test** (see Howell, 1992; Chapter 14).

EXERCISE 10

WITHIN SUBJECTS EXPERIMENTS WITH TWO FACTORS

BEFORE YOU START

We suggest that you read Section 9.6 before proceeding. In this exercise, we consider the ANOVA of within subjects factorial experiments, that is, factorial experiments with crossed treatment factors and repeated measures on all factors.

THE TWO-FACTOR WITHIN SUBJECTS ANOVA

A two-factor within subjects experiment

An experiment is carried out to investigate the effects of two factors (independent variables) upon the recognition of symbols briefly presented on a screen, as measured by the number of correct identifications over a fixed number of trials. The factors are *symbol* (with levels Digit, Lower Case, Upper Case) and *font* (with levels Gothic, Roman). Each of the six subjects in the experiment is tested under all six combinations of the two treatment factors. The results are shown in Table 1.

Table 1. Results of a two-factor within subjects experiment

	Digit		Lower case		Upper case	
	Gothic	Roman	Gothic	Roman	Gothic	Roman
S1	2	6	18	3	20	5
S2	4	9	20	6	18	2
S3	3	10	15	2	21	3
S4	1	12	10	9	30	10
S5	5	8	13	8	20	8
S6	6	10	14	10	16	6

Preparing the SPSS data set

Enter the data into the **Data Editor** grid in the manner described in Section 9.6.

Exploring the data

Check for any distribution problems by using the boxplot option of the **Explore** procedure, as in Exercise 9.

Running the two-factor within subjects ANOVA

To run the ANOVA, follow the procedure described in Section 9.6.3 .

Output listing for the two-factor within subjects experiment

The output listing for the two-factor repeated measures ANOVA is explained in Section 9.6.4 .

- **Examine the present listing and interpret the implications of the results of the tests for main effects and the interaction in terms of the aims of the study.**

EXERCISE 11

MIXED (SPLIT-PLOT) ANOVA:

TWO-FACTOR EXPERIMENT WITH REPEATED MEASURES ON ONE FACTOR

BEFORE YOU BEGIN

Readers should study Chapter 10 carefully before proceeding with this exercise.

THE TWO-FACTOR MIXED FACTORIAL ANOVA

An experiment on the effects of ambient hue and sound on performance in a vigilance task

In an experiment investigating the effect of the colour of the ambient light upon performance of a vigilance task, subjects were asked to press a button when they thought they could discern a signal against a background of random noise. The experimenter expects that the ambient colour would have varying effects upon the detection of different kinds of sound. Three types of signal were used: a horn, a whistle and a bell. Each signal was presented 30 times in the course of a one-hour monitoring session, during which the subject sat in a cubicle lit by either red or blue light. The dependent variable was the number of correct presses of the button. For theoretical purposes, it was necessary to use different subjects for the different colour conditions; on the other hand, it was considered that there would be advantages in testing each individual with all three kinds of signal. In this experiment, therefore, the factor of *colour* was between subjects; whereas the other factor, *signal*, was within subjects. The results are shown in Table 1.

Table 1. The results of a two-factor mixed factorial experiment

			Horn	SIGNAL Whistle	Bell
COLOUR	Red	S1	25	18	22
		S2	22	16	21
		S3	26	19	26
		S4	23	21	20
		S5	19	18	19
		S6	27	23	27
	Blue	S7	19	12	23
		S8	21	15	19
		S9	23	14	24
		S10	20	16	21
		S11	17	16	20
		S12	21	17	19

Preparing the SPSS data set

Recast the data of Table 1 into a form suitable for entry into the **Data Editor**. You will need to define a grouping variable *colour* and three variables for the scores: *horn*, *whistle*, and *bell*. The last three variables will be the three levels of the within-subjects factor *signal*, which is not defined until the ANOVA procedure is actually being run. Follow the procedure described in Section 10.2.3.

Exploring the data set

Since there is a grouping variable, use the **Means** procedure to obtain means and standard deviations.
Examine the table of means. Plot the profiles of cell means against the different signals for those subjects who performed under red and blue illumination.

- **Are there signs of main effects or an interaction?**

Procedure for the two-factor mixed ANOVA

Run the procedure as described in Section 10.2.4.

Output listing for the two-factor mixed ANOVA

The main features of the output are explained in Section 10.2.6.

- **Write down the values of F and their associated p-values. Relate these findings to the experimental hypothesis.**

EXERCISE 12

MIXED (SPLIT-PLOT) ANOVA:

THREE-FACTOR EXPERIMENT WITH REPEATED MEASURES ON TWO FACTORS

BEFORE YOU START

Before proceeding with this exercise, you should study Section 10.3. From the procedural point of view, the analysis of mixed experiments with three factors is a fairly simple extension of the procedure for two-factor mixed experiments. In general, however, the interpretation of data from factorial experiments becomes increasingly problematic as more factors are added. In particular, where there is a complex design with repeated measures on some factors but not on others, the naming of the factors must be carried out with special care.

A MIXED FACTORIAL A x (B x C) EXPERIMENT

The data

Imagine an experiment investigating the recognition of shapes under sub-optimal conditions on a monitor screen. There are three shapes (*shape1*, *shape2*, *shape3*), each of which can be either *open* (outline) or *filled*. Each subject in the experiment is tested under all six combinations of these two treatment factors, which can be labelled *shape* and *shade*. The between subjects factor *group* is the type of observer used: one group consists of *psychology students*, the other of *engineering students*. The dependent variable is the number of correct identifications over a fixed series of trials. The results are shown in Table 1.

Table 1. Results of a three-factor mixed factorial experiment with two within subjects treatment factors

		FACTORS Shape: Shade:	Shape 1 Open	Filled	Shape 2 Open	Filled	Shape 3 Open	Filled
	Psychology	S1	2	12	3	1	4	5
	Students	S2	13	22	5	9	6	8
		S3	14	20	8	7	5	7
GROUP								
	Engineering	S4	12	1	3	9	6	10
	Students	S5	11	2	8	10	5	9
		S6	12	7	2	4	4	10

Preparing the SPSS data set

Recast the results in Table 1 as described in Section 10.3.1. The data will comprise seven variables: a grouping variable and a variable for each combination of the two treatment factors. Define the variables appropriately, remembering to label the values of the grouping variable. Enter and save the data.

Exploring the data

Use the **Means** procedure to obtain tables of cell and marginal means. In a three-factor experiment, there is the possibility of a three-way interaction among all three factors. A three-way interaction is said to occur when the interaction between two factors is heterogeneous across the levels of a third factor. This definition might suggest that the presence of a three-way interaction might be rather easy to discern in a three-way table of cell means by simply comparing graphs of two-way interactions at the different levels of a third factor. In fact, the interpretation of graphs drawn from the cell means of three-way tables requires considerable practice. This is because, just as two-way tables of means (and their graphs) reflect the presence of main effects as well as the interaction, three-way tables (and their graphs) reflect the presence of two-way interactions as well as any three-way interaction that might be present. To the untrained eye, two-way graphs may look heterogeneous; but this may arise entirely from the presence of two-way interactions.

From the listing from **Means**, graph the two-way interactions between two of the factors at the different levels of the third factor. Do this by drawing two graphs side-by-side, one for *psychologists* and the other for *engineers*. With the three levels of *shape* on each x-axis and the values of the means on the y-axes, mark in the *open* means with dots and the *filled* means with crosses. Connect up the dots and connect up the crosses with lines in each graph.

- **Do the patterns of lines seem similar? If not, a three-way interaction may be present.**

Running the ANOVA procedure

The procedure is merely outlined in Section 10.3.1, but is a straightforward extension of the routine for the two-factor mixed experiment.

Output listing for the A x (B x C) mixed factorial experiment

Look for the table of 'Tests of Between-Subjects Effects' for the factor *group*. For the various 'Tests involving ..... Within-Subject Effect', **Mauchly** tests will appear for factors with more than two levels (ie the *Shape* factor and for the *shape* x *shade* interaction); check that the p-values are greater than 0.05.

- **Write down the F ratios (and p-values) for the three factors, their two-way interactions and the three-way interaction. Do the values of F confirm the patterns you saw earlier in your graphs among the treatment means?**

As always where there are repeated measures factors, special care is needed when interpreting an F ratio that is significant with a p-value just below 0.05.

EXERCISE 13
THE PEARSON CORRELATION

BEFORE YOU START

Before starting to work through this practical exercise we recommend that you read Chapter 11. The Pearson correlation r is one of the most widely used (and abused) of statistics. Despite its apparent simplicity and versatility, however, it is only too easy to misinterpret a correlation. The purpose of the present exercise is not only to show you how to use SPSS to obtain correlations but also to illustrate how misleading a given value for r can sometimes be.

THE PROJECT

A famous data set

This exercise involves the analysis of four sets of paired data, which were contrived by Anscombe (1973). Each set yields exactly the same value for the **Pearson correlation**. The scatterplots, however, will show that in only one case are the data suitable for a Pearson correlation: in the others, the Pearson correlation gives a highly misleading impression of the relationship between the two variables.

The data are presented in Table 1. The four sets we shall examine are $X1$ and $Y1$, $X1$ and $Y2$, $X1$ and $Y3$, and $X2$ and $Y4$.

Table 1. Anscombe's four data sets

Subject	X1	X2	Y1	Y2	Y3	Y4
S1	10.0	8.0	8.04	9.14	7.46	6.58
S2	8.0	8.0	6.95	8.14	6.77	5.76
S3	13.0	8.0	7.58	8.74	12.74	7.71
S4	9.0	8.0	8.81	8.77	7.11	8.84
S5	11.0	8.0	8.33	9.26	7.81	8.47
S6	14.0	8.0	9.96	8.10	8.84	7.04
S7	6.0	8.0	7.24	6.13	6.08	5.25
S8	4.0	19.0	4.26	3.10	5.39	12.50
S9	12.0	8.0	10.84	9.13	8.15	5.56
S10	7.0	8.0	4.82	7.26	6.42	7.91
S11	5.0	8.0	5.68	4.74	5.73	6.89

Preparation of the SPSS data set

Name the variables as shown in the data table above (omit subject numbers), enter the data and then save them in the file **anscombe.sav** (this file will be used again in Exercise 15). If the numeric format does not include decimals, click on the **Type** button and enter 2 into the **Decimal Places** box.

Exploring the data

Obtain scatterplots of the four data sets, as described in Section 11.2.2. The plots can be produced either one at a time by choosing **simple scatterplot** or, more dramatically, by opting for a **matrix scatterplot**, which is a grid of scatterplots normally used when one is plotting all pairwise combinations of several variables. In the present exercise, however, we only want the plots of $Y1$, $Y2$ and $Y3$ against $X1$ and of $Y4$ against $X2$. It is best to obtain the plot of *Y4* against *X2* separately.

If the matrix scatterplot is selected and variables *X1*, *Y1*, *Y2* and *Y3* are transferred to the **Matrix Variables** box, only the first column of plots, those with *X1* on the horizontal axis, will be of interest.

- **What do you notice about the scatterplots in the first column? Which one is suitable for a subsequent calculation of a Pearson correlation? What is wrong with each of the others?**

Return to the **Graphs** menu (it might be necessary to click on **Window**, and select the **anscombe.sav** window), and set up a simple scatterplot with *X2* and *Y4* (see Section 4.3.4.2 or 11.2.2).

- **Is the plot suitable for a Pearson correlation?**

The plot of *Y1* against *X1* shows a substantial linear relationship between the variables. The thinness of the ellipse indicates that the **Pearson correlation** is likely to be high. This is the kind of data set for which the Pearson correlation gives an informative and accurate statement of the strength of linear relationship between two variables. The other plots, however, are very different: that of *Y2* against *X1* shows a perfect, but clearly nonlinear, relationship; *Y3* against *X1* shows a basically linear relationship, which is marred by a glaring outlier; *Y4* against *X2* shows a column of points with a single outlier up in the top right corner.

Obtaining the Pearson correlations corresponding to the four scatterplots

Using the procedure described in Section 11.2.3, obtain the correlations between *X* and *Y* for the four sets of paired data.

The listing will include, in addition to the correlations of *X1* with the various *Y*s, the correlations among the four *Y* variables. The latter can be ignored.

- **What do you notice about the value of *r* for each of the correlations with *X1*?**

Return to the dialog box, click on the **Reset** box, and select *X2* and *Y4* for the remaining calculation.

- **What do you notice about the value of *r* in comparison with the values of *r* involving *X1*?**

The big surprise is that in all cases, the **Pearson correlation** has the same value (*0.817*), even in the case where there appears to be no systematic relationship between *X* and *Y* at all! Anscombe's data strikingly illustrate the need to inspect the data carefully to ascertain the suitability of statistics such as the Pearson correlation.

REMOVING THE OUTLIERS

It will be instructive to recalculate the **Pearson correlation** for the data set (*X1*, *Y3*) when the values for Subject 3 have been removed. The outlier is the value *12.74* on the variable *Y3*. Use the **Select Cases** procedure to select cases which do not have a value of *12.74* on *Y3*. Since none of the other values exceed 10, it is simplest to eliminate any cases with a value greater than 10.

Return to the **Scatterplot** and **Bivariate Correlations** dialog boxes for *X1* and *Y3* (ignore the other variables) to re-run these procedures using the selected cases. Check that in the listing, only 10 rather than 11 cases have been used. You should find that the Pearson correlation for *X1* and *Y3* is now +1, which is what we would expect from the appearance of the scatterplot.

CONCLUSION

This exercise has demonstrated the value of exploring the data first before calculating statistics such as the **Pearson correlation**. While it is true that Anscombe's data were contrived to give his message greater force, there have been many misuses of the Pearson correlation with real data sets, where the problems created by the presence of outliers and by basically non-linear relationships are quite common.

EXERCISE 14
OTHER MEASURES OF ASSOCIATION

BEFORE YOU START

Please read Section 11.3 before proceeding with this practical exercise. The **Pearson correlation** was devised to measure a supposed linear association between quantitative variables. There are other kinds of data (ordinal and nominal), to which the Pearson correlation is inapplicable. Moreover, even with interval data, there may be considerations that debar the use of the Pearson correlation. Fortunately, other statistical measures of strength of association have been devised and in this exercise, we shall consider statistics that are applicable to ordinal and to nominal data.

ORDINAL DATA

The Spearman rank correlation

Suppose that two judges each rank ten paintings, A, B, ..., J. Their decisions are shown in Table 1.

Table 1. The ranks assigned to the same ten objects by two judges.

	Best									Worst
First Judge	C	E	F	G	H	J	I	B	D	A
Second Judge	C	E	G	F	J	H	I	A	D	B

It is obvious from this table that the judges generally agree closely in their rankings: at most, the ranks they assign to a painting differ by two ranks. But how can their level of agreement be measured? The information in this table can be expressed in terms of numerical ranks by assigning the counting numbers from 1 to 10 to the paintings in their order of ranking by the first judge, and pairing each of these ranks with the rank that the same painting received from the other judge, as shown in Table 2.

Table 2. A numerical representation of the orderings by the two judges in Table 1

Painting	C	E	F	G	H	J	I	B	D	A
First Judge	1	2	3	4	5	6	7	8	9	10
Second Judge	1	2	4	3	6	5	7	10	9	8

This is not the only way of representing the judgements numerically. It is also possible to list the objects (in any order) and pair the ranks assigned by the two judges to each object, entering two sets of ranks as before. Where the measurement of agreement is concerned, however, the two methods give exactly the same result.

Define two variables, *judge1* and *judge2*, and enter the ranks assigned by the judges into the two columns. Obtain the **Pearson correlation** between the two sets of ranks. This is the value of the **Spearman rank correlation**.

Use of the Spearman rank correlation where there is a monotonic, but non-linear, relationship

Consider a common problem. Table 3 shows a set of paired interval data. On inspecting the scatterplot, we see that there is a **monotonic relationship** between the two variables: that is, as X increases, so does Y. On the other hand, the relationship between X and Y is clearly non-linear, and the use of the **Pearson correlation** is therefore inadvisable.

Table 3. A set of paired interval data showing a monotonic, but nonlinear, relationship

Y	1.00	1.58	2.00	2.32	2.58	2.81	3.00
X	2.0	3.0	4.0	5.0	6.0	7.0	8.0

Enter these values into the **Data Editor**, calculate the **Pearson correlation** and obtain the scatterplot.

- **Describe the shape of the scatterplot and write down the value of the Pearson correlation.**

Since there is a perfect (but non-linear) relationship between X and Y ($Y = \log_2 \{X\}$), the degree of association is understated by the Pearson correlation coefficient.

Another approach (and arguably a better one) is to convert X and Y to ranks using the **Rank Cases** procedure within the **Transform** menu, and then calculate the Pearson correlation using the resulting ranks. Do this and compare the two values of r.

- **Which value of r is the truer expression of the strength of the relationship between X and Y ?**

Kendall's correlation coefficients

The association between variables in paired ordinal (and interval) data sets can also be measured by using one of **Kendall's correlation** coefficients, **tau-a**, **tau-b** or **tau-c** (see Section 11.3.1.2). (When there are no tied observations, **tau-a** and **tau-b** have the same value.)

With large data sets, **Kendall's** and **Pearson's correlations** give rather similar values and tail probabilities. When the data are scarcer, however, Kendall's statistics are better behaved, especially when there is a substantial proportion of tied observations, and more reliance can be placed upon the Kendall tail probability. Kendall's correlations really come into their own when the data are assignments to predetermined ordered categories (rating scales and so on).

There are two ways of obtaining **Kendall's correlations** in SPSS:

(1)   In the **Bivariate Correlations** procedure, mark the **Kendall's tau-b** check-box.

(2)   Use the **Crosstabs** procedure (See Section 11.3.2.2).

Use the **Bivariate Correlations** procedure to obtain **Kendall's tau-a** (there are no ties) for the data in Tables 2 and 3.

MEASURES OF ASSOCIATION STRENGTH FOR NOMINAL DATA

In an earlier exercise, we considered the use of the **chi-square statistic** to test for the presence of an association between two qualitative variables. Recall that, provided that the data are suitable, the **Pearson correlation** measures the strength of a linear association between two interval variables. In that case, therefore, the same statistic serves both as a test for the presence of an association and as a measure of associative strength. It might be thought that, with nominal data, the chi-square statistic would serve the same dual function. The chi-square statistic, however, cannot serve as a satisfactory measure of associative strength, because its value depends partly upon the total frequency.

To illustrate the calculation of measures of association for two-way contingency tables, we can recall an earlier example, concerning the possibility of a gender difference in the choice of objects by children. The data were as shown in Table 4.

Table 4. The choices between two objects of 50 children

		Boys	Girls
	A	20	6
Object			
	B	5	19

Prepare the data set for the **Crosstabs** procedure (Section 3.5) and run **Crosstabs** (Section 11.3.2.2). This time, however, select **Phi** and **Cramer's V** within the **Nominal Data** box of the **Crosstabs: Statistics** dialog box.

- **Write down the values of the chosen measures of association between the qualitative variables of Gender and Choice.**

EXERCISE 15
SIMPLE, TWO-VARIABLE REGRESSION

BEFORE YOU START

Before proceeding with this exercise, please read Chapter 12.

THE REGRESSION PROJECT

Purpose of the project

In this exercise, we shall look at some of the pitfalls that await the unwary user of regression techniques; in fact, as we shall see, all the cautions and caveats about the **Pearson correlation** apply with equal force to regression. In Exercise 14, Anscombe's specially contrived data set (whose columns were named $X1$, $X2$, $Y1$, $Y2$, $Y3$, $Y4$) was saved in a file named **anscombe.sav**. Scatterplots and correlation coefficients were obtained for the pairings $(X1, Y1)$, $(X1, Y2)$, $(X1, Y3)$ and $(X2, Y4)$. All sets yielded exactly the same value for the Pearson correlation. When the scatterplots were inspected, however, it was seen that the Pearson correlation was appropriate for only one data set: in the other sets, it would give the unwary user a highly misleading impression. One problem with the Pearson correlation is that it is very vulnerable to the leverage exerted by atypical data points, or **outliers** as they are termed. It can also show large values with monotonic but nonlinear relationships. All this is equally true of the parameters of the regression equation. In this exercise, we return to Anscombe's data to investigate the statistics of the regression lines for the four sets of paired data.

Preparation of the data set

No preparation should be necessary: simply recall Anscombe's data set in file **anscombe.sav** to the **Data Editor** window.

Running the simple regression procedure

Following the procedure described in Section 12.2, obtain the regression statistics of $Y1$, $Y2$ and $Y3$ upon $X1$ and of $Y4$ upon $X2$. For present purposes, the plotting of the scatterplot of *ZPRED and *ZRESID should provide illuminating tests of the credibility of the assumption that the data are linear. Full details of preparing the **Linear Regression** dialog box are given in Section 12.2.1.

Since we want to carry out regression upon all four (X,Y) data sets, it will be necessary to prepare the

Regression dialog box for the first pair to include a scatterplot of *ZPRED and *ZRESID, and then change the variable names on subsequent runs for the remaining three pairs. After each run, you should record the value of **R Squared** and the regression equation, and note the shape of the scatterplot.

Output listing for the simple regression analyses
The main features of the output listing of a simple regression analysis are fully explained in Chapter 12.

- • **Compare the regression statistics for all four bivariate data sets. What do you notice about their values?**

EXERCISE 16
MULTIPLE REGRESSION

BEFORE YOU START
The reader should study Section 12.3 before proceeding with this exercise.

THE PROJECT

A problem in reading research
Reading comprises many different component skills. A reading researcher hypothesises that certain specific kinds of pre-reading abilities and behaviour can predict later progress in reading, as measured by performance on reading tests taken some years after the child's first formal lessons. Let us, therefore, label the dependent variable (DV) in this study *progress*. While they are still very young indeed, many children evince a considerable grasp of English syntax in their speech. Our researcher devises a measure of their syntactic knowledge, *syntax*, based upon the average length of their uttered sentences. Some researchers, however, argue that an infant's prelinguistic babbling (which we shall label *vocal*) also plays a key role in their later reading performance. At the pre-reading stage, some very young children can acquire a sight vocabulary of several hundreds of words. The ability to pronounce these words on seeing them written down is known as Logographic reading; but many authorities do not accept logographic reading. Our researcher, who views the logographic strategy as important, includes a measure of this skill, *logo*, in the study.

Preparing the data set
Fifty children are studied over a period beginning in infancy and extending through their school years. Their scores on the four measures, the DV *progress* (P), and the three IVs *logo* (L), *vocal* (V) and *syntax* (S), are listed in the appendix to this exercise. Since it would be very laborious for you to type in all the data during the exercise, we must hope that your instructor has already stored them in a file which you can access. Let us suppose that the data are available in the file **reading.sav**.

Exploring the data
Use **Descriptives** to list means and standard deviations and **Explore** to plot the boxplots of all the variables. These procedures will obtain the statistics for each variable and the distribution of the scores.
Regression is most effective when each IV is strongly correlated with the DV but uncorrelated with the other IVs. Although the correlation matrix can be listed from within the regression procedure, it is often more useful to scrutinise the matrix before proceeding with a regression analysis in order to make judgements about which variables might be retained and which dropped from the analysis. For example, it might be advisable to make a choice between two variables which are highly correlated with one another.
Use the **Bivariate Correlations** procedure to compute the correlation matrix. Notice that the DV *progress* shows substantial correlations with both *logo* and *syntax*. On the other hand, there is no appreciable correlation

between *logo* and *syntax*. The remaining variable (*vocal*) shows little association with any of the other variables; although there is a hint of a negative correlation with *logo*.

Running the multiple regression analysis

Run the multiple regression of *progress* upon the three regressors, by following the procedure in Section 12.3. Use both the simultaneous (**Enter**) and stepwise (**Stepwise**) procedures.

Output listing for the multiple regression

The main features of a multiple regression output listing, both for the simultaneous and forward stepwise methods, are explained in Section 12.3 .

- Do the decisions of the multiple regression procedure about which variables are important agree with your informal observations during the exploratory phase of the data analysis?

Appendix to Exercise 16
The data

P L V S	P L V S	P L V S	P L V S
65 75 34 48	46 55 75 32	65 50 75 68	34 32 42 27
58 29 18 67	51 31 50 66	71 65 23 64	54 64 55 32
42 40 43 38	61 69 59 46	60 56 52 44	81 82 60 69
55 55 9 48	45 19 71 59	17 10 64 20	77 66 50 79
68 81 41 54	53 48 44 45	55 41 41 55	57 30 20 54
59 28 72 68	46 45 29 45	69 51 14 62	80 82 65 58
50 39 31 42	25 28 58 28	47 49 46 59	89 51 52 48
50 26 78 56	71 70 51 54	53 14 53 77	50 34 45 60
71 84 46 50	30 55 42 25	50 40 51 31	69 49 72 72
65 71 30 52	62 53 52 57	80 45 59 90	71 69 57 60
34 30 30 20	47 20 78 69	51 18 22 61	39 25 81 49
44 71 79 22	60 46 80 67	79 58 13 82	
47 62 26 30	70 66 40 61	51 43 31 50	

EXERCISE 17
FACTOR ANALYSIS

BEFORE YOU START

Before proceeding with this practical, please read Chapter 15.

THE PROJECT

A personality study
Two hundred subjects are given a battery of personality tests, comprising the following items:
Anxiety; Agoraphobia; Arachnophobia; Extraversion; Adventure; Sociability.

Preparing the data set
Although the first step would normally be to enter the data for the 200 subjects into the **Data Editor** grid, there is obviously not time for you to do that in this Exercise. We shall therefore input a correlation matrix directly. Unfortunately, this cannot be done by using the dialog box interface: instead, **SPSS Syntax** must be used, as described in Section 15.2.3.
The **R matrix** is shown in Table 1.

Table 1. The R matrix

	Anxiety	Agora	Arachno	Advent	Extrav	Sociab
Anxiety	1.0000	0.8560	0.7845	0.0820	0.0560	0.0995
Agora	0.8560	1.0000	0.8271	0.0564	0.0283	0.0752
Arachno	0.7845	0.8271	1.0000	0.0624	0.0369	0.0795
Advent	0.0820	0.0564	0.0624	1.0000	0.8652	0.8396
Extrav	0.0560	0.0283	0.0369	0.8652	1.0000	0.8560
Sociab	0.0995	0.0752	0.0795	0.8396	0.8560	1.0000

Procedure for the factor analysis
The preparation of the syntax for the running of a factor analysis with a correlation matrix as input is fully described in Chapter 15. Follow the procedure described there.

Output listing for the factor analysis
- Construct your own table from the rotated factor matrix in the listing, showing the loadings of each of the variables on the two factors that have emerged from the analysis. State clearly whether there is a tendency for different groups of variables to load upon different factors.

EXERCISE 18
LOGLINEAR ANALYSIS

BEFORE YOU START

Before you proceed with this practical, please read Chapter 13.

THE PROJECT

Helping behaviour: the opposite-sex dyadic hypothesis

In the literature on helping behaviour by (and towards) men and women, there is much interest in three questions:

(1)   Are women more likely to receive help?
(2)   Are women more likely to give help?
(3)   Are people more likely to help members of the opposite sex? (This is known as the **opposite-sex dyadic hypothesis**.)

A male or female confederate of the experimenter approached male and female students who were entering a university library and asked them to participate in a survey. Table 1 shows the incidence of helping in relation to the sex of the confederate and that of the subject.

Table 1. Results of an experiment to test the opposite-sex dyadic hypothesis

CONFEDERATE (sex of)	SUBJECT (sex of)	HELP Yes	No
Male	Male	52	35
	Female	21	43
Female	Male	39	40
	Female	23	75

Exploring the data

Before carrying out any formal analysis, however, a brief inspection of the contingency table may prove informative. First of all, we notice that, on the whole, help was more likely to be refused than given; moreover, the females helped less than did the males. In view of the generally lower rate of helping in the female subjects, therefore, there seems to be little support for the hypothesis that females help more. Finally, turning to the third question, although the male subjects did help the male confederate more often, the female subjects tended to be more helpful towards the male confederate. This provides some support for the opposite-sex dyadic hypothesis.

Procedure for a loglinear analysis

In order to answer the three research questions, these results will be subjected to a **hierarchical loglinear analysis** (following the **backward elimination** strategy), with a view to fitting the most parsimonious **unsaturated model**. Prepare the data set exactly as described in Section 13.2.2. There are three variables in the contingency table:

(1)   Confederate's Sex (*confsx*).

(2)   Subject's Sex (*subjsx*).

(3)   Subject's Response (*help*).

Since there must be a coding variable for each of these, plus another variable of cell counts (*count*), the data set will comprise four variables in all. Prepare four columns in the Data Editor grid, adding appropriate extended variable names and the value labels of the coding variables. Run the loglinear procedure as described in Section 13.2.2.

Output listing for the loglinear analysis

The main features of the output listing for a hierarchical loglinear analysis are described in Section 13.2.3. The listing reports tests of models in which one of the two-way interaction terms has been left out. It can be seen that only the interaction between *confsx* and *subjsx* can be removed so that the increment in the **L-R chi-square** has a p-value not less than 0.05. That term, therefore, is dropped from the model. The final model has two interaction terms: *confsx*help* and *subjsx* help*.

- **Note down the value of the L-R chi-square associated with the best-fitting model. This is a measure of the failure of the model to predict the cell frequencies.**

Finally the listing shows a table of 'Observed, Expected Frequencies and Residuals'. Notice how small the residuals are.

If there is time, you might test the hypothesis of total independence of all three variables, using the procedure described in Section 13.2.4.

CONCLUSION

It should be quite clear from the foregoing comparisons that the final loglinear model is a very considerable improvement upon the model of total independence. Loglinear models provide a powerful tool for teasing out the relationships among the variables in multi-way contingency tables.

EXERCISE 19
PREDICTING CATEGORY MEMBERSHIP:
DISCRIMINANT ANALYSIS

BEFORE YOU START

Before proceeding with this practical, please read Chapter 14.

The purpose of discriminant analysis is, given the independent variables *IV1*, *IV2*, . . ., *IVp*, to find a linear function (*D*) of the IVs such that when a **one-way ANOVA** is carried out to compare the categories of the qualitative dependent variable with respect to *D*, the ratio $SS_{between}/SS_{total}$ is as large as possible. The function *D* will be of the general form:

$$D = b_0 + b_1 (IV1) + b_2 (IV2) + . . . + b_p (IVp)$$

As in multiple regression, it is possible to identify those variables that make significant contributions to the predictive process and drop the others from the final function. There are many other parallels between the two statistical techniques.

Recall that in one-way ANOVA, the total sum of squares (SS_{total}), which is a measure of the total dispersion of the scores around the grand mean, can be partitioned into two components:

(1) $SS_{between}$

(2) SS_{within}

The first of these components is the dispersion of the group means around the grand mean; the second is the dispersion of the scores around their group means. The three sums of squares are related according to the identity:

$$SS_{total} = SS_{between} + SS_{within}$$

Other things being equal, the ANOVA is more likely to show significance if the ratio ($SS_{between}/SS_{total}$) is close to unity: that is, the group means show large dispersion, whereas the individual scores lie close to their group means.

The quantity ($SS_{between}/SS_{total}$) is known as the **correlation ratio (eta squared)**. The correlation ratio is the oldest of various ANOVA measures of the strength of the effect that a treatment factor exerts upon the dependent variable. This can be expressed in another way. In the univariate case (ie there is just one dependent variable), the ratio SS_{within}/SS_{total} is the value of a statistic known as **Wilks' lambda**. Wilks' lambda is the complement of the ratio $SS_{between}/SS_{total}$: that is,

Wilks' lambda + correlation ratio (eta squared) = 1

The smaller the value of Wilks' lambda, the more chance there is of a significant ANOVA result, because the relatively small dispersion of the individual scores around their group means implies a relatively large dispersion among the group means.

In discriminant analysis, the question of whether a function can be found which reliably discriminates among the categories of the dependent variable is answered by a **chi-square test** of the value of **Wilks' lambda**, rather than an ANOVA. The two tests, however, will lead to the same decision about H_0 . For each of the categories of the dependent variable, there will be a (supposedly normal) distribution of D for the members of that category. The distributions will usually overlap, of course; but the goal of discriminant analysis is to find values for the constants (b_0 , b_1 , . . ., b_p) in the discriminant function such that the overlap among the distributions of D is minimised. In other words, the idea is to spread out the distributions of D to the greatest possible extent. If there are only two categories in the dependent variable, only one discriminant function can be constructed.

THE PROJECT

Prediction of reading success at the school-leaving stage

Just before they leave school, students in the most senior class of a school are regularly tested on their comprehension of a difficult reading passage. Typically, only 50% of students can perform the task. We shall also suppose that, for a substantial number of past pupils, we have available data not only on their performance on the comprehension passage but also on the very same variables that were investigated in the exercise on multiple regression, namely, the reading-related measures that we have referred to as *logo*, *syntax* and *vocal*, all of which were taken in the very earliest stages of the children's education.

The full data set is given in the appendix of this exercise. As with the multiple regression example, we can only hope that the data have already been stored in a file with a name such as **discrim.sav**, the contents of which you can access by using the **Open** procedure. Table 1 shows the first and the last few lines of the data set.

Table 1. Part of the data set

Logo	Syntax	Vocal	Comprehension
10	20	64	1
28	28	58	1
.	.	.	.
82	69	60	2
51	48	52	2

The rightmost variable is a coding variable whose values, *1* and *2*, denote, respectively, *failure* and *success* on the comprehension task.

Exploring the data set

Before moving on to the main analysis, a preliminary exploration of the data will bring out at least some of the important features. For example, if a particular variable is going to be useful in assigning individuals to categories, one might expect that, if its scores are subdivided according to category membership, there should be a substantial difference between the group means; if, on the other hand, there is no such difference, that would suggest that the variable will play a minimal role in the final discriminant function. To investigate these differences, **one-way ANOVAs** can be used to compare the group means on the various independent variables. These tests, however, are requested by options within the **Discriminant** procedure. We shall therefore return to the descriptive statistics when we come to prepare the dialog box.

Since discriminant analysis assumes that the distribution of the independent variables is multivariate normal, we shall also need to look at their empirical distributions to ascertain the credibility of that assumption.

Use the **Explore** procedure to plot boxplots for the predictor variables.

- **Study the output and note whether the boxplots reveal any outliers. Do the side-by-side boxplots show anything of interest?**

Procedure for discriminant analysis

Run the discriminant analysis as described in Section 14.2.2.2. There, however, we recommended the **Stepwise** method of minimisation of **Wilks' lambda**. In the present example, because of its simplicity, it is better to use the default method known as **Enter**, in which all the variables are entered simultaneously. Since **Enter** is the default method, there is no need to specify it.

Output listing for discriminant analysis

The main features of the output for a discriminant analysis are explained in Section 14.2.3.

The first table shows the number of cases in each of the categories of the variable group.

The next table, headed 'Wilks' lambda (U-statistic) and univariate F-ratio', shows the F-ratios (and their associated p-values) for the comparisons between the groups on each of the three independent variables.

The value of **Wilks' lambda** given in each of the ANOVAs is equal to one minus the square of the **point-biserial correlation** of each variable with the dependent variable: lambda is the complement of the correlation ratio.

- **Which variables have significant F ratios and which do not?**

There now follows the first of the tables showing the output of the discriminant analysis proper. Its title is 'Canonical Discriminant Functions'. Because there are only two groups, there is only one function.

The most important entries in the table are the statistic **lambda**, its **chi-square value** and the associated **p-value**. You will notice immediately that the value of lambda is smaller than the value for any of the three IVs considered separately. That is well and good: the discriminant function *D*, which uses the information in all the IVs should do a better job than any one IV alone. Here there is an obvious parallel with multiple regression, in which the predictive ability of the multiple regression equation cannot be less than the simple regressions of the target variable on any one regressor alone. Just as, in multiple regression, predictions can only improve when more regressors are added, the addition of another variable to the discriminant function can only improve its efficacy (although, in the case of the variable *vocal*, the improvement is negligible). Since, however, two of the IVs can each discriminate reliably between the groups, the result of the chi-square test of lambda in the discriminant analysis table is a foregone conclusion. As expected, the p-value is very small. The discriminant function *D* can indeed discriminate reliably between the two groups on the basis of performance on the independent variables.

Ignore the table of standardized Canonical Discriminant Function Coefficients.

A more useful table is the next one, labelled 'Structure Matrix: Pooled-within-groups correlations between discriminating variables and canonical discriminant functions'.

- **Are the correlations as you expected?**

The next table, entitled 'Unstandardized Canonical Discriminant Function Coefficients', gives the values of the parameters of the discriminant function D. The entries in the first three rows are presented in what is known as scientific notation, in which a term such as 'E-01' means 'multiplied by ten to the power of -1', which is the same as 'divided by ten to the power of +1'. So divide the numbers in the first row by ten, and the third row by 1000 (i.e. 10^3).

Examine the 'All-groups stacked histogram' to ascertain the success of the discriminant function in minimising the overlap between the distributions of D in the two groups. Notice that, although the groups are generally well separated, some 2s intrude into the area dominated by the 1s and vice versa. This means that, if category membership is unknown, SPSS will misassign some of the cases to the wrong group.

We have shown that the discriminant function D discriminates effectively between the two groups; but how effectively does it do this? This is shown by the **Confusion Matrix**, which appears under the heading: 'Classification Results'.

- **Note down the percentage of grouped cases correctly classified, the percentage of correct group 1 predictions and the percentage of correct group 2 predictions.**

CONCLUSION

This exercise is intended to be merely an introduction to the use of a complex and sophisticated statistical technique. Accordingly, we chose an example of the simplest possible application, in which the dependent variable comprises only two categories. The simplicity of our interpretation of a number of statistics such as **Wilks' lambda** breaks down when there are more than two categories in the dependent variable. For a treatment of such cases, see Tabachnick & Fidell (1989).

Appendix to Exercise 19
The Data

10	20	64	1	45	45	29	1	43	50	31	1	56	44	52	2	84	50	72	2
28	28	58	1	62	30	26	1	48	45	44	1	69	46	59	2	70	54	51	2
55	25	42	1	20	69	78	1	14	77	53	1	53	57	52	2	65	64	23	2
30	20	30	1	49	59	46	1	64	32	55	1	75	48	34	2	69	60	57	2
32	27	42	1	39	42	31	1	55	48	9	1	71	52	30	2	66	79	50	2
25	49	81	1	26	56	78	1	41	55	41	1	50	68	75	2	58	82	13	2
40	38	43	1	40	31	51	1	30	54	20	2	81	54	41	2	45	90	59	2
71	22	79	1	34	60	45	1	29	67	18	2	51	62	14	2	82	58	65	2
19	59	71	1	31	66	50	1	28	68	72	2	49	72	72	2	82	69	60	2
55	32	75	1	18	61	22	1	46	67	80	2	66	61	40	2	51	48	52	2

REFERENCES

Anderson, A. J. B. (1989). *Interpreting Data: A First Course in Statistics.* London: Chapman and Hall.

Anscombe, F. J. (1973). Graphs in statistical analysis. *American Statistician, 27,* 17 - 21.

Cohen, J., & Cohen, P. (1983). *Applied Multiple Regression/Correlation Analysis for the Behavioral Sciences. 2nd Edition.* Hillsdale, N. J.: Lawrence Erlbaum.

Cook, R.D. & Weisberg, S. (1982). *Residuals and Influence in Regression.* London: Chapman and Hall.

Darlington, R. B. (1968). Multiple regression in psychological research and practice. *Psychological Bulletin, 69,* 161 - 182.

Delucchi, K. L. (1983). The use and misuse of chi-square: Lewis and Burke revisited. *Psychological Bulletin, 94,* 166 - 176.

Everitt, B. S. (1977). *The Analysis of Contingency Tables.* London: Chapman and Hall.

Gravetter, F. J., & Wallnau, L. B. (1992). *Statistics for the Behavioral Sciences: A First Course for Students of Psychology and Education. 3rd Edition.* St. Paul: West.

Greene, J., & D'Oliveira, M. (1982). *Learning to Use Statistical Tests in Psychology: A Student's Guide.* Milton Keynes: The Open University Press.

Hartwig, F., & Dearing, B. E. (1979). *Exporatory Data Analysis.* Sage University Paper Series on Quantitative Applications in the Social Sciences, 07-016. Newbury Park, CA: Sage.

Howell, D. C. (1992). *Statistical Methods for Psychology. 3rd Edition.* Belmont, CA: Duxbury.

Kim, J., & Mueller, C. W. (1978a). *Introduction to Factor Analysis: What It Is and How To Do It.* Sage University Paper Series on Quantitative Applications in the Social Sciences, 07-013. Newbury Park, CA: Sage.

Kim, J., & Mueller, C. W. (1978b). *Factor Analysis: Statistical Methods and Practical Issues.* Sage University Paper Series on Quantitative Applications in the Social Sciences, 07-014. Newbury Park, CA: Sage.

Kirk, R. E. (1982). *Experimental Design: Procedures for the Behavioral Sciences. 2nd Edition.* Belmont: Brooks/Cole.

Lewis, D., & Burke, C. J. (1949). The use and misuse of the chi-square test. *Psychological Bulletin, 46,* 433 - 489.

Lovie, P. (1991). Regression diagnostics: a rough guide to safer regression. In P. Lovie & A. D. Lovie, *New Developments in Statistics for Psychology and the Social Sciences.* London and New York: The British Psychological Society and Routledge.

Meddis. R. (1984). *Statistics Using Ranks: A Unified Approach.* Oxford: Basil Blackwell.

Microsoft (1992). *Microsoft Windows User's Guide and Getting Started.* U.S.: Microsoft Corporation.

Myers, J. L. (1979). *Fundamentals of Experimental Design. 3rd Edition.* Boston: Allyn and Bacon.

Neave, H.R. & Worthington, P.L. (1988). *Distribution-Free Tests.* London: Unwin Hyman.

Norussis, M. (1993). *SPSS for Windows: Base System User's Guide: Release 6.0.* Chicago: SPSS Inc.

Reynolds, H. T. (1984). *The Analysis of Nominal Data. 2nd Edition.* Sage University Paper Series on Quantitative Applications in the Social Sciences, 07-007. Newbury Park, CA: Sage.

Siegel, S. (1956). *Nonparametric Statistics.* New York: McGraw-Hill.

Tabachnick, B. G., & Fidell, L. S. (1989). *Using Multivariate Statistics. 2nd Edition.* New York: Harper and Row.

Tukey, J.W. (1977). *Exploratory Data Analysis.* Reading, MA: Addison-Wesley.

Upton, G. J. G. (1978). *The Analysis of Cross-tabulated Data.* Chichester: John Wiley.

Upton, G. J. G. (1986). Cross-classified data. In A. D. Lovie (ed.) *New Developments in Statistics for Psychology and the Social Sciences.* London and New York: The British Psychological Society and Methuen.

Winer, B. J. (1971). *Statistical Principles in Experimental Design. 2nd Edition.* Tokyo: McGraw-Hill Kogakusha.

INDEX

H

Hanging or freezing 9
Hard copy 2
Hard disk 3
Hardware 2
Help drop-down menu
    in SPSS 79
    in Windows 17
Hierarchical loglinear model 191
High density disk 3
Homogeneity of covariance 124
        Mauchly test 124
Homogeneity of variance 120

I

Independent samples t-test 91
Independent-Samples T Test procedure 91
Independent variable 23
Input 2
Interaction 110, 256
Interactive processing 2
Interval data 51

K

Kendall's tau correlations (tau-a, tau-b, tau-c) 163
Keyboard 4
KMO (in Factor analysis, the Kaiser-Meyer-Olkin
    measure of sampling adequacy) 219
Kruskal-Wallis test (k-sample median test) 104

L

Latent root (see Eigenvalue)
Least Significant Difference test 249
Level (see Average)
Level (of a factor in ANOVA) 81
Levene's test (of homogeneity of variance) 92, 93
Leverage (exerted by outliers) 91, 241
Likelihood ratio (L.R.) chi-square 191
Linear association 153
Line graph 116
List Cases procedure 53
Logging in and logging out (of a network) 10
Loglinear, meaning of 191
Loglinear analysis 189
    comparison with ANOVA 189
    small expected frequencies 192
Long term storage 2
Lower case 5

M

Main effect (in ANOVA) 110
Mainframe (computers) 1
Mann-Whitney test 94
MANOVA (multivariate analysis of variance) 77
Marginal
    frequencies 191
    means 109
Mauchly sphericity test 124
Means procedure 60, 115
    (see also
    Compare Means, Descriptives and
    Explore procedures)
Menu (see also Drop-down menus) 16
Missing data 35
Missing values (system-missing & user-missing) 35
Mixed (split-plot) designs 139
Mouse 13
    clicking 13
    click-and-drag operations 13
    shapes of screen pointer 13
MS-DOS (Microsoft Disk Operating System) 7
Multiple comparisons 98, 102
Multiple correlation coefficient R   171
Multiple regression 171
Multivariate analysis of variance (see MANOVA)
Multivariate statistics 77 (see also MANOVA)
Multiway contingency tables 78

N

Network (of computers) 3
Newman-Keuls test 103
Nominal data 51
Nonparametric tests 93, 104, 238, 241
    (see also
    Binomial test
    Chi-square test
    Cochran Q test
    Friedman test
    Kruskal-Wallis test
    McNemar test
    Mann-Whitney test
    Sign test
    Wilcoxon test)
Normality of distribution
    in ANOVA 104
    in t-tests 86
Null hypothesis 84
Number lock [**Num Lock**] key 6
Number pad 5